More Praise for *Create Your Own Future:*
How to Master the 12 Critical Factors of Unlimited Success

Here in one book is a complete blueprint for success, achievement, increased income, rapid promotion, and better results in every area of your life. Buy it now and read every word!
—Robert G. Allen, Bestselling Author,
Multiple Streams of Income and
Multiple Streams of Internet Income

I've read many of Brian's books, and this could be his best work ever! Anybody who reads this book can't help but become more successful. His concepts are not only real and proven, they can be implemented the very next day!
—Allan D. Koltin, CPA, President and CEO,
Practice Development Institute (PDI)

Brian Tracy is one of the smartest, most inspirational men I've ever met. This book is a ticket to a better future for you. Buy it now.
—David Horowitz, Author

If you are looking for some inspiration and direction, you have to read *Create Your Own Future* by Brian Tracy. As in the past, Brian Tracy has again mastered motivation and the power of visualization in this important new work.
—William B. Bennett, Partner,
Manulkin, Glaser & Bennett

Two of my closest friends told me Brian Tracy literally saved their professional and personal lives. After reading *Create Your Own Future*, I can see how. A must read.
—David A. Kekich, CEO,
Trans Vio Technology Ventures

Brian Tracy offers a blueprint for success based on experience, not theory. You cannot lead where you haven't been; Brian has been there. A must read for anyone interested in influencing their own destiny.
—James H. Amos, Jr., President and CEO,
Mail Boxes Etc.

Brian Tracy has seen the future and it works.
—Sally C. Pipes, President and CEO,
Pacific Research Institute

A pleasure to read . . . stimulating and informative, with enough creative insights to suit every taste. There are so many compelling thoughts that it deserves a second reading; so much that needs to be taken seriously and applied. This book makes it clear that if it's going to be it's up to me.
—Michael Wolff, Partner, Eisner LLP

Another Brian Tracy winner! Within the pages of this book lies a formula for uncharted success where there are no limits!
—H. J. (Jim) Graham, President and CEO,
Cyber Broadcast One, Inc.

An easy, engaging read for anyone who really wants to live a more fulfilling life.
—Rick Metcalfe, President and CEO,
Asset Marketing Systems

If you can only read one book to supercharge your life and career, this is it. *Create Your Own Future* puts your destiny squarely in your own hands.
—Raymond J. Faltinsky, President and
Cofounder, FreeLife International

Brian's book helped me add value to my life, what I give to others and my future! Brian shows us how to make luck predictable.
—Thomas Winninger, Author, *Price Wars*

Create Your Own Future brings together in one book the best ideas and strategies for success ever discovered. You can use this as a guide to personal greatness in the years ahead.
—Sidney Friedman, President and CEO,
Corporate Financial Services

Brian Tracy, as usual, brings unique insights and practical ideas in *Create Your Own Future* that will be useful today and for years to come.
—Frank Kolhatkar, Partner, Deloitte & Touche

Brian Tracy's book *Create Your Own Future* is a winner . . . just like he is! Read it, because it could change your life.
—Mac Anderson, Founder, Successories

This amazing book shows you how to step on your own accelerator and develop the knowledge, skills, and contacts you need to double your results–faster than you can imagine!
—Tom Ferry, President, The Mike Ferry
Organization, Real Estate Resource Center

Create Your Own Future

How to Master the 12 Critical Factors of Unlimited Success

Brian Tracy

JOHN WILEY & SONS, INC.

Published by John Wiley & Sons, Inc., Hoboken, NJ
Published simultaneously in Canada.

ISBN 0-471-25107-0

Printed in the United States of America.

10 9 8 7 6 5 4 3 2

*This book is lovingly dedicated
to the most important people in my life:
my wonderful wife Barbara
and our four incredible children—
Christina, Michael, David, and Catherine (the Great).*

You have made it possible for me to create my own future.

Contents

Introduction:
There Are No Limits

"If we did all the things we are capable of doing,
we would literally astonish ourselves."
—Thomas Edison

Once upon a time, a long time ago, in a land far away, there lived an old man in a house on top of a hill. He had dedicated his entire life to study and meditation. He was known far and wide for his intelligence, sensitivity, and wisdom. Politicians, businesspeople, and dignitaries came to visit him and ask him questions. His answers were always correct. He seemed to have a special faculty that enabled him to cut to the essence of any problem or issue. When his answers and solutions were implemented, the result was always excellent. His fame soon spread throughout the land.

In the village below the hill was a group of boys who played together. Sometimes they climbed the hill to visit the old man and ask him questions, for which he always seemed have the correct answer. Over time, it became a little game, with the boys continually trying to think of a question that the old man could not answer. But they were never successful.

One day, the ringleader of the group, a boy named Aram, called the others around him and said, "I have finally found a way to stump the old man. Here in my hand, I have a bird. We will go and ask the old man if the bird is alive or dead. If he says that it is *dead*, I will release it and it will fly away. If he says that it is *alive*, I will crush it, and the bird will be dead. Either way, he will at last have been proven wrong."

Excited about the prospect of finally catching the old man with a wrong answer, they hurried up the hill. The old man watched them coming and noticed the eager looks on their faces. Then Aram stepped forward and asked, "Old man, I have a bird here in my hands. Is it alive or is it dead?"

The old man looked at their mischievous, expectant faces and then quietly said, "Aram, it is in *your* hands."

You Are the Master of Your Own Destiny

The point and moral of this story is that almost everything that happens to you is *in your hands*. Your destiny is very much up to you. Your future is largely determined by yourself, by your own choices and decisions. What you achieve is the result of what you do, or fail to do, day by day and year by year.

When I was 21, in the middle of a cold, cold winter, I sat in my small one-room apartment and contemplated my future. It didn't look very promising. I was a high school dropout working as a construction laborer, too broke to even go out the week before payday. Suddenly, I had a revelation. Just like the story about the old man, I realized that everything that happened to me from that moment onward was in my own hands. No one else was going to do it for me. I was responsible.

You Can Create Your Own Future

The management guru Peter Drucker wrote, "The very best way to predict the future is to create it." Everyone wants to be happy, healthy, popular, prosperous, and successful in whatever they do, but the only way for you to achieve and enjoy all that is possible for you is to *create your own future*. And the good news is that there have never been more opportunities, in more different areas, for you to fulfill your dreams and goals than there are today. Your chief aim in life should be to take full advantage of everything that your world has to offer.

There are basically two types of people in our world, the *active* and the *passive*. Only about 10 percent are proactive, and although they are very much in the minority they are the movers and shakers in every area. They are the people who take their lives into their own hands and *make* things happen. They accept complete responsibility for themselves and the results of their actions. They dare to go forward in the face of risk and uncertainty. When you decide to create your own future, you join this vital minority. You begin to push to the front of the line in your own life.

The majority of people tend to be passive in their responses and reactions to life, constantly wishing and hoping that something good will happen to them. They buy lottery tickets, watch television endlessly, and complain about their situations. They resent successful people, but they are not willing to make the efforts that others have made to achieve what they have achieved. They live their lives like people waiting for a bus on a street where no buses go.

Hope Is Not a Strategy

Hope is not a strategy for success. Your life is too precious and important to be left to chance. Your greatest responsibility is to take command of your future and shape your destiny the way you want it, to do something wonderful with your life.

In the years since that moment of awareness in my small apartment, I have traveled and worked in more than 80 countries. I have started, built, managed, or turned around 22 different businesses. I have served as a consultant or trainer for more than five hundred companies, and taught more than two million students and seminar participants these strategies for success in business and personal life. In the following pages, I will share with you the best ideas I have ever discovered to help you create the kind of future you both desire and deserve.

Sometimes, in my seminars, I will ask, "Is there anyone here who would like to double their income?" Almost instinctively, they all raise their hands.

"Well," I say. "I have good news for you. I can guarantee that everyone here is going to double their income, *if you just live long enough*.

If your income increases at the rate of inflation, about three percent per year, and you work another 20 to 25 years, you will definitely double your income."

"So, doubling your income is not the real question, is it? The real question is, 'How fast can you do it?'"

Step on Your Own Accelerator

If you are like me, you are impatient about getting results. Once you have decided to do something new or different, especially to create your own future, you want to get on with it as quickly as possible. That's good. That's the way it should be.

In this book, I show you how to step on the accelerator of your own life, and how to achieve your goals faster than you ever dreamed possible. I will share with you a series of practical, proven methods that work for everyone who uses them, and give you the most powerful and popular tools and techniques for personal and career success ever discovered, the same strategies used by all successful people, in every field.

Join me on a journey to discover and explore the vast, uncharted regions of your own potential. Decide today to create your own future.

Success Is Predictable

*"It is our duty as men and women to proceed
as though the limits to our abilities do not exist."*
—Pierre Teilhard de Chardin

The great question of philosophy has always been, "How shall we live in order to be happy?" The greatest minds of all time have dedicated years, often entire lifetimes, seeking the answers to this question. Your ability to ask and answer this question correctly for *yourself* is the key to everything that happens to you and to everything that you accomplish. The worst use of time and life is to work hard to climb the ladder of success only to find that it is leaning against the wrong building.

I did not graduate from high school. I fooled around and left school in the half of the class that makes the top half possible. Because of my limited education, the only work I could find was at laboring jobs. For years, I traveled from place to place, washing dishes, working in sawmills and on construction sites, slashing brush with a chain saw as part of a logging crew, and working on farms and ranches.

When the laboring jobs ran out, I got a job in straight commission sales, going from door to door and office to office. I wasn't afraid to work, but hard work alone was not enough. I lived from sale to sale, barely making a living. Then, one day, I did something that changed my life.

Learn from the Experts

I went to the top salesman in my company, a man who was selling and earning at least five times as much as I was, and I asked him, in frustration, "What are you doing differently from me?"

He was selling the *same* product out of the *same* office at the *same* price to the *same* people under the *same* competitive conditions. Yet he was selling vastly more than me, and in less time as well. Again I asked him, "What are you doing differently from me?"

And he told me. First, he sat down with me and asked how I was selling already; what kind of results I was getting. He listened patiently and then he told me how he did it. He explained the importance of asking questions and understanding the real needs and problems of the prospect before attempting to sell anything. He showed me how to present my product as the best possible choice for a particular customer. He explained the best answers to the most common concerns that prospects ask, and he showed me how to ask for a buying decision.

It turned out that earlier in his career, he had been thoroughly trained at a large company in the process and methodology of professional selling. He had mastered the skills of the basic sales process and then adapted them to his current products. He had discovered that, like riding a bicycle or driving a car, the system of selling, once learned, could be transferred to another product, service, or industry, and it would work just as well.

This principle hit me like a thunderbolt. It changed my life. Just imagine! There were reasons for everything that happened, for success or failure in any area. If there was something I wanted, I just had to find out how other people had achieved it. Within reason, if I just did what they did, I would eventually get the same result.

Here is my first rule: *If you do what other successful people do, nothing can stop you from eventually getting the same results they do. And if you don't do what they do, nothing can help you.*

I was on my way! In the years to come, I worked in many different businesses at a variety of jobs. Each time I started in a new field, I immediately buckled down and learned everything I could about the rules of success in that business, then applied what I had learned, adapting it to my current job until I got the same or better results than others had achieved.

The Great Question

As I began moving up, I started asking another question, "Why is it that some people are more successful than others?" Why is it that some people have more money, better jobs, happier families, vibrant health, and exciting lives, and others not? Why do some people drive newer cars, wear nicer clothes, and live in better homes? These people always seem to have money in their pockets and in their bank accounts. They dine in fancy restaurants, take beautiful vacations, and live more enjoyable, satisfying lives. Why was this?

The answer I got back was that these people were somehow *luckier* than the average, as if they had been born with a special gene or chromosome that others lacked. Even people who have achieved greatly often attribute their success to "luck."

However, I felt that something was *wrong* with this explanation. Were people who started off with limited backgrounds and eventually succeeded just lucky? If people worked hard, studied continuously, and pulled themselves up into positions of prominence by their own application and effort, was this a matter of luck?

Did this explanation mean that people who had come from all over the world, arriving with no friends, no language skills, no money, and no opportunities, and who had then become successful, were just lucky? Did this mean that people who started off with nothing, who, over the course of their working lifetimes, became financially independent, self-made millionaires, or even billionaires, were just lucky? This explanation didn't make sense to me.

The Statistics Don't Lie

According to the IRS, there are more than five million *millionaires* in the United States, most of them self-made. There are almost 300 billionaires, most of whom started with little or nothing. More than 100,000 people become millionaires in the United States each year, at a rate of approximately one every five minutes. Are all these people just lucky?

The Breakthrough in Philosophy

In about 350 B.C., the Greek philosopher Aristotle propounded what has come to be recognized as the foundation law of Western philosophy and Western thought. At a time when most people believed in the various gods who lived on Mount Olympus and the causeless, chaotic influences of flowers, rocks, trees, and the elements on human life, Aristotle instead propounded his "Principle of Causality." He said that we live in an orderly universe, governed by great unchanging laws. He insisted that there is a reason for everything that happens, whether we know the law or principle behind it or not.

Today, we call this the "Law of Cause and Effect." We accept it as an essential way of interpreting what happens in our world. But in Aristotle's day, it was a remarkable idea, a breakthrough in thought. It revolutionized the study of philosophy and guided the great thinkers through the centuries right up to the present age. It was commonly believed that *all Western thought for 2000 years was merely a footnote to Aristotle.*

Simply put, the Law of Cause and Effect says that everything happens for a reason. It says that for every effect in your life there is a cause or a series of causes, whether you know them or agree with them or not. Nothing happens by chance.

This law says that if there is anything you want in life, any *effect* that you desire, you can probably acquire it. You simply find others who have achieved the same result or effect that you desire. You then discipline yourself to do the same things that they did, over and over, until you eventually get the same results and rewards. It is completely predictable and largely under your control.

What Are the Odds?

In my thirties, I applied for and was accepted into an executive MBA program at a major university. For four years, including evenings and weekends, summers and winters, I invested more than 4,000 hours studying the cause and effect relationships that determined business success or failure. It was during this time that I was first exposed to an arcane subject called probability theory. What I learned in this class profoundly influenced my thinking and answered many of my questions about luck.

Probability theory teaches that there is a *likelihood* that any particular event will occur. This likelihood or probability can often be calculated with great accuracy, and sometimes not. The entire worldwide insurance industry, involving billions of dollars in premiums and trillions of dollars in coverage, is based on actuarial tables, which are simply applications of probability theory.

In life insurance, actuaries know that there is a likelihood that a certain person of a certain age and medical history will die in a certain time period. But because it is not possible to determine who that person might be, all persons in that class can be insured at a price that makes it possible to provide death benefits to the few people who actually die during the life of the policy. This is called pooled risk.

The Law of Probabilities

The Law of Probabilities is the critical factor in explaining luck. This law says that *for every event, there is a probability of that event occurring under certain circumstances.*

Where the level of probability can be established with some accuracy, the level of predictability can be dramatically increased. For example, if you flip a coin, it will come down heads 50 percent of the time and tails 50 percent of the time. The probability of a head or a tail is 50 percent, no matter how many times you flip the coin. You may flip the same coin five thousand times, and on every flip of the coin, the probabilities remain 50 percent. You can, therefore, predict the outcomes over time with complete accuracy.

You Can Improve Your Likelihood of Success

Become Brilliant on the Basics

If you want to achieve success in any field, and you have clear, written plans that you follow and work on each day, you are much more likely to attain it. If you then study thoroughly and apply yourself to developing the knowledge and skills necessary to excel in your field, you will increase your probabilities of success. If you associate with the right people, manage yourself and your time extremely well, move quickly when opportunity presents itself, persevere in the face of obstacles, you will get the breaks.

Willingness to take intelligent risks in the pursuit of your clearly defined, intensely desired goals, puts you on the side of the angels. You will increase all the possible probabilities in your favor. You will achieve the same level of success in one or two years that other people may not achieve in 10 or 20 years of less focused, less directed behavior. You will create your own future. And it's not a matter of luck!

Look for Every Opportunity to Reduce Uncertainty

In physics, Heisenberg's Uncertainty Principle had a profound influence on science and eventually earned him a Nobel prize. This principle states that, even though it is scientifically possible to determine exactly how a class of particles will behave *in general*, it is not possible to predict exactly *which* of those particles will behave that way *specifically*. As a result, there always exists a degree of uncertainty in physics, no matter how sound the general theory.

In human terms, it is possible to predict that about 5 percent of Americans will achieve a net worth of $1 million or more in the course of their working lifetimes. But it is not possible to determine in advance exactly *which ones* it will be. We can only be sure about the degree of probability.

In terms of health, happiness, and longevity, a certain percentage of people are going to lead wonderful lives, raise happy, healthy children, make a real contribution to their work and their communities, and live to be 80 or 90 years old. We just don't know for sure exactly who they will be.

Here is the key to creating your own future: Whatever you want, do everything possible to *increase the probabilities* of your achieving it. Even one small factor can spell the difference between success and failure.

Your primary goal should be to increase the likelihood that you will be one of those remarkable people who achieves greatly and makes a real difference with his or her life. And this is very much in your own hands.

To realize your full potential, free yourself as much as possible from randomness and uncertainty. Organize your life in such a way that the probabilities of achieving your goals are extremely high. Learn the cause and effect relationships between what you want and how to get it.

Take complete control over every part of your life and create your own future. You must leave nothing to chance.

Chance versus Luck

When people achieve great success faster than others, they are immediately accused of having good luck. When people make a mess of their lives, largely due to their own shortcomings, they dismiss it as bad luck. A leading politician said recently, "All of life is like a casino. Some have succeeded greatly at the gaming tables of life, others not. Those who have been successful should be forced to share their winnings with those who have not done as well."

One of the reasons for this confusion about the reasons for success and failure is that most people don't understand the difference between chance and luck. Chance refers to *gambling*, to casinos, to blackjack, poker, slot machines, and horse racing. In games of chance, the outcome is almost completely out of your control. You have little or no influence over the result. Your level of risk in gambling is so high that your chances of winning over the long term are almost zero.

Luck, however, is something completely different from chance. What we call luck is really the Law of Probabilities in action. Whenever you see a person who has succeeded greatly, you see the result of many events that have happened in the past to achieve a particular outcome in the present moment. The lucky individual has done many things that, in combination, dramatically increased the likelihood that his or her desired goal would be achieved.

If you examine the history of any great success, and review the many actions that preceded it, you will see a definite pattern emerge. You will see that the successful individual did many little things, sometimes for years, which made the final success possible.

The Basic Success Principle

Here is a rule: *There is a direct relationship between the number of different things you attempt and your likelihood of eventual success.*

If a new salesperson gets up early each morning, plans his day, works steadily all day long, talks to as many prospects as possible, follows up persistently, and continually works on himself to improve his selling skills by reading, audio learning, and regular attendance at sales courses and seminars, he is going to be far more successful than another salesperson who fails to do these things. His high earnings will not be a matter of luck but rather of design.

If you get a good education, thoughtfully match your career choice with your natural talents and abilities, and continually work to upgrade your skills and the value of your contribution to your company, your eventual success will not be the result of luck.

Play the Averages

An additional luck factor is the Law of Averages, which is an extension of the law of probabilities. This law says that *although you cannot predict which one of a series of events will be successful, by the Law of Averages you know that by doing a certain thing a certain number of times, you will achieve your goal.*

If you read more books, you are much more likely to read something that can help you in your work or personal life. If you make more sales calls, you will be much more likely to meet the prospect who has an immediate need for what you are selling. If you continually innovate and try new methods to achieve your goals or solve your key problems, you are going to be vastly more successful than someone who plays it safe and tries nothing new or different.

What Do You Really Want?

Everyone wants to be happier, healthier, and more prosperous, and get more out of life than they do today. No matter how much you accomplish, you always want *more*, and this is a good thing. Your desire for continuous self-betterment keeps you growing and developing toward the realization of your full potential.

But today, in a world of almost unlimited opportunities, only a few people, by their own admission, are really living up to what they are truly capable of in their day-to-day lives. Most people have an uneasy feeling that they could be doing far better than they are doing today, if only they knew how.

Success, however you define it, is not an accident. It is not a result of good luck versus bad luck. Even if you have not taken the time to clearly identify the steps you took or failed to take to get you from where you were to where you are today, a definite process has brought you to where you are at this minute. And the fact is that these actions and behaviors of yours could have brought you to no other place.

You are where you are and what you are because of yourself. Your choices and decisions over the months and years have inevitably determined the condition of your life at this moment. The most wonderful part of this fact is that, at any time, you can start making different choices and decisions for your future. You can start taking different steps, and as a result, you will inevitably arrive at a different place from where you are today.

The Luck Factors

The Law of Probabilities is what enables you to create your own future with a high level of accuracy and predictability. You need only learn and practice the specific behaviors that increase your likelihood of success, however you define it, and you can take complete control of your destiny. You can achieve anything you really want in life.

These various actions, behaviors, and strategies, all of which increase your probabilities of greater success, are what I call *luck factors*. Over the years, in studying thousands of successful people, I have identified dozens of these factors. Any one of them, if you are not yet using it, can change your life, and sometimes it can do it overnight.

As the result of using the luck factors in your life, success becomes *predictable*. You will dramatically increase the amount of what others call luck in your life, if you continually do the things that other lucky people do.

Starting from Nothing

A seminar participant of mine named Ivan Strigorsky, a Russian immigrant, told me his story not long ago. After the collapse of the Soviet Union, his dream was to come to the United States. After several years of trying and failing, over and over, he finally got a visa and a plane ticket. He arrived in New York with everything he owned in a cardboard box tied up with string. He could not speak a word of English.

He found his way to the neighborhood in New York called "Little Russia," where a large number of Russian immigrants lived. In his first year in the United States, the only job he could get was delivering pizza out of a Russian pizza place to other Russians within the radius of a few blocks.

But Ivan had one tremendous advantage that many other people lack. He was absolutely convinced that America was a land of opportunity and that he was completely responsible for taking advantage of those opportunities. No one would do it for him. He had to make his own luck.

He also knew that the key to success in the United States was the ability to speak English fluently. To master this new language, he began listening to my audio programs on success and achievement, on sales and personal management. He listened to those of other success authors and narrators, as well. He read our books and articles on personal and business effectiveness. He learned English and learned basic success principles at the same time. All these ideas were new to him and he absorbed them like a sponge. He had never heard them growing up in the Soviet Union.

At the end of his first year in the United States, his English was good enough for him to get a job in sales with a printing company. At the end of his second year, he was doing so well selling printing services for others that he decided to start his own company as a printing broker. In his third year, he sold $2 million worth of printing services and made more than $400,000 in personal income. And his success had nothing whatever to do with luck.

You Make Your Own Luck

There are millions of men and women in the United States who have come from difficult backgrounds, with every conceivable type of handicap and liability, but who have gone on to build wonderful lives for themselves. Often, people around them ascribe their good fortunes to *luck*. But if you talk to these people and you trace their stories from where they began to where they are now, you will find that luck had little to do with their success. And, it has little to do with yours.

The Law of Cause and Effect cuts in both directions. It also says that if there is an effect in your life, such as lack of money, overweight, problems in your relationships, an unsatisfying job or career, or any other difficulty, you can trace that effect back to the things that you did to cause it, and by removing the causes, you can begin to remove the effects, sometimes immediately.

Practice the Proven Principles of Success

In its simplest terms, successful, happy, healthy, prosperous people are those who have discovered the principles that govern our lives and have designed their lives so that they live in harmony with those principles. As a result, they experience far more joy and satisfaction in life. They accomplish far more in a few years than the average person does in a lifetime.

You've heard it said, in Poker, "The winners laugh and tell jokes while the losers say, 'shut up and deal!' " In the world around you, the winners are busy and actively working toward achieving their goals while average people are putting in as little work and contribution as they can and hoping for a lucky break. Winners always ascribe their success to hard work and application. Mediocre people always ascribe their failures to bad luck.

Actions Have Consequences

Another version of the Law of Cause and Effect is the Law of Action and Reaction. First propounded and explained by Sir Isaac Newton, this law states that, "For every action, there is an equal and opposite reaction." Put another way, *actions have consequences*.

This is important. At the beginning of any project, you can decide on your action. You can control what you do. But once you have launched a particular action, the consequences are often out of your hands. Once you have done or said a particular thing, the consequences take on a power and a force of their own. This is why successful people are more *thoughtful* about the potential consequences of what they say and do than the average person. Unsuccessful people, on the other hand, tend to be thoughtless, even careless, about their statements or behaviors, and what might happen as a result of them.

The key to enjoying more of what people call luck is for you to engage in *more* of the actions that are more likely to bring about the consequences that you desire. At the same time, you must consciously decide to *avoid* those actions that will not bring about the consequences you desire or, even worse, will bring about consequences that you don't want.

If you are in sales, the daily actions of prospecting, presenting, following up, and working continuously to cultivate leads and referrals will ultimately bring about the consequences of sales success, higher income, personal pride, and greater satisfaction from your career. The more of these actions you engage in, the more pleasurable consequences you will enjoy. Your success will be largely under your control. It will not be a matter of luck at all.

If you are in management, the daily actions of careful planning, organizing your work before you begin, selecting the right people for the job, delegating properly, supervising intelligently, and vigorously executing your required tasks will bring about success in your work. It will have nothing to do with luck.

The Law of Sowing and Reaping

Another version of the Law of Cause and Effect comes from the Old Testament: the Law of Sowing and Reaping. This law says, "Whatsoever a man soweth, that also shall he reap." This law says that whatever you put in, you get out. It also says that whatever you are reaping today is a result of what you have sown in the past. Your life today, in every respect, is the result of your past decisions and behaviors.

The Laws of Cause and Effect, Action and Reaction, Sowing and Reaping, are timeless truths, universal principles that have existed since the beginning of history. They are often referred to as the iron laws of human destiny. All lasting success, happiness, and high achievement comes from organizing your life in harmony with these timeless principles. When you do, you will achieve satisfaction and enjoyment at levels seldom experienced by the average person. You will take complete charge of creating your own future. And of course, people will start to refer to you as lucky.

ACTION EXERCISES
What You Can Do Now

1. Develop your own personal definition of happiness. What sort of activities or conditions do you enjoy more than anything else?

2. Go to one of the top people in your field and ask that person for advice that will help you to be more successful.

3. Identify the *luckiest* events that have happened in your life and then trace back the various actions you took that contributed to them.

4. Determine the cause and effect relationships between something you want and the best way of getting it. What are they?

5. Take one specific action immediately that can increase the likelihood that you will achieve one of your goals. Do it now!

Principle 1—Your Potential Is Unlimited

"If one advances confidently in the direction of his dreams
and endeavors to live the life he has imagined, he will meet
with a success unexpected in common hours."
—Henry David Thoreau

Your mind has all the power you need to get you anything you really want in life. Your ability to harness the incredible, creative, and constructive capacities of your thinking determines everything that happens to you. When you unlock your mental powers, you will accomplish more in a few months than many people do in several years.

Thought Is Creative

Perhaps the most important corollary of the Law of Cause and Effect is this: *Thoughts are causes, and conditions are effects.*

Your mind is the most powerful force in your universe. You are where you are and what you are because of your habitual ways of thinking. Your thoughts are creative, and they ultimately create your reality. As Emerson said, "A man becomes what he thinks about most of the time." Therefore, if you change your thinking, you change your life. You actually become a different person and get different results.

The greatest thinkers of all time, dating back to the earliest religions, philosophers, and metaphysical schools, have all emphasized the power of the human mind to shape individual destiny.

Become a Magnet for Good Luck

The Law of Attraction explains perhaps the most important luck factor of all. This law, first written about 3000 B.C.E., says that *you are a living magnet, and you inevitably attract into your life the people, circumstances, ideas, and resources in harmony with your dominant thoughts.*

The Law of Attraction falls under the Law of Cause and Effect. The Law of Attraction explains almost every circumstance of your life. People who think and talk continually about what they *want* seem to attract more and more of those very things into their lives. People who talk about what they don't want, the things they fear or worry about, or people who are angry and resentful, continually attract negative and unhappy experiences into their lives as well.

The Law of Attraction is in itself *neutral*, as are all of these other laws and principles. It is objective, not subjective. Natural laws do not play favorites. They are no respecters of persons. They function automatically and unemotionally. They only affect you either positively or negatively, depending on whether you use them constructively or destructively.

Perhaps the most important lesson you will ever learn is this: To be successful and happy, you must think and talk only about the things you want. At the same time, you must discipline yourself not to think and talk about the things you don't want. This may sound simple and obvious, but it is often the most difficult of all exercises in self-control and self-mastery.

You Will See It When You Believe It

The Law of Belief is another luck factor that you can use to your advantage. The Law of Belief states that *whatever you believe with conviction becomes your reality.*

William James of Harvard wrote that, "Belief creates the actual fact." In the New Testament it says, "According to your faith, it is done unto you." In the Old Testament it reads, "As a man thinketh (or believeth) in his heart, so is he." Throughout history, people have recognized that our beliefs play a major role in the way we see the world, and in the way we think and behave.

If you absolutely believe that you are destined to be a great success in life, you will think and behave accordingly, and you will make it come true. If you confidently believe that you are a lucky person, and that good things are continually happening to you, your belief will become the actual fact of your life.

You See What You Already Believe

Once upon a time, two shoe salesmen, from different companies, were sent to an African country to explore the market for shoes. The first shoe salesman hated the assignment and wished he didn't have to go. The second shoe salesman loved the assignment and saw it as a great opportunity for advancement in his company.

When they each arrived in the African country, they studied the local market for shoes. Then they both sent telegrams back to their head offices. The first salesman, who didn't want to be there, wrote, "Trip has been wasted. No market in this country. Nobody wears shoes."

The second salesman, who saw this as a real opportunity and believed that he could make something of it, said in his telegram, "Wonderful trip. Market opportunities unlimited. No one wears shoes."

You Create Your Own Reality

There is a short poem that says, "Two men looked out through prison bars. One saw the mud, the other saw the stars."

Shakespeare wrote, "Nothing is but thinking makes it so."

Your beliefs *do* become your realities. The Law of Mind, a corollary of the Law of Belief, says that, *Thoughts objectify themselves. Thoughts held in mind produce after their kind.* The results of your habitual ways of thinking eventually appear in the world around you. All you have to do is to look around you to see the truth of these timeless principles.

By Their Fruits

In the New Testament, Jesus says, "By their fruits, ye shall know them." You can tell what a person thinks about *most of the time* by looking at the fruits of his or her life. A happy, healthy, prosperous person with good friends and family is invariably a person who thinks about his life in positive terms, most of the time. He absolutely believes that happiness and success are in the natural order of things for him.

Harvard University did a study a few years ago and made three predictions for that year. These predictions, as it turned out, seemed to be true for every year thereafter. The Harvard study predicted that first, in the coming year, there would be more *changes* than ever before. Second, in the coming year, there would be more *competition* than ever before. Third, in the coming year there would be more *opportunities* than ever before. The fourth conclusion, which was contained in a footnote, said that those who do not adjust to the rapid rate of change, respond to the increase in competition, or take advantage of the new opportunities available would be out of their jobs within two years.

The Opportunities of Tomorrow

The truth about opportunities is that there are more of them today than ever before, but they are different from the opportunities of the past. There are more opportunities for more people to achieve more of their goals of health, happiness, and financial independence today than have ever existed in all of human history. But to take advantage of them, you will have to adjust and adapt to the new realities of your situation, whatever they are.

One of the greatest luck factors of all, which few people realize or appreciate, is the factor of being born and living in our world as it exists at this moment. Most of the major illnesses have been eliminated, there are no major wars or revolutions, inflation is under control, unemployment is down, and the possibilities for positive, creative people are virtually unlimited.

We are entering into a new Golden Age that has been dreamed about throughout history. Your goal must be to take full advantage of all the wonders of the modern world to design and create your own future.

Of course, there will always be social, political, and economic problems to contend with. The problems of world terrorism create new feelings of uncertainty and insecurity. But these ups and downs are inevitable. They are challenges that we will rise to and eventually meet successfully. The good news is that for you, the possibilities are unlimited.

There Are No Limits

Your greatest limits are not *external*. They are internal, within your own thinking. They are contained in your personal self-limiting beliefs. These are the beliefs that act as the brakes on your potential. These are the beliefs that cause you to sell yourself short, and to settle for far less than you are truly capable of.

Many people think that they are not smart enough, creative enough, or talented enough to get the things they want. But the fact is that most of these beliefs have no basis in reality. They are simply not true. There are very few limits on what you can really accomplish, except the ones you accept in your own mind. As Henry Ford said, "If you believe you can do a thing, or you believe you cannot, in either case, you are probably right."

Here is an important point: You cannot intensely desire something without simultaneously having the ability to attain it. The existence of the desire itself is usually proof that you have within you everything you need to fulfill that desire. Your job is simply to find out *how* to do it. Your job is to identify all the things that you can do to increase the probabilities and improve the averages that you will achieve your goal, as you desire it, and on schedule.

Expect the Best

The Law of Expectations contains and explains another luck factor. This law says that, *whatever you expect, with confidence, becomes your own self-fulfilling prophecy*.

Perhaps the most powerful and predictable motivator of all is an attitude of positive expectations. People are most motivated to act when they are convinced that their actions will lead to a successful, positive outcome. They take action because they confidently expect good things to happen as a result of what they do.

One way to manufacture your own mental force field of positive expectations is to start off each morning by saying, "I believe something wonderful is going to happen to me today!" Repeat this affirmation several times until your entire mind is charged up with confident expectancy. "I believe something wonderful is going to happen to me today."

At the end of the day, do a brief review and think over the events of the past few hours. You will be amazed to notice the great number of wonderful things, large and small, that actually did happen to you when you mind was supercharged with this power of confident expectation.

Successful people are characterized by this attitude of positive self-expectancy. They expect to succeed more often than they fail. They expect to win more often than they lose. They expect to gain something from every experience. They look for the good in every situation. They see the glass as half full rather than as half empty. Even when things go wrong for them, they look into the temporary setback or reversal for the lessons they can learn and the advantages they can gain from the experience.

The Success Secret of the Wealthiest 500

Napoleon Hill, in his study of 500 of the richest men in America, concluded that one characteristic that they all had in common was this attitude of positive expectancy. They made a habit of looking into every obstacle or setback for an equal or greater advantage or benefit. And they always found it. You must do the same.

When you start any new career or a business, you should confidently expect to succeed. You should confidently expect that people will buy your products or utilize your services. You should confidently expect that your bank or others will provide the funds that you require. You should confidently believe that you will attract the very best people to help you realize your business dreams. This expectant attitude goes before you like a shining light, throughout the day, affecting everybody that you come in contact with.

When you have a setback or difficulty, no matter what it is, look upon it as a valuable lesson, and try to learn as much from it as possible. Refuse to consider the possibility of failure. Remain open minded and flexible. Be prepared to try new things and abandon old methods that are not working. Resolve in advance that you will never give up. And if you think this way all day long, what do you think will eventually happen to you?

Your beliefs about yourself and your world create your expectations. Your expectations determine your attitude. Your attitude determines your behavior and the way you relate to other people. And the way you behave toward and relate to other people determines how they relate to and behave toward you.

The more confident and positive you become, the more you will believe yourself destined for great success. You will generate a more powerful force field of attraction around you. You will draw more people and opportunities into your life to help you achieve your goals at a faster rate. You will create your own future, and people will continually call you lucky.

Use All Your Mental Powers

Your subconscious mind can be another luck factor, when you use it correctly. The Law of Subconscious Activity says, *whatever thought or goal you accept in your conscious mind will be accepted by your subconscious mind as a command or instruction.*

Your subconscious mind, the sending station of the power of attraction, once programmed with your goals, will then begin drawing into your life the people and resources you need to achieve them. Your subconscious mind will make your words and actions fit a pattern consistent with your self-concept, with your dominant thoughts and ideas about yourself. Your subconscious mind will determine your body language and the ways that you interact with other people. The commands you have given to your subconscious mind by your habitual ways of thinking will affect your tone of voice, your energy levels, your enthusiasm, and your attitude.

Your subconscious mind is extraordinarily powerful. It works 24 hours per day. Once you begin using it in achieving your goals, you will begin to move forward at a speed that you cannot now imagine.

Activate Your Reticular Cortex

In your brain, there is a small finger-like organ called the reticular cortex. This reticular cortex is like a telephone switchboard that accepts and forwards calls from the outside. Your reticular cortex takes in information and passes it on to your conscious mind, as well as to your subconscious mind. Your reticular cortex, or *reticular activating system*, works on the basis of commands that you have given it about what you want and what is most important to you.

For example, if you decide that you want a red sports car, you will begin to see red sports cars everywhere. This desire or goal will activate your reticular cortex and make your mind highly sensitive to red sports cars. You will become aware of red sports cars wherever you go. You will see them turning corners and parked in driveways. You will notice pictures and advertising for red sports cars. And you will attract people and ideas that will help you to finally acquire a red sports car. Was there ever anything you really wanted for a long time that you didn't eventually get, often in the most amazing way?

If you decide that you want to become *financially independent*, you will immediately develop a heightened awareness to information, people, and opportunities that can help you financially in some way. You will begin to attract into your life people who have ideas and advice for you. You will come across books and articles that answer key questions. You will find yourself taking actions that help you achieve the financial independence you desire.

Program Your Mind for Success

You act on the outside consistent with the way you are programmed on the inside. This programming can be accidental and random or it can be deliberate and purposeful. When you take charge of the *suggestive* influences in your life, you activate another luck factor, and you can control your own programming with affirmations that you repeat over and over.

The power of repeated affirmation actually changes your thoughts, feelings, and behaviors. Just as you become what you think about most of the time, you also become *what you say to yourself and believe*. Whatever goals you repeat, over and over, in a *positive, present tense, personal* way will be accepted by your subconscious mind as commands. Your subconscious mind will then go to work to attract these goals into your life.

For example, when you repeat an affirmation such as, "I earn $50,000 per year! I earn $50,000 per year! I earn $50,000 per year!" over and over, you program this command deeper and deeper into your subconscious mind. Eventually, this goal is accepted by your subconscious mind and begins to take on a power of its own. Very soon, things will start to happen inside you and around you to help make this goal a reality.

You will find that people who are described as lucky are always talking confidently about the things that they want and about the specific things they can do to get them. They recognize that, just as you become what you think about, *you get what you talk about*, as well. So they make sure that what they talk about is what they truly want, and not what they *don't want*.

Your Outer Life Reflects Your Inner Life

The Law of Correspondence explains one of the most powerful of all luck factors. This timeless principle underlies and explains almost everything that happens to you. It says that *your outer world tends to be a mirror image of your inner world*. What is going on outside of you is a reflection or manifestation of what is going on inside of you. And it cannot be otherwise.

When you stand in front of a mirror and you see your reflection, you know that this picture is determined by what you are presenting to the mirror. When you look at each part of your life, you will see your own attitudes and beliefs reflected back to you. *You do not see the world the way it is, but the way you are.* The person you are inside primarily determines what is happening to you on the outside.

Your character and your personality largely determine the quality of your relationships with other people. Your attitude and the way people react to you is largely determined by your own beliefs and expectations and your attitude toward yourself. Your inner level of desire and determination creates your outer world of success and financial achievement. People are poor on the outside primarily because they are poor on the inside.

Your levels of health and fitness on the *outside* are largely determined by the way you think about your health and fitness on the *inside*. People who think about food all the time tend to be overweight and unfit. People who think about health and fitness all the time tend to be thin, trim, and highly energetic. Health and fitness always begin with your thinking.

The Law of Mental Equivalence

The summary principle of all of these mental laws, and perhaps the most important luck factor of all, is the Law of Mental Equivalence. This law says that *what you experience in your life is the mental equivalent of what you create in your mind*.

Your main aim is, therefore, to create within yourself the mental equivalent of what you wish to enjoy on the outside. To enjoy greatly, and to achieve greatly, you must build up within yourself the consciousness of success, health, happiness, prosperity, and personal achievement consistent with what you really want. You must create your desired reality *in your mind* before you can experience it in your world. And you have complete control over your own mind.

You can start at any time to create this mental equivalent. It is not your past thoughts or your future thoughts that determine your life and your destiny. It is only the thoughts that you think right now, in the present moment. You are not bound by the mistakes of the past or the uncertainties of the future. Your potential is unlimited because you are *free to choose* your thoughts at this moment, and what you think at this moment determines the future direction of your life.

Grab the Steering Wheel of Your Own Life

If you are driving down the road, and you turn the wheel of your car sharply in one direction or the other, that is the direction that you will go at that moment. If you keep your car moving in that new direction, that will determine where you end up. Your future is not determined by how you drove yesterday, or how you drive tomorrow. It is determined by what you think and do right now.

You cannot control the entire world. You cannot control all the intricate and infinite details of modern life. You cannot control all the years that lie behind or the years that lie ahead, but you can control this present moment. Fortunately, this is all that you need to do to create your own future and achieve all the success that is possible for you.

Control the Influences That Affect You

Your mind is continually changing, based on what is going on in the world around you. The information and influences that you allow into your mind during the day have a major impact on the evolution and direction of your thinking. These changes in your thinking can either be conscious, deliberate, and positive or they can be random, haphazard, and negative.

The *power of suggestion* influences the way you think, feel, and behave. It affects the person you are and the person you become. The influences bombarding your mind each day are creating a force field of attraction that is either bringing you things you want or things you don't want.

Because you tend to be sensitive to your environment, you must take control over the influences that you allow to reach your conscious mind. Just as you would only eat healthy nutritious foods if you wanted to be superbly fit physically, you must only take in healthy, nutritious mental influences if you want to be superbly fit mentally, as well. You should read inspiring material, listen to positive audio programs, watch uplifting educational video programs, and associate with positive people. You must guard your mental integrity as a sacred thing.

Take Charge of Your Life

Another factor that is guaranteed to increase the number of lucky breaks you get in life is the *acceptance of complete responsibility* for yourself, and for everything that happens to you. The mark of excellent people is that they refuse to make excuses, blame others, or complain about their situations. Instead, they say, over and over, "I am responsible!"

In the final analysis, since you become what you think about, and only you can think your thoughts, you *are* completely responsible for every aspect of your life. You are where you are and what you are because you have decided to be there. If there is any part of your life that you don't like, you are responsible for changing it.

The acceptance of responsibility is the great liberator. It puts you completely in charge of your life, and of everything that happens to you. Since your thinking controls your destiny, by taking charge of your thoughts, you can control the rest of your life.

By deciding to think only about the things you want, you can become an extremely lucky person. You will activate your reticular cortex (the part of your brain that alerts you to things that are important to you) and get it working for you. You will program your subconscious mind. You will increase the probabilities that you will achieve the success you desire. Meanwhile, you can stop doing the things that are holding you back. You can decide to reject any ideas that limit your belief in your own potential.

If you buy a brand new, beautifully engineered car from the dealership and take it out on the road and it runs beautifully, do you ascribe it to luck? Of course not! The fact is that whether it is a sophisticated piece of sound equipment, a hand crafted watch, or a beautiful automobile, you know that each of them was built according to specific laws of mechanics, physics, and electricity. The fact that they run beautifully is not luck.

It is the same with you. When you begin applying these luck factors to your life, you will start to achieve extraordinary things. You will surge ahead of the people around you. You will enjoy greater success and accomplishment than you ever imagined. You will create a wonderful future for yourself. And it will be the result of design, not luck.

ACTION EXERCISES
What You Can Do Now

1. Resolve today that you are going to think and talk about only those things that you really want in your life. What are they?

2. Challenge your self-limiting beliefs; identify the negative ideas you have that are holding you back, and then act as if they weren't true.

3. Expect the best in every situation. Imagine that you have been guaranteed great success in everything you do, and act accordingly.

4. Identify your biggest problem or source of worry today. What can you learn from it that will make you better and stronger in the future?

5. Program your mind for success by repeated personal affirmations of your goals in the present positive tense—I can. . . .

6. Control the suggestive influences in your environment; continually feed your mind with positive books, audios, people, and conversations.

7. Discipline yourself to look for something good or helpful in every experience. You will always find it.

Principle 2—Clarity Is Critical

"The greatest thing that a man can do in this world is to make the most possible out of the stuff that has been given him. This is success and there is no other."

—Orison Swett Marden

Perhaps the most important of all luck factors is knowing exactly what you want, in each area of your life. The primary reason for great success is clear, specific, measurable goals and plans, written down and accompanied by a burning desire to accomplish them. Knowing what you want dramatically increases the probabilities that you will get it.

The primary reason for underachievement and failure is fuzziness and confusion about goals. Failure comes from the inability to decide exactly what you want, what it will look like, when you want it, and how you will attain it. As motivational speaker Zig Ziglar says, the great majority of people are "wandering generalities" rather than "meaningful specifics." The fact is that *you can't hit a target that you can't see.* If you don't know where you're going, you will probably end up somewhere else. You have to have goals.

A person without goals is like a ship without a rudder, carried whichever way the tides and wind are blowing. A person with clear, specific goals is like a ship with a rudder, sailing straight and true to its destination.

It is amazing how fast you change your luck by becoming intensely goal oriented. As a wealthy friend of mine once said, "Success is goals, and all else is commentary." Goals may not be the only reason for success, but no success is possible without them!

There Are No Coincidences

Some people believe in coincidences. They believe in the power of random events to make and shape a person's life. But the fact is that in most cases, coincidences don't just happen. They can almost always be traced back to previous events and mental preparation, as explained earlier in this book.

Rather than coincidences, there are, instead, a variety of different probabilities that particular events will occur. According to the Law of Averages, if you try enough different things, like billiard balls rolling around the table, one or two of them are going to bang into each other. But this coming together of different events is based on law, not luck or coincidence.

Look for Serendipity in Everything

There are two important principles that are essential luck factors, and have been so throughout history. The most successful men and women experience them regularly. An understanding of these principles can open your eyes to potentials and possibilities that you may have never understood or been aware of in the past.

The first of these luck factors is the principle of Serendipity. Serendipity has been best described as the "capacity for making happy discoveries along the road of life." The principle of Serendipity comes from the fairy tale of the three princes of Serendip. These three princes traveled around, coming upon experience after experience of misfortune and seeming disaster in the lives of others. But as a result of their visits and the happy discoveries they made, the disasters or tragedies were turned into greater successes and happinesses than before.

On one occasion, the three princes came to a farmhouse where an unfortunate accident had taken place. The farmer's only son had been thrown from the farmer's only horse and had broken his leg. The horse had then run off and could not be found. The farmer was quite distressed, but the three princes told him not to worry, "It's too soon to judge; something good will happen."

This country happened to be involved in a war at that time with a neighboring country. The next morning, a squad of soldiers arrived at the house to forcefully conscript all young, able-bodied men into the army. As it happened, the farmer's only son had a broken leg so he was spared from conscription.

Later that day, representatives of the government came by to seize all horses that could be used by the army. But since their only horse had run off, again the farmer was spared. Later, the army lost a great battle and most of the men and horses were killed. What appeared to be an unfortunate event, the breaking of the leg and the escape of the horse, turned out to be the salvation of the farmer.

Some time later, after the war, the horse came home of its own accord, leading several other wild horses. The son's leg soon mended. And the farmer was happy. An apparent disaster turned out to be a series of blessings in disguise. This sort of thing will happen to you as well, over and over, if you allow it and you look for it.

In another story, the three princes of Serendip came across a wealthy landowner whose entire estate had been washed away by a flood. Everything he had accumulated in his lifetime was destroyed. As you can imagine, he was distraught and depressed. But the three princes of Serendip convinced him that something good would turn up.

As they walked across the land where all the soil had been washed away by the flood, they found a precious stone, then another, and another. It turned out that the flood had revealed countless precious stones that made the landowner wealthier than he had ever imagined.

Develop an Attitude of Positive Expectancy

The key to understanding serendipity is the principle of *positive expectations*. This principle says that the more confidently you expect something good to happen, the more likely it is to occur. The one common denominator of a serendipitous event is that it only occurs when you are completely confident that all will work out for the best, and when you are looking for something good in every setback or difficulty. Then, surprisingly, all kinds of happy occurrences take place, many of which initially appear as failures or unfortunate events. They later turn out to be exactly what needed to happen for you to achieve your ultimate goal.

Your Current Situation Is Exactly What You Need

Here is an important philosophical principle: *Your situation today is exactly what you need, at this moment, for your own personal growth and development.* Every part of your life is exactly as it should be. Every difficulty you are facing or dealing with today contains within it possibilities that you can turn to your own advantage to achieve the kind of life that you want for yourself.

You may be working for a difficult boss in an industry where the competition is fierce, the margins are low, and your potential future seems limited. If you are not careful, you may become negative about your job and worry about your current situation. But if you realize that, according to the principle of Serendipity, it is exactly what you need at this moment, you can look into it for the benefit or advantage it might contain.

You can ask yourself, "If I was not doing this job, knowing what I now know about the job and its future, would I get into this field in the first place?" If your answer is "No," then your next question could be, "If I could do anything I really wanted, what would it be?"

Whatever it is, you can use your current experience as a springboard to higher and better experiences rather than just sitting there, wishing and hoping that things will improve. You only learn the right course for you by following the wrong course temporarily.

Think about the Future

Another luck factor is explained in the rule that *It doesn't matter where you are coming from; all that really matters is where you are going.*

The past is dead. It cannot be changed. It serves only to give you guidance and wisdom so that you can make better decisions in the future. All that matters is where you are going from this moment forward. You can't allow yourself to cry over spilled milk. Look upon the past as a sunken cost, as an investment in your life that is irretrievable. You can't get it back. Then, focus your attention on the future horizon of your own possibilities and begin moving in that direction.

The Principle of Synchronicity

This timeless principle explains perhaps the most important luck factor of all. It is intertwined and connected with many of the other principles in this book. It has been known about for thousands of years and is called *synchronicity*. It actually goes above and beyond, and works on a different plane than, the Law of Cause and Effect.

The Law of Cause and Effect says that every effect in your life has certain specific causes that you can relate to each other. The principle of Synchronicity on the other hand says that things will happen in your life that have no direct cause–effect relationship. Synchronicity happens when events that occur in your life are linked, not by causality, but by *meaning*. There will be no direct or discernible connection between events except for the meaning they have in relation to one of your goals.

A Hawaiian Vacation

Imagine that you get up one morning and talk with your spouse about how nice it would be to take a vacation to Hawaii. But you know you can't afford it and you couldn't get the time off, anyway. Nonetheless, the idea of going to Hawaii is very attractive to you. It stimulates your mind. Your emotions of desire and interest are aroused by the idea of a Hawaiian vacation.

Any thought you *emotionalize*, including the idea of going to Hawaii, is passed from your conscious mind to your subconscious mind, the seat of the Law of Attraction. As a result, you begin to send out positive vibrations that start to attract into your life people and circumstances that will make that thought a reality. You begin to activate the principle of synchronicity.

You go to work that day fantasizing about someday taking a trip to Hawaii with your spouse. Completely unexpectedly, your boss calls you in a couple of hours later and tells you that, because you've been doing such a great job, and that because the company is now in the slow season, there would be no problem if you wanted to take a week or two off as your vacation.

At lunchtime, a friend of yours tells you about a new travel agency that puts together Hawaiian vacation packages, including hotel, airfare, and ground transportation, at really great prices. In fact, your friend has a brochure that has a description of exactly the island that you wanted to visit and a hotel that would be ideal for you. And the price is less than $2,000 for both of you for an entire week in Hawaii.

That night, you get home, and there is an income tax refund in the mail for an unexpected overpayment that amounts to—you guessed it—about $2,000!

Notice what has happened. You had a very clear, emotionally charged idea of taking a trip to Hawaii with your spouse. That day, three events occurred, none of them having any connection with each other, but all of which worked together to enable you to achieve your goal in less than one day.

Get Yourself into the Zone

This sort of synchronous event will begin to happen to you regularly once you get into the zone. This is the mental state where you feel and perform at your best. (Being "in the zone" is a common phrase in athletics.) When you emotionalize your mind, clarify your thoughts, intensify your desires, and approach your life with an attitude of confident, positive expectations, all sorts of serendipitous and synchronous events begin to occur in your life. The only relationship that these events have to each other is the *meaning* that you give them by the thoughts you think.

Alas, if your thoughts are fuzzy, confused, and contradictory, these principles cannot work for you. This lack of clarity is the primary reason that most people are unhappy and unsuccessful. They have enormous potential powers but they are failing to use them to their best advantage because they don't understand how they work.

Getting a Better Job

Here's another example of synchronicity, a true story. A friend of mine was unhappy in his job. He and his wife talked about how much better off he would be if he could get a better job in a different field. They discussed his wanting to work for a smaller company, where there were more opportunities for pay and promotion based on merit, rather than a rigid salary structure that put a ceiling on what he could earn.

The next night they went out for dinner at a nice restaurant. But the restaurant was full and they had lost his reservation. So instead of going home, they went to a nearby restaurant that had one table free. At the next table was a friend of his that he hadn't seen for some time. This friend and his wife were having dinner with another couple. The male member of the other couple was the president of a rapidly growing business in town. They had just been talking about how hard it was to find ambitious people who were looking for opportunity rather than security. They began chatting from table to table, and the first thing that the young man said was that he was looking for a job that had greater opportunities for advancement.

The president gave him his business card and asked him to call the following week. He called, made an appointment, went through an interview process and got the job. A year later he was earning twice as much. He and his wife had moved to a nicer home, bought a new car, and were living a much better life.

Most people would say that this was an example of luck, but you know by now that it was an example of *synchronicity*. The young man was clear, confident, and optimistic about what he wanted. As a result, he triggered a series of forces in the universe that not only canceled one reservation and opened another, but also sat him at exactly the right table at the right time next to the right person, who had the right opportunity for him at that time of his life.

The young man could have stayed at home that night, reading the newspaper and watching television. In that case, probably nothing would have happened. Then, he could tell everyone he was stuck in a crummy job because he had bad luck. But he made his own good luck by taking action, just as he would have made his own bad luck by doing nothing. You and I are doing the same sort of thing every day, with every decision we make and every action we take.

The Power of Strategic Thinking

Clarity is a critical luck factor. The clearer you are about what you want, the more rapidly you will attain it. When you are absolutely clear about your goals, you activate all the powers of your mind to help you to achieve them. You develop a better sense for the specific activities you can engage in to move you faster toward them. You can make better and faster decisions about the allocation of time and resources. This is true in both personal and business life.

For example, businesses with clear, written strategic plans are far more successful than businesses that are operating from the seat of their pants. It may take a good deal of time, perhaps many hours and even many days, to write out a strategic plan. But once completed, the strategic plan becomes a blueprint for the future of the company. It gives the company a clear track to run on, and benchmarks against which to measure success. A strategic plan allows the company, and everyone in it, to focus on high value activities.

The purpose of strategic planning in business is to increase the *return on equity*, the financial return on the capital invested in the business. A good strategic plan enables the people in the company to focus on those few things the company can do to get the highest returns from the people and resources at work in the business.

As an individual, you will also be more focused and effective when you have a *personal* strategic plan. However, instead of attempting to increase your *return on equity*, your aim in personal strategic planning is to increase your *return on energy*.

Just as a company has financial capital to invest in its business activities, you have *human* capital to invest in your life. Your human capital is *mental, emotional, and physical*. Your goal is to get the highest possible return on your investment of yourself in your work and in your personal life.

Don't Be Like Columbus

Everyone wants to be happy. But I have found that almost every unhappy person, if you probe deeply enough, will confess to having no real goals. Unhappy people have no clear sense of meaning and purpose in life. They are like Columbus, who set off for the new world not knowing where he was *going*. When he got there, he didn't know where he *was*. And when he got back, he didn't know where he had *been*. This is how most people live their entire lives.

Success Is Not an Accident

Instead of practicing the principles of control and self-determination, most people live unconsciously by the Law of Accident. This law says that *failing to plan means planning to fail*.

People who live by the Law of Accident believe that life is a series of random, haphazard events, like the throwing of dice or the turning of a roulette wheel. They believe that "It's not what you know, but who you know." They say things like, "You can't fight City Hall."

People who live by the Law of Accident are those who buy lottery tickets, go to casinos, invest in get-rich-quick schemes, penny stocks, and investments that they don't know anything about. They are always hoping for a lucky break and never getting one. People who live by the Law of Accident are usually the most envious of those who are successfully living by the Law of Control, or the principle of goal orientation.

Different Rewards for the Same Job

In every industry, there are people who are doing very much the same job but who are earning far more or far less than others. It is quite common for me to meet two people, selling the same product, out of the same office, under the same competitive conditions, to the same people, at the same prices, but one of them is earning up to ten times as much as the other. There is very little difference between them in age, education, experience, intelligence, or any other factor, yet one person, sometimes the younger person, is earning several times as much as the other person. What is the reason for this?

You already know part of the answer. It is because the more successful person has done many little things to increase the probabilities of success in his or her particular field. The less successful person has *failed* to do these things. Just as you reap what you sow, you fail to reap what you don't sow. If you don't put it in, you don't get it out. If you do not trigger the action, you don't get the reaction.

Almost invariably, the highest paid people in America, in every field, have personal strategic plans. These people are intensely goal oriented. They know exactly what they want. They have written plans and blueprints, with schedules and action plans to achieve them. They work on them every day.

The clearer you are about what you want, and the more confident you are about achieving it, the more you will activate the Laws of Belief, Expectations, Attraction, Correspondence, and Mental Equivalence. The more positive you are, the more you enjoy the phenomena of serendipity and synchronicity. The greater clarity you have, the more your life becomes a continuous series of happy events and circumstances that move you toward your goal, and move your goal toward you.

Take Control of Your Life

The *principle of control* is a vital luck factor. This principle, based on years of psychological research, says that *You feel positive about yourself to the degree to which you feel you are* in control *of your own life; you feel negative about yourself to the degree to which you feel that you are* not in control, *or that you are controlled by external forces or other people.*

There is a direct relationship between high performance and happiness on the one hand and a sense of control in your life on the other. The more you feel that you are in charge of what is happening to you, the more personal power you experience. The more you feel that you are the architect of your own destiny and the master of your own fate, the happier and the more positive, energetic, and purposeful you become.

However, if you feel that your life is controlled by your boss, your bills, your health, your relationships, your upbringing, your race or any other factor, you will feel out of control. You will feel anxious, negative, and angry. You will feel like a victim, innocent of your situation and unable to change it. You will lash out and blame other people for your problems. You will resent successful people and be envious of anyone who is doing better than you are. You will, in effect, set yourself up for failure because you will attract into your life more and more of the people and circumstances that reflect your negative frame of mind.

The Starting Point of Success

The starting point of success and happiness is for you to take control of your life. The wonderful thing about goals is that they give you a sense of control over the *direction* of change in your life. Goals give you the feeling that you are in the driver's seat, that you have your hands on the wheel. Goals make you feel that your life is going in the direction you want it to go.

The more you feel in control of every part of your life the more positive and optimistic you become. The more positive and optimistic you become, the more you activate all the mental laws and principles in your life and the more luck you will seem to experience.

The Power of Purpose

Another luck factor is *intensity of purpose*. As Benjamin Disraeli said, "*The secret of success is constancy of purpose.*"

All really successful people are extremely focused and purposeful. If you find two people with roughly the same abilities, the one who *wants* it the most—the more intense of the two—is the one who will almost always be more successful. Decide exactly what you really want in each area of your life, and then focus intensely, like a laser beam, on achieving it. Resolve to stay at it, no matter how long it takes. Decide in advance that you will never give up.

Start with the Inner Game

In designing your personal strategic plan, start from the *inside* and work outward. Start from the inner core of your being, your innermost values and convictions. You then organize every aspect of your daily life and activities so that your behavior and your daily actions are congruent with your fundamental, unifying principles.

In this area of goals, begin with yourself. *What are your values?* What do you believe in? What do you stand for, and equally important, what would you not stand for?

Do you believe in the values of honesty, sincerity, generosity, compassion, caring, love, forgiveness, and truth? Do you believe in the values of integrity, personal excellence, creativity, freedom, and self-expression? Do you believe in the values of friendship, self-discipline, work, self-development, and success? What are *your* values?

Your ability to ask and answer these questions for yourself is the starting point of maximum achievement and personal greatness. These answers are indispensable to unlocking your full potential, and to your determining exactly what it is you really want in life. When you know who you really are *inside*, only then can you decide what you really want on the *outside*.

You need about three to five core values to build a great life and character. You can add others later. But these are enough for a personal strategic plan. Once you have selected your core values, you should then organize them by importance. Which is most important to you? Which comes second? Which comes third? And so on.

How can you tell your true values? It is simple. You always express your values in your *actions*. You demonstrate to yourself and others what you truly believe by looking at what you do, especially when you are *under pressure*. Whenever you are forced to choose between one action and another, you will always select the action that is consistent with your dominant value at that moment.

If a person says, "My family is my most important value," this means that, when forced to choose, he will always pick his family. If a person says that health is his key value, he will always act to maintain the health and well-being of both himself and the people he most cares about.

But remember, it is not what you say, or wish, or hope, or intend, or plan to do or be someday. It is only what you *do* that counts. Your actions tell yourself and everyone around you who you really are. This principle is as true in business and political life as it is in personal relationships and life.

What Is Your Vision for Your Future?

Once you have determined your values, you then move on to create your personal *vision*. Your vision is a picture of your ideal life sometime in the future. You create your vision for yourself, your family, your career or business, by imagining that you have *no limitations* whatsoever. Imagine that you could wave a magic wand and create a perfect future. What would it look like?

Leaders are different from average people in that they have *vision*. Men and women who are going somewhere with their lives have a clear vision of what it will look like when they get there. The development of a compelling, exciting vision for your future is one of the most important steps you take in creating your own future.

As an exercise, imagine that you won $10 million cash, after taxes, or that you inherited it from a long lost relative. What would you do *differently?* How would you design your perfect life? Imagine that if you can just be clear about what it will look like, this ideal future life is guaranteed to you. With this vision guiding you, you then think about what you could do every day to make it a reality.

Leaders Have Vision

One of the qualities of leaders in every field is that they have a vision of an ideal, exciting future for themselves, their families, and their organizations. They allow themselves to dream. They create a picture of what is possible rather than allowing themselves to get stuck with what exists at the present moment. George Bernard Shaw, the famous English playwright, once wrote, "Most men look at the world and ask 'why?' I look at the world and ask 'why not?' "

There are thousands of men and women all over America who have risen to great heights from humble beginnings. Many of them came from foreign countries and started with no advantages at all. But the one thing they did have was dreams. And they believed that they had the ability to achieve their dreams. Because they intensely believed in themselves, and were determined to do whatever was necessary to fulfill their dreams, they activated all of the mental laws and principles we have talked about. In a few short years, everyone around them was talking about how *lucky* they were to be so successful.

Create a Mission Statement

Once you have a vision for your ideal future, you can write out your personal mission statement. Your mission is different from your vision. While your vision is an ideal *image* of a desired future state, your mission is a specific *statement* of the kind of person you want to become sometime in the future. Your mission statement describes how you want to make a difference with your life, and how you are going to make a difference in the lives of other people.

When Albert Einstein was asked the purpose of human life, he replied, *"Why, it must be to serve others. What other purpose could there be?"*

Your mission statement also tells how you would like to be described by others in the future. Stephen Covey suggests that you write out your personal mission statement as if you were writing your own obituary. Define your mission as the way you would like to be remembered, with the description that you would want a trusted friend to read at your funeral.

Your personal mission statement serves as a guide for your behavior toward other people throughout your life. It is an expression of your values in action. For example, if one of your values was honesty, your mission with regard to honesty could be, "I am completely honest with myself and others in every situation, no matter what the cost. I always keep my word and I can be trusted implicitly under all conditions."

You also need a mission statement for your work. This mission statement for your business and your career should be in harmony with your personal mission statement, but be more specific in certain ways. It should be both measurable and achievable. You should be able to accomplish a business mission, like a military mission, and then go home.

For example, at one time the mission statement of AT&T was to "Bring a telephone within the reach of every person in America." It took AT&T almost 80 years to achieve that goal. That mission statement guided the activities of one of the world's most successful companies for almost a century. Once it was achieved, however, AT&T needed a new mission, which they failed to develop. They have floundered ever since.

Your business mission could be something like the following: "I am an outstanding professional salesperson, among the top 10 percent in my industry. I give the very finest quantity and quality of service, reliability and honest dealing with every customer, and as a result I earn more than $50,000 per year in my field."

This is a mission statement that defines the level of income you want to attain in your field, the kind of work that you are going to do to attain that level, and how you will measure that you have achieved your goal. An objective third party could look at your behavior and your results and tell you how close you are to fulfilling your mission.

The One-Two Combination

The wonderful thing about having both a vision and a mission statement is that by thinking about them, and reviewing them regularly, you activate and cause all the mental laws to work in your life. You actually start to become the kind of person that you have imagined, and you begin creating the ideal future you have dreamed about. You take charge of shaping your own character and your own destiny.

Remember, you *do* become what you think about most of the time. When you think about yourself continually as an absolutely excellent human being, in time you will become very much like that excellent person you have imagined. When you think about your perfect future, you will soon attract into your life everything you need to make it come true for you.

The Fire of Desire

You can improve your probabilities of achieving great success by increasing the intensity of your desire for your goal. The only real limitation on what you can accomplish is *how badly you really want it*. Your desire determines your destiny. It is the fire of desire that determines your intensity of purpose. When you have a burning desire to achieve a goal of any kind, you will be both pulled by it and driven toward it. *Desire is the fuel in the furnace of ambition*. Desire is the power in your personality. The primary reason people accomplish great things is because they are passionate about what it is they really want. They become irresistible and unstoppable.

Desire comes from deep within you. It is rooted in the depths of your personality and your true values. The only way that you can have an intense, burning desire for a specific goal, personal or otherwise, is for that goal to be an expression of your true values and consistent with your vision of the person you really want to become in your life.

Create Your Own Dream List

Here is a wonderful exercise for you. Take a piece of paper and begin to create your own personal dream list. Let your mind float freely. Imagine that you have no limitations. Imagine that you have all the time, all the money, all the resources, all the intelligence, all the education, all the experience, and all the contacts in the world. Imagine that you could do, be, or have anything in your life. Write down everything you would want in your life if you had no limitations whatsoever on your potential.

Be sure to decide what you really want before you decide what is possible. Don't fall into the trap of limiting yourself in advance by thinking of all the reasons why it's not possible before you even begin writing. Put the word *possible* aside for now and just allow yourself to dream.

Make a List of Your Goals

Once you've finished your dream list, take another sheet of paper and write today's date at the top. Then make a list of at least 10 goals that you want to accomplish in the next 12 months. This is one of the most powerful goal achieving exercises you will ever learn. It is both simple and powerful, and all it requires is a piece of paper, a pen, and a few minutes of your time

A full 97 percent of adults have no written goals. When you make out a list of 10 goals that you want to accomplish in the next 12 months, you move yourself into the top 3 percent of people living and working today. By the simple discipline of committing your goals to paper, you join the elite.

Interestingly enough, if all you did was to write out a list of 10 goals, and then put that sheet of paper away somewhere where you wouldn't find it for a year, your whole life would change. At the end of 12 months, when you opened up that sheet of paper, you would be astonished to find that as many as 8 of your 10 goals had been achieved in the most remarkable ways.

You would notice amazing incidences of synchronicity and serendipity behind the attainment of each of your goals. You would see a remarkable string of interconnected coincidences that you could not have predicted or planned. But the bottom line is this: You will have accomplished 8 of your 10 goals in ways that you cannot now even imagine. And all it costs for you to make this exercise work in your life is a piece of paper, a pen, and about 10 minutes.

A Proven Life Changer

I have given this exercise to tens of thousands of people all over the world. I have never had anyone come back to me and say that it didn't work. In fact, many people say that their entire lives changed after they did this exercise, sometimes in as little as 30 days. And the more successful you are already, the faster and greater will be your results when you write down these 10 goals.

Not long ago, I gave a talk to a room full of high-powered financial executives. During the morning session, I recommended that they each write out 10 goals for themselves before the end of the day. At the beginning of the afternoon session, I asked them how many had already written down their 10 goals? Fully 60 percent of the audience had already completed them by lunchtime! By the end of the day more than 90 percent of them had their goals done. And I am quite sure that they all had their goal lists complete before they went to bed that night.

Over the next 12 months, that division went on to break every sales record in the company. The people in that room became some of the top money earners in the industry. They still talk about this exercise and rewrite their goals every year. They consider goal writing to be their secret weapon. It can be yours as well.

Determine Your Major Definite Purpose

Once you have a list of 10 goals, go through it and ask yourself, *"Which one goal on this list would have the greatest positive impact on my life if I accomplished it?"*

Whichever it is, take that goal and write it at the top of another sheet of paper. This goal now becomes your *major definite purpose* for the foreseeable future. This becomes the goal that you think about and work on most of the time. This becomes the central organizing principle of your activities.

Definiteness of purpose enables you to set better priorities, make better decisions, and do more of those things that will help you achieve your goal. By writing down 10 goals, selecting your most important goal, and deciding upon that as your major definite purpose, you move yourself into the top 1 percent of adults in our society.

Make a Plan to Achieve Your Goal

Below your goal on that sheet of paper, write out every single action that you can possibly think of that you could do now or in the future to achieve that goal.

This is an important exercise. The more different actions that you can think of to take that will help you achieve your goal, the greater clarity you will have. You will become more convinced that your goal is attainable. You will become more confident and determined. You will be more eager to get started and to keep going when you have a list of activities to work on.

When you write down your goal the first time, you may experience doubts and misgivings. Although you wish and hope for that goal, you may be doubtful and even critical of your ability to achieve it. But when you begin to plan out the necessary steps you need to take, starting today, you begin to see your goal in a whole new light.

The greater the detail with which you plan the achievement of your goal, the more achievable it appears. By writing out your goals and plans, you plant them deeper into your subconscious mind. You increasingly believe that they are possible for you to achieve. You start to attract ideas, people, and resources that help you to achieve them.

Take Action on Your Plan

Once you have a list of activities, select at least one and take action on it immediately. From the first time you take action on your list, you will begin to see progress. This progress will motivate you to take additional actions. You will begin to experience examples of synchronicity in the events and circumstances that surround you. You will feel more in control of your life.

By writing, planning, and working toward your goal, you will activate your reticular cortex. You will be more aware of people and possibilities around you that can help you to achieve that goal. You will have more energy and focus. You will be more clear and positive. You will begin to create your own future. And all it takes is a piece of paper and a few minutes of your time.

Winners Ask the Right Questions

Here is a key difference between winners and losers. The *loser* hears about this exercise of writing down 10 goals, selecting one, and then working on it every day, but then asks, "What if it doesn't work?"

But that's the wrong question. The right question to ask, the question the winner asks is, "What if it *does* work?"

If it doesn't work, all it costs you is a piece of paper and a few minutes of your time. However, if this 10-goal method works, it can change your life forever. Of course, if it doesn't work, you will be one of the few people among countless thousands for which this exercise has not worked. In fact, you would probably have to be an extremely determined person to stop this exercise from working, in spite of yourself.

However, the fact is that it *does* work. And it works faster than you could imagine. Give it a try and see for yourself.

Miracles Do Happen

A financial advisor attended my seminar in Phoenix, Arizona on a Saturday morning. He flew back to Houston that afternoon. The following Thursday he phoned my office and spoke to my secretary. Then he wrote me a letter in some detail that told what he had done after he had left the seminar. This is what happened to him.

He said that he had heard about goals many times before but he had avoided writing them down. He decided that, as a result of my recommendation, he would write down 10 goals for the next 12 months, which he did on the plane ride home on Saturday afternoon. He said that by Sunday night at 7 o'clock, in less than 24 hours, he had already accomplished 5 of the 10 one-year goals he had set for himself. And these were both financial and family goals.

So he quickly wrote out five more goals so that he had a list of ten goals to start the week. By Thursday evening at 5 o'clock when he called my office, four days later, he had already accomplished 5 more of his new list of 10 goals.

In his letter he said, "I can quite honestly say that I have accomplished more in six days with clear, written goals, than I really expected to achieve in an entire year. I was simply amazed!"

I have files full of letters from people who have written and told me similar stories. I never go to a seminar that someone doesn't come up and tell me of an experience just like this. I could do an entire audio program or book based on stories of people who went home and wrote down their 10 goals, made plans to accomplish them, and got busy. Their whole lives were different as a result.

The Principle of Accelerating Acceleration

Once you have your goals written out, there are a series of powerful mental techniques that you can use to move yourself faster toward your goals and to move your goals more rapidly toward yourself. The *principle of accelerating acceleration* is a powerful luck factor that you can use for goal attainment. This principle says that whatever you are moving toward begins moving toward you as well. Like attracts like. In a way, this is a corollary of the Law of Attraction, but with one important difference.

When you first set a new, big goal and begin moving toward it, your progress will often be quite slow. You may be frustrated and think of giving up. The bigger your goal, the further away it will seem. You may have to work on it for a long time before you see any progress at all. But this is all part of the process of goal attainment.

The *20/80 rule* helps to explain the principle of accelerating acceleration. For the first 80 percent of the time that you are working toward your goal, you will only cover about 20 percent of the distance. However, if you persist and refuse to give up, you will accomplish the final 80 percent of your goal in the last 20 percent of the time that you spend working on it.

Many people work for weeks, months, and even years toward a big goal and see very little progress. They often lose heart and give up. But what they didn't realize is that they had laid all of the groundwork necessary and were almost at the take-off point. They were just about to start accelerating toward their goal, and their goal was about to start moving at a greater speed toward them.

This principle of accelerating acceleration seems to apply to almost every big goal that you set for yourself. You must therefore decide in advance that you will never give up. This decision is one of the most powerful of all luck factors.

Create Affirmation Cards for Each Goal

Here is another powerful exercise you can practice to increase the speed at which you attain your goals. Write each of your goals on a three-by-five-inch index card, one card per goal. Write each goal in a *personal, present tense, and positive* affirmative statement. This method is like putting your foot onto the accelerator of your own life.

For example, you could write goals like, "I weigh 156 pounds." "I earn $50,000 per year." "I speak Spanish fluently and well." Write each of your goals in large letters on a single three-by-five-inch index card and carry the cards around with you.

Read and reread these goal cards each morning when you get up, and each evening before you go to bed. As you read these goals, visualize and imagine the goal as if it were already attained. Create an exciting mental picture of your goal as a reality. See it as vividly and as clearly as you possibly can.

Here is the multiplier: Combine the mental picture of your goal with the same *feeling* or emotion that you will enjoy when you achieve your goal. As you think about that beautiful car you want to drive, imagine the feeling of happiness and pleasure that you will have when you drive away in that car.

Many top salespeople use this exercise to visualize being the top salesperson for their company, and winning the top award at the national sales convention. They visualize and imagine themselves walking up onto the stage and receiving the award from the president. They hear the applause of the audience. They create within themselves the feeling of pride and satisfaction that they will enjoy when they attain that award. And over and over, these people go on to become the top performers in their organizations.

One of the most important of all success principles in creating your own future is the power of concentration. This principle says that *whatever you dwell upon grows and increases in your world.*

The more you think about, talk about, visualize, and emotionalize a desired goal, the more of your mind works to draw that goal toward you, and to move you toward that goal. *Anything you can hold in your mind on a continuing basis, you can have.* Your ability to concentrate singlemindedly on a key goal sharpens all your mental abilities, increases your creativity, and releases energy for goal attainment.

The clearer you are about your goals, the more you activate all of your mental powers. You create a force field of energy around yourself that causes wonderful things to happen to you. You attract amazing opportunities and possibilities that other people describe as luck.

The fact that you are reading this book means that you are already in the top 10 percent, perhaps the top 5 percent of people living today. You are among what has been called the *talented tenth*. You are a member of the elite.

The fact that you have come this far with this book means that you are in a special class, almost all by yourself. You are in the winner's circle. And it doesn't matter where you are in life or how much you are earning today, *all that matters is where you are going.*

The commitment that you are making to your life and to your future by determining your values, your vision, your mission, and your goals is the best indicator of where you are going to be in the years ahead. If you just continue in the same direction that you are going now, you will accomplish extraordinary things, and nothing will stop you. You will soon become known as one of the *luckiest* people in your personal world.

ACTION EXERCISES
What You Can Do Now

1. Review some of your successes and note the examples of serendipity and synchronicity that have happened for you in the past. How could you cause them to happen again?

2. Determine your vision of your ideal future and lifestyle; if your life were perfect in every way, what would it look like?

3. Sit down and write out your own personal dream list. Imagine that you have all the time, money, and ability in the world. What would you really want?

4. Make a list of 10 goals that you would like to accomplish in the next one or two years; write them in the present tense, as if they have already been accomplished.

5. Select the one goal that would have the greatest positive impact on your life if you were to achieve it. Make this your major definite purpose, and think about it all the time.

6. Make a plan to achieve your major goal, complete with deadlines and subdeadlines, as well as measures and priorities.

7. Take action immediately on your goal; do something every day to move you toward it. And resolve that you will never give up!

Principle 3—Knowledge Is Power

"Blessed is the man who finds wisdom, the man who gains understanding, for she is more profitable than silver and yields better returns than gold. She is more precious than rubies; nothing you desire can compare with her."
—Bible, Proverbs 3:13–15

There is a race on today and you are in it. The only question is whether you are going to win or lose. And this is largely up to you. One advantage you have is that the great majority of people aren't aware that they are in a race. They are simply *strolling* along. They don't understand how competitive our world is today, and they don't realize how important it is to win.

There is a story from East Africa that makes this point. Every morning on the Serengeti Plains of Africa, a gazelle awakens. The gazelle knows that in the day ahead, he must run faster than the fastest lion if he wants to survive. And every morning on the Serengeti Plains, a lion awakens. The lion knows that he must run faster than the slowest gazelle if he wants to eat that day.

The moral of the story is that, whether you see yourself as a gazelle or a lion, when the sun comes up, *you'd better be running*.

Join the Information Age

It took 6,000 years of recorded history for man to move from the agricultural age into the industrial age, which officially began about

1815. By 1950, the majority of workers in the developed countries were industrial workers. But by 1960, in less than 150 years, the industrial age was over. We had entered into the Service Age. There were more people working at delivering services of all kinds than there were in manufacturing.

By the late 1980s, just 20 years later, we had left the Service Age, in terms of employment, and we had entered into the Information Age. There were more people working in the generation and processing of information than in any other area. As we move into the twenty-first century, we are already in the Communications Age. There are now more people employed in the generation and communication of information, ideas, entertainment, news, or education, than there are employed in any other single industry.

Just imagine! It took 6,000 years to go through the Agricultural Age, 150 years to pass through the Industrial Age, 20 years to move through the Service Age, 20 more years to pass through the Information Age, and we are now in the Age of Communication.

We have gone from muscle power to mind power, from brute power to brainpower. We have evolved from a focus on making and moving things to a focus on the creation and dissemination of ideas and knowledge. For the rest of your life, the knowledge content of your work, and your ability to communicate it, is largely going to determine the value of what you do, the amount of money you earn, and the overall quality of your life.

The Primary Source of Value

According to Moore's Law in computers, information processing capacity doubles every 18 months. At the same time, the cost of information processing drops by 50 percent. This is a staggering increase in efficiency! If the cost and efficiency of a new Lexus automobile had improved at the same rate as the improvement in computing capacity, a new Lexus today would cost $2.00, get 700 miles per gallon of gas and travel at 500 miles per hour. In fact, a new Lexus automobile today has more computer systems in it than the Apollo 13, which was the most advanced moon rocket of its time.

In a new automobile today, more money is spent on the electronics and the knowledge and information systems that run it than is spent on steel.

We have moved into the Information Age so quickly, with knowledge as the primary source of value, that most of the major institutions of society have not yet caught on or caught up. This is one of the great challenges, and opportunities, of our time.

What Is a Company Worth?

A friend of mine has a company that increased its sales from $1 million to $10 million per year over a period of five years and tripled its profits at the same time. Its bank then cut off its line of credit, categorizing the company as a high-risk organization. Why? Because the company had extremely high sales volume but it had not increased its fixed assets—its furniture, fixtures, buildings, cars, computers, and so on—at the same speed that it had increased its growth. The bank did not understand that *brainpower* is the company's primary resource, and that it can be used in an infinite number of ways to create wealth with virtually no investment at all in fixed assets.

Financial institutions today are often baffled at the fact that a $100 million factory can be rendered obsolete by technological change in as little as a year. When a bank today asks for collateral, it has no way of measuring the most valuable assets of the company, the knowledge that exists between the ears of the people who work there. The entire organization could burn to the ground tomorrow but the brainpower could walk across the street and start over again in a few hours.

Just a few decades ago, if a factory burned down, it was out of business. It might never be rebuilt. Sometimes an entire community built around that manufacturing plant would collapse. Today that is no longer the case.

The Winning Edge

The *Winning Edge Concept* is one of the most important ideas of the twentieth century. It says that small differences in knowledge and ability can lead to enormous differences in results. Here is an example: If a horse runs in a horse race and comes in first by a nose, it wins *ten times* as much as the horse that comes in second, by a nose. Does this mean that the horse is ten times faster? Is it twice as fast? Ten percent as fast?

No. The horse is only a *nose* faster, but a nose translates into ten times the prize money.

When a company gets the business in a competitive market, it is often only a tiny bit better than the company that failed to get the business. But the company that wins gets 100 percent of the sale, 100 percent of the profit, and the salesperson gets 100 percent of the commission. Is the company or salesperson 100 percent better than the company or salesperson who loses the deal? No. The company or salesperson has merely developed the "winning edge." And that makes all the difference.

One small piece of information that you have that your competitors lack can be all that it takes for you to gain the winning edge in a particular transaction. An executive said recently, "Our ability to learn and apply new ideas faster than our competition is our only real source of sustainable competitive advantage."

Lifelong Job Security

There is a good deal of talk today about insecurity in the labor force. People are being laid off by the thousands every month, in both good times and bad. This trend will continue, with massive lay-offs every year for the indefinite future. Rapid changes taking place in knowledge and information are creating new products and services, and rendering many current products and services obsolete. When demand shifts, people have to move quickly to jobs producing what customers want today, rather than what they wanted yesterday.

The sum total of human knowledge is doubling every two to three years. This means that you could take all the knowledge accumulated in human history, from every country and in every form, and put it into a huge pile. Three years from now, at most, there would be a pile of new knowledge next to it that is equal to or greater than the first pile.

Knowledge multiplies exponentially. A new piece of knowledge can be combined and recombined with other pieces of knowledge to create still more knowledge. By early in the twenty-first century, the total accumulated knowledge of mankind in certain areas will be doubling every year.

In personal terms, this means that today your knowledge must double every two to three years just for you to stay *even* at your current level of ability, at your current income, in your current field of work. If your personal knowledge is not increasing at the same speed that general knowledge is increasing in your field, you will be in great danger of becoming obsolete.

The main reason that people are laid off is that companies need new forms of knowledge and skill, and they need more knowledgeable people in newer, more specialized areas. Just as some companies are announcing lay-offs of thousands of people, other companies are hiring thousands of people, in different positions, with different knowledge, performing different tasks.

The Law of Integrative Complexity

The Law of Integrative Complexity explains an important luck factor that can help you to achieve vastly more than the average person. This law states that, "In every group of individuals, the person who can absorb, integrate, and apply the greatest quantity of essential information will eventually dominate all the other individuals within that group."

To put it another way, the Law of Integrative Complexity says that the more knowledge and experience you have relative to the particular needs of your organization, the more capable you will be to help the group to succeed and achieve its goals. Power, position, influence, and prestige tend to gravitate toward the person who acquires and then uses his or her knowledge the most effectively for the benefit of all.

Knowledge and experience give you the ability to recognize patterns in new situations that arise. The more repeating patterns you can recognize, the faster you can make decisions and take action in any given set of circumstances. The person with the greatest pattern-recognition ability will always rise to the top of any organization of value. His or her judgment and contribution will be of greater value and have greater impact on other people and on the results of the organization than anyone else.

Get Ahead and Stay Ahead

For example, the top salespeople tend to remain the top salespeople year after year. Why is this? It is because they have worked many weeks, months, and years to become increasingly knowledgeable and skilled at selling ever more of their products or services to ever more sophisticated and demanding customers.

As a result, like runners taking a lead and increasing it as the race goes on, the top salespeople pull ahead, and often way ahead, of their competitors by learning to recognize more and more patterns in more and more complex and varied sales situations. This enables them to identify a potential selling situation quickly. They immediately know what to do and say to get the additional business. As a result, they sell more and more.

With each additional sale, they acquire even more experience. This increased experience, and the patterns that accompany it, enable them to sell even more, faster and with greater ease, in the future. You've heard it said, "Nothing succeeds like success." This is what happens in virtually every competitive field.

Don't Rest on Your Laurels

With the rapid expansion of knowledge in your field, your existing store of knowledge is becoming obsolete at a more rapid rate than ever before. If you were to take a trip around the world in a catamaran and be gone for a year or two, when you got back, you would find that 30 percent, 40 percent, or even 50 percent of all the knowledge that you had accumulated that justified your salary and position in your business was no longer valid or of any use any more. You might even have to start over. Your business or industry might no longer exist.

In some fields, the rate of knowledge obsolescence is far faster than in others. For example, the knowledge of a historian or librarian, which are fields that change slowly, may take 10 or 20 years, or even longer to become obsolete. The knowledge of a stockbroker, of prices, market dynamics, interest rates, economic conditions, and so on, may become obsolete in a few days or even a few hours.

One significant political or economic event can so affect opinion polls as to make all the accumulated knowledge regarding the outcome of an election obsolete over night, and create a whole new scenario.

The Future Belongs to the Competent

If you want to be lucky, you must never forget that the future belongs to the competent. The future does not belong to the well meaning, the sincere, or the merely ambitious. It belongs to those who are very good at what they do. The future belongs to the people with the critical knowledge of how to get results, and those who are adding to their knowledge base every day.

There is an old saying that *the rich get richer and the poor get poorer*. Today, however, it is not a contest between those who have more and those who have less. It is a competition between those who know more and those who know less. The most significant differences in income in America are between those who are continually increasing their levels of knowledge and skill and those who are not.

To move ahead faster, especially in your financial life, you must remember that *to earn more, you must learn more*. You are maxed out today at your current level of knowledge and skill. Your glass ceiling is within yourself. If you want to increase your income and your earning ability, you have to learn new information, ideas, and skills that you can apply to your work to create added value for your company and your customers.

Knowledge Is Power

It has often been said that knowledge is power, but the fact is that only *applied* knowledge is power. Only knowledge that can be utilized to bring about a benefit that someone will pay for is power in today's economy.

How do you determine the value of a piece of new knowledge? Simple. Valuable knowledge increases your ability to get results for other people. Valueless knowledge does not. There are enormous quantities of knowledge taught in universities that are absolutely true, but totally *useless* in the real world, because they cannot be translated into a value that someone will pay for.

One of the problems facing college graduates is that they are often shocked to find out that they have spent three or four years learning about subjects that no one but themselves really cares about. No employer is willing to pay them for a degree in archeology or anthropology. This is why fully 80 percent of college graduates find themselves working outside their fields of study within two years of leaving school. They finally have to find something to do that actually benefits other people.

Open Every Door

As I mentioned earlier, I started off with very few advantages in life. But I had one thing going for me: *reading*. As a boy, I loved to read. As an adult, I got hooked on reading and learning. Over the years, I found that virtually every successful person in America who has started with nothing and worked his or her way up has done it through a commitment to study and personal development.

One of the most empowering of all rules is this: *You can learn anything you need to learn to achieve any goal you can set for yourself.*

This is one of the great principles of success. Properly applied, this means that there are no real limitations on what you can accomplish. If you are clear about your goal, you can then identify the knowledge that you will need to achieve it. When you learn what you need to learn, and then apply that knowledge, the achievement of your goal becomes almost inevitable.

Just imagine! You can start off with nothing but an intense desire to be successful and then, by the process of self-study and self-development, you can learn anything you need to learn to achieve any goal you can set for yourself.

You Can Start with Nothing

Today, an immigrant from another country can come to America and walk up to customs with no luggage. This immigrant can have the ability to create a $100 million industry in his mind and he can still say to the customs officer, "Nothing to declare." He can walk into this country with pure brainpower and go on to achieve great success in our society.

Not long ago, I had dinner with a group of business people in Palo Alto, California, not far from Silicon Valley. The Chinese gentleman next to me had come over from Taiwan 15 years ago on a scholarship to study engineering at Stanford University. He told me that after graduation, he had decided to stay. I asked him what he was doing now. He told me that he had an electronics business.

Of course, I immediately thought of consumer electronics, a high volume, low margin type of business, selling televisions and stereos. I asked him how it was going. He told me that his electronics business was quite successful, but they expected to do better in the future. I politely asked him how big his business was today. He told me that they had just passed $1 billion in sales and had more than 2,000 employees. By "electronics business" it turned out that he meant computer components and motherboards that he supplied to most of the major computer manufacturers in the United States and abroad.

He and one partner, also from Taiwan, owned the entire company. He had arrived in America less than 15 years ago, gotten an education, continued upgrading his skills, started a business, and built a billion-dollar corporation with brainpower and perseverance.

Steve Jobs and Steve Wosniak did the same with Apple Computer, starting in a garage with an idea. In the greatest success story of the age, Bill Gates created Microsoft out of an idea that he and Paul Allen had when they were at university. He went on to become the richest self-made billionaire in the world. And he did it on pure brainpower.

You Don't Need to Be a Genius

Please don't get the idea that you have to be some kind of high-tech computer whiz with a Ph.D. from Stanford or Harvard to be successful in the information age. Ninety percent of all fortunes are still made in ordinary businesses selling familiar products and services in local markets to regular customers. All you really need is an idea that is 10 percent new to start a fortune. All you need is a new piece of knowledge, a new idea, a new insight, and the willingness and ability to apply it in the marketplace, and you can become a big success in our economic system.

Abraham Lincoln once wrote, "I will study and prepare myself, and someday my chance will come."

Luck is what happens when preparation meets opportunity.

It is amazing how many people are sitting around waiting for a lucky break. But people do not just have lucky breaks. They *make* their own lucky breaks. They create their lucky breaks by preparing so thoroughly for their opportunity that when it does come along they are ready to grab it and run with it, like a fumble in a football game, toward the goal lines. Napoleon Bonaparte said, "Opportunity? What is opportunity? I create my own opportunities!"

Earl Nightingale once said that, "If your opportunity comes and you are not prepared for it, it will only make you look foolish."

By the Law of Attraction, whenever you pay the price and put in the preparation, you attract into your life an opportunity to use your knowledge and skills at the level you are prepared for.

Another way to increase your luck is explained in Jesus' *parable of the talents*. This parable says, "Oh good and faithful servant, you have been faithful over small things; I will make you master over large things." In modern terms, this means that, if you develop your natural talents and abilities, doors will open for you to use them.

You will seldom develop a useful talent or ability without sooner or later getting an opportunity to apply that talent or ability to some good purpose. By some strange power, you will draw into your life the people, circumstances, opportunities, and resources necessary for you to use that talent for your benefit and for the benefit of others.

Ideas Are the Keys to Your Future

You can dramatically increase the odds in your favor by constantly seeking new ideas to help you to achieve your goals. The fact is that, "Your success will be in direct proportion to the quality and quantity of ideas that you can generate to improve your current circumstances."

Ideas are the keys to the future. Ideas are the primary source of value today. Ideas are the cream of knowledge rising to the top. They represent a synthesis of information crystallizing into a usable concept. The more ideas you generate, the more likely it is that you will discover the right idea at the right time for you.

The Value of Ideas

But remember, ideas in and of themselves have no value. It is only your ability to take an idea and to apply it in such a way that you can bring about some result or improvement that adds worth to the idea. You must personally make the idea worth something.

I am always amazed when people write or phone me and try to sell me their new idea. I ask them, "What is it?" They say that they can't tell me the idea until I have paid them for it. I try to explain to them that their ideas are of no value by themselves. They are often shocked. They think that their idea has value just because *they* thought of it.

The fact is that 99 out of 100 ideas don't work, at least not in their original form. This is why you have to generate a lot of ideas if you are going to come up with the one that makes a difference. There is a direct relationship between the *quantity* of ideas and the *quality* of ideas. And the one idea that does work only has value when it is combined and re-combined with a variety of other ideas and information to achieve some worthy end.

Superior Knowledge Is a Key Luck Factor

Regarding the luck factor of superior knowledge, you have a distinct advantage. The great majority of people drift along, generally unaware that their knowledge is limited and that whatever knowledge they have is becoming obsolete with each passing day. They spend much of their time socializing at work and at home, watching television and generally living as easy a life as possible.

However, the small, enlightened minority, like yourself, who realize that we are in a race for useful knowledge, have the winning edge. You are already ahead of the pack because you know what you need to do to move to the top of your field.

What Is an Education Worth?

Some statistics on the value of education were just released by the U.S. Department of Labor. The researchers found that a person who completes high school would earn about $600,000 over the course of his or her working lifetime. But a person with a two-year community college degree will earn about $1,000,000 in his or her lifetime. This works out to an additional $400,000 more than a high school certificate, or about $200,000 more of lifetime income for each additional year of study. This is about $5,000 more per year. And it gets better.

A university graduate with a four-year diploma will earn about $1,400,000 on average, over the course of his or her lifetime. A person with a master's degree, equal to approximately five or six years of college education, will earn about $2,000,000 in his or her lifetime. A person with a Ph.D., which requires two to four additional years, will earn an average of $3,000,000.

Every additional year of schooling after high school will increase your annual income from 8 percent to 25 percent per year, depending upon the relevance of the courses that you take. Often, people who attend community colleges or technical schools earn more than people who graduate from universities. This is because what they learn at a community college is immediately applicable to getting results that a business will pay for. People who learn practical subjects are more valuable more quickly to an employer.

Investing in yourself is perhaps the highest pay-off investment that you can make. Imagine, one additional year of community college adds $200,000 to your lifetime earnings. You can increase your earning ability, your ability to get results, by 10 percent or 20 percent more per year as the result of each additional year of education, if you study the right subjects.

Build to the Sky

If you want to know how high they are going to build an office building, you can tell by looking at how deep they dig the foundation. The depth of the foundation determines how high the structure can be erected. But once a building is complete, the builders cannot go back and add another 10 or 20 floors onto the building by digging the foundation deeper. It's not physically possible. The building height is fixed by the depth of the original foundation.

The same principle applies to you, but with one great exception. You can tell how high you will rise in life by how deeply you dig your foundation of practical knowledge and skill. Unlike a building, you can continually deepen your foundation. You can continually increase the height of your personal performance by continually increasing the depth of your knowledge and skill. And there are no limits.

What Determines the Quality of Your Thinking?

You attract good luck by the quality of your thinking, and the quality of your thinking is determined by your commitment to continuous learning. The more you feed your mind with new knowledge, new insights, new ideas, and new information, the more you magnetize your mind. You then attract into your life all kinds of opportunities and possibilities to use your abilities at a higher level to achieve more and more of your goals.

Leaders Are Readers

The key to expanding your knowledge is *reading*. Perhaps not all readers are leaders, but all *leaders are readers*. How much should you read? According to the research, the highest paid Americans read an average of two to three hours per day. The lowest paid Americans don't read at all.

In fact, the statistics are shocking! According to the American Booksellers Association, 80 percent of American families did not buy or read a single book in the last year. Seventy percent of American adults have not been into a bookstore in the last five years. Fifty-eight percent of adults never read another book after they leave school, including 42 percent of university graduates.

According to *USA Today*, 43.6 percent of American adults read below the seventh grade level. For all intents and purposes, this means that they are functionally illiterate. Fully 50 percent of high school graduates can neither read their graduation diplomas nor fill out an application form for a job at McDonalds.

Many large companies that advertise continually in search of qualified people are forced to reject as many as 95 percent of all applicants because of their lack of basic reading skills.

My friend Charlie Jones says, "*You will be in five years where you are today except for the people you meet and the books you read.*" I would add to that that you will be in five years where you are today except for the audio programs you listen to, the courses you take, and the other sources of information you absorb. You just can't learn too much about how to succeed in your field.

Movies versus Books

In 2001, the most successful year in movie history, $8 billion was spent in the film industry. This amount makes the movie industry one of the biggest in the country. If you look around, you will see movie stars and movie industry news in every newspaper and on half the magazines on every news rack. They are the constant subject of news and entertainment on television and radio. It is as though we are immersed in a movie culture.

But what you probably don't know is that each year, Americans spend more than $25 billion on books. In fact, the twenty-first century has been dubbed "The Age of the Book." More than 100,000 books are published each year. Amazon.com has more than 3,000,000 titles available.

If you go into the home of a wealthy person, what is one of the first things you see? And the answer is, a library! The wealthier the homeowners, and the larger the home, the more likely it is that they will have a fully stocked library.

If you go into the home of poor people, what is the very first thing you see? That's right! The biggest television they can afford!

Now, here's a question for you. Did the owners of large homes become wealthy and then buy the books? Or, did they buy the books and read them, and then become wealthy? I think the answer is clear. People buy the books, study and apply them, become increasingly proficient, and are eventually paid very well.

Reading Opens Every Door

Robert fooled around at school and was nonetheless allowed to graduate from high school without learning to read. He was upset to find that the only jobs he could get were minimum-wage laboring jobs, digging ditches, planting trees, and sweeping floors. He came from a good home and a good neighborhood, but all he could get was dead-end jobs. And all his friends who passed out of high school without learning to read were in the same situation.

After a year and a half of this frustrating work, he came to me and asked for my advice. I told him that he needed to increase his education. He told me that he didn't like to read. Reading big paragraphs actually made him tired, he said. I told him that he had better go to a community college and take a course in reading. If he didn't, he would be trapped in low-wage jobs forever. He was reluctant to follow my advice, but he was even more opposed to continuing to work as a laborer.

He finally enrolled in and attended a community college at night for two years. He learned how to read proficiently. With his new skills, he enrolled in a technical school and took a degree in biomedical electronics. It took him two more years before he graduated with a certificate.

But then, his life changed completely. He was immediately hired by a large hospital supply company to sell medical instrumentation to hospitals and clinics. Within five years he was earning more than $50,000 per year. He had a home, a new car and a great life. He told me later that the advice I gave him to learn to read and improve his education was the turning point in his life.

How to Read Effectively

Here are some ways for you to upgrade your knowledge through reading. They have been successful for me and for thousands of other people who are now highly paid leaders in their industries.

The very best books to read are those written by men and women who are actively working in their fields. They are books written by experts, by practitioners of their crafts. Stay away from books written by university professors and management consultants. These people simply do not have the in-depth understanding that comes from working day after day and year after year in a particular field.

A book written by an expert can be incredibly valuable. You can buy a book full of practical, proven ideas that someone else has taken 20 years to learn and another two or three years to write and publish. For the price of a book, you can get the knowledge that may have cost someone else a lifetime of experience and thousands of dollars to accumulate. All you need is one good idea from one book to change the whole course of your life.

Here's an important point. Every problem that you could ever have has already been solved by someone, somewhere. And the solution that that person has found to your problem is written in a book or magazine and is available to you if you can find it.

If there is an idea out there that can help you, that can save you thousands of dollars and months or years of hard work, and you don't have the idea, it is as if that idea didn't exist. What you don't know can hurt you, and hold you back. This is why successful people are always searching for new information and ideas.

You may have to be exposed to 100 ideas before you discover the one idea that you need at that moment to make a major difference in your life and work. You increase your luck, and put the odds of success in your favor, by continually seeking and gathering as many new ideas and insights as you can. You need a large *quantity* of ideas to find the one *quality* insight that can help you at that moment, in that situation.

Buy your own books. Build your own library. Don't check them out of a public library and then return them. When you read a book, underline the key points with a colored pen or highlighter. Make the book your own property.

When I first started buying and marking up my own books, I found that it might take me a few hours to read a book the first time, but then I could read all of the key points through in less than an hour. Now, I quickly read a book and then go back and dictate all the most valuable ideas to be typed up and reviewed later. This dramatically increases the speed at which I learn and remember.

Learn Speed Reading

Speed reading is a skill that you can learn with practice. There is a complete description of the speed reading process on my audio program, *Accelerated Learning Techniques*, but let me give you a simple method here that can double and triple the speed at which you read any book.

It is based on what is called the OPIR Method, or O-P-I-R. These four letters stand for *overview, preview, in-view, and review*. Here's how you use this technique.

Before you plunge into a book, always start with an *overview*. Read the front of the book and the back. Read the biography of the author and make sure that this is a person who really knows what he or she is talking about. Read the contents and ask yourself whether or not these ideas are of interest to you. Read the appendix and the index quickly to see what information sources the author used. If you get a good feeling about the book and you think that it has some value for you, you go to the next stage.

The second stage of rapid reading is the *preview* stage. This is when you take the book and page through it from cover to cover, one page at a time. You read the chapter headings and paragraph headings. Look at the graphs, charts, and diagrams. Read the first lines of as many paragraphs as you can. Read a couple of paragraphs through to get a feeling for the style of the author. Determine whether you are comfortable with the book and whether you enjoy the way the author expresses himself or herself.

Save Hours in Reading a Book

The best way to save several hours on a book is to throw it away and not read it at all. One of the best of all time savers is to decide in advance that the book is not of sufficient value for you to spend your time reading it.

After you have completed the overview and the preview, and you feel that you want to read the book, ask yourself, "Why?" When you ask yourself this question, it forces you to think about *what you can gain* from the book and how you can apply it to your life or work. This is called *reading on purpose*. The more relevant and applicable new information is to you at this moment, the more likely it is that you will remember it when you are finished.

The third stage of reading is the *in-view*. If you are reading a non-fiction book, start with the chapter that is the most interesting to you; then stop if you don't feel like proceeding. Sometimes, an excellent book will only have one or two chapters that are relevant to you and your life right now.

The fact is that, if the information is not immediately helpful to you, you will forget it anyway, so why read it in the first place?

As you proceed with the in-view, make as many notations as possible. Underline key sentences and phrases with a colored pen or marker. Use exclamation points, stars, and quotation marks in the margins. Circle key ideas. Make it easy for you to come back and find the facts that you thought most important.

The final stage of the OPIR method is to *review* the book. No matter how smart you are, you have to go over key points three or four times before they stick in your memory. But once you have marked up a book properly, you can flip through it quickly in as little as an hour and get the essence of the entire book.

Keep Current with New Knowledge

Where do you get the best business books? Simple. Join the various book clubs advertised in the business magazines. Order the books that they offer at a reduced introductory rate, and add to your library by buying one or two of their choices each year. In no time at all, you will be one of the best-informed people in your circle.

Another way to keep current is to subscribe to *Soundview Book Summaries*. This is an organization that summarizes two or more top business books every month. They hire professionals who condense the key points of the book into an easily readable four- to eight-page report. You can keep abreast of the best that is being written for business people by getting a key synopsis of these books each month.

You can also subscribe to *Fast Track*. This organization summarizes two business books on audio each month. You can listen to these summaries, with all the key points, in your car. I have learned a lot of great ideas from these summaries without ever having had to read the entire book.

If you want to keep current, it is important that you subscribe to the key magazines and publications in your field. If you are in business, you should subscribe to *Fortune* and *Forbes*. If you are in sales, you should subscribe to *Personal Selling Magazine*. If you are in senior management, you should be taking the *Harvard Business Review* and the *Sloan Business Review*.

The best way to find out what to read is to ask the most successful people in your field what *they* read. What books would they most recommend? What magazines do they enjoy the most and read the most regularly? By the Law of Cause and Effect, if you read what the very best people read, you will soon know what the very best people know. You will develop the winning edge in your field.

Save Time Reading Magazines

With magazines, use the rip-and-read method to save time. Here is how it works. Go to the table of contents of the magazine. Note the articles that you feel would be important to you. Go straight to those articles and tear them out. Throw the rest of the magazine away. Put the torn-out articles into a file and put the file in your briefcase. Then, whenever you have a few moments, pull out your rip-and-read file and read through the articles with a red pen or highlighter.

There are two types of reading, *maintenance* reading and *growth* reading. Maintenance reading consists of the current magazines and publications that keep you up to date with your field. Growth reading, on the other hand, consists of the books you read that actually *increase* your knowledge in your field. They enable you to grow rather than to stay even.

Enroll in Automobile University

Listen to audio programs in your car, and when you are exercising. The average car owner in America drives 12,000 to 25,000 miles each year. This is the equivalent of 500 to 1,000 hours that you spend in your car. Use this time well. Turn your car into a learning machine, a *university on wheels*.

Remember, when you are traveling during work time or going to and coming from work, you are not on vacation. You can't afford to waste time. You do not have the luxury of driving around listening to music. Driving time is working time as well. Keep your mind active and growing by continually learning new ideas as you move around.

You can get the equivalent of three to six months of 40-hour weeks, or between one and two full-time university semesters, by just listening to audio programs in your car as you drive from place to place. You can become one of the smartest and highest paid people in your field by using audio learning to its fullest advantage.

Attend Courses and Seminars

Take every seminar and course that you can. Go to courses taught by practical authorities, by experts in their fields. Take courses that are taught by people who are actually in the field practicing in their professions during the daytime.

Be perfectly selfish when you enroll. Take only those courses that are the most relevant and which can be the most helpful to you *immediately*. The faster that you can apply a piece of new information, the more likely it is that you will retain it for life.

One good idea is all you need to give yourself an edge in a competitive situation. Because of competition, most of the courses and seminars offered today are loaded with good ideas. They are usually taught by highly skilled professionals who jam a lot of value-packed information into a short period of time.

Many people have doubled and tripled their productivity and their incomes as a result of attending a single seminar. You simply cannot afford *not* to commit yourself to continuous learning. One key idea from one seminar can save you a year of hard work.

Fish Where the Fish Are

Make it a regular practice to attend trade shows, conventions, and exhibitions, especially those that are specific or relevant to your field. I have spoken at many annual conventions and association meetings over the years and found that the very best and highest paid people in their industries are always at the conventions. They are always touring the exhibition floors. They are always in the front rows at the key sessions given at those conferences. And you must do the same thing that the top people do if you want to be one of the top people as well.

Every change or improvement in your life comes as a result of your mind *colliding* with a new idea. Your aim must be to increase the probabilities that you will bump into the right idea or insight at the right time for you. You put luck on your side by consciously and deliberately placing yourself in the crossfire of new information and ideas.

Ask for Ideas and Inputs

Perhaps one of the most important things you can do to rise to the top of your field in the Information Age is to *ask* people for advice and for inputs. Ask top people for recommendations on books, audio programs, and courses. Ask them for answers to questions and for solutions to problems. One good piece of advice from someone who has had a similar experience can save you weeks and months of hard work and enormous amounts of money.

Benjamin Franklin once said that there are two ways that we can get our knowledge, *we can either buy it or we can borrow it*. By buying it, we pay full price in terms of time and treasure. But by borrowing it, we get it from others who have already paid full price to learn it.

By continually bombarding your mind with new information and ideas, you activate all the mental laws and trigger all the luck factors we have discussed so far in this book.

Your goal is to become one of the most knowledgeable experts in your field. You will then become one of the most valuable and highest paid people in your industry. You will rise rapidly and be promoted steadily. You will move into the top 10 percent of income earners, with all the prestige, recognition, and respect that goes with it. You will live in a larger house, drive a nicer car, and have a bigger bank account. And when people accuse you of being lucky, you can simply tell them, "The more I learn, the luckier I get."

ACTION EXERCISES
What You Can Do Now

1. Identify the critical knowledge that is essential for success in your field; how can you increase your store of this knowledge?

2. Determine the specific things you can do to develop the winning edges in your work; which are the most important for productivity and profitability, and how can you improve in these areas?

3. Develop a reading plan to keep you both current with and ahead of your field; schedule regular times each day to upgrade your knowledge.

4. Investigate additional courses and seminars you can take to stay abreast of your field; enroll in and attend three or four seminars each year.

5. Take a speed-reading course and practice until you can read and remember 1,000 words per minute or more.

6. Go to your boss and to the most successful people in your field and ask them for advice on what to read and listen to, and what courses to attend. Follow their advice, and then ask for more recommendations.

7. Turn your car into a mobile classroom; listen to educational audio programs as you drive around rather than wasting this precious time. Never stop learning.

Principle 4—Mastery Is Magical

"The man who comes up with a means for doing or producing anything better, faster or more economically has his future and his fortune at his fingertips."

—John Paul Getty

You have the ability, right now, to exceed all your previous levels of accomplishment. You have within you at this moment the talents you need to *be, do, and have* far more than you have ever achieved in your life to date. This is because you can learn any skills that you need to learn, to do any job you need to do, to achieve any goal that you can set for yourself.

When a violinist plays a perfect piece of classical music in a concert, or when the three tenors—Pavarotti, Domingo, and Carreras—sing exquisite opera, no one ascribes their accomplishments to *luck*. When a craftsman builds a beautiful piece of furniture, elegant and refined in every detail, obviously a superb piece of work, no one explains or dismisses his achievement as having been a matter of good luck.

In every case, when you see someone do something in an excellent fashion, you recognize and appreciate a work of *mastery*. You know that many weeks, months, and even years of hard work and detailed preparation precede an excellent performance of any kind.

My friend Og Mandino, author of books that have sold in the millions, once told me that many people say his books are *easy to read.*

He said that the reason they were easy to read is because they were so hard to write. Og told me that he would write and rewrite a single paragraph as often as fifteen times so that it flowed smoothly on the page for the reader.

My good friend, Nido Qubein, one of the top professional speakers in America, told me that he would often invest as many as one hundred hours of planning, preparation, and rehearsal for a one-hour talk that he would only give once to a single audience.

Business Success Is Not an Accident

When professional salespeople carefully analyze their market, identify their ideal prospects, use the telephone and fax to set up and confirm appointments, arrive punctually and fully prepared, establish a high level of rapport, make excellent presentations for their product or service, and walk away with the orders, no one can ascribe their accomplishments to luck. In every case, they are examples of excellent performance.

There is tremendous *resentment against achievement* in the world today. In a highly competitive society, it takes many years to achieve excellence and to earn the rewards that accrue to top performance. Unfortunately, most people are not willing to make these efforts. Rather than pulling themselves up, they prefer to pull others down. Instead of making progress, they make excuses. They rationalize and justify their poor performance and poor results. They do this by ascribing the success of others to luck, whereas their own failure has been unlucky.

You know the truth. We live in a universe governed by law, not chaos. There is a reason for everything, and great success in any field is largely the result of high standards and high overall levels of performance in that field. It has been the same throughout human history and is even truer today in every area of human endeavor.

The Two Metaphors for Success

There are two metaphors for success that are continually used throughout our society: *sports and business*. In both areas, recognition and rewards go to those individuals and organizations that achieve excellence in competition. We salute and praise those who win in competitive sports. We purchase the products and services of those companies who we feel offer us the very best for the money we pay. In each case, quality and excellence are the measures we use to choose and reward the best performers. It has never been otherwise.

The fact is that the market only pays extraordinary rewards for extraordinary performance. The market pays ordinary rewards for ordinary performance, and below average rewards, unemployment, and insecurity for below average performance.

Two Mental Illnesses

There are two mental illnesses that are rampant across America, and much of the industrialized world today. The first is the *something-for-nothing* disease and the second is the *quick-fix* disease. Either of these can sabotage your success but both of them, in combination, can be fatal.

The something-for-nothing disease is contracted by people who think that they can get more out than they put in. They think that they can put in a dollar and get two dollars back. They are constantly looking for opportunities to get something they want without paying full price. They want to go through the revolving door of life on someone else's push.

People with the something-for-nothing disease are trying to violate the basic laws of the universe, the Laws of Sowing and Reaping, Action and Reaction, Cause and Effect. They try to violate one of the great success principles: *Never hope to succeed by attempting to violate universal laws.*

Violating universal laws is the same as attempting to violate the Law of Gravity. You may have heard the story of the person who jumps off a 30-story building to commit suicide. As he falls past the fifteenth floor, someone leans out of the window and shouts, "How's it going?" The individual, hurling toward the earth, shouts back, "So far, so good!"

Every person who is trying to get out more than they put in is in a similar situation. He may appear to be doing well in the short term, but he is plummeting rapidly toward a rude awakening in life. Don't let this happen to you.

Looking for Short Cuts

The second mental illness is the quick-fix disease. This is contracted by people who are looking for fast, easy ways to achieve their goals. They look for short cuts to acquire key skills that actually take many months and years of hard work to master. They search for quick ways to solve problems that may have taken them many months or years to develop.

These people become suckers for the latest get-rich-quick idea. They buy lottery tickets and sign up for pyramid schemes. They buy penny stocks and invest in things that they don't know anything about but which promise a quick return. These people often waste many years of hard work and savings searching for the will-o'-the-wisp of quick, easy success.

The Practice of Service

Dedicating yourself to serving others is the way of life that will bring you more *luck* than you can imagine. The commitment to service helps you to focus on contributing value to those people whose satisfaction determines your own success. This is the rule: *Your rewards in life will always be equal to the value of your service to others.*

The universe is always in balance. You get out what you put in. If you want to increase the quality and quantity of your rewards, you must focus on increasing the quality and quantity of your service to others.

One of the best questions that you can ask yourself, every single morning, is, "How can I increase the value of my service to my customers today?"

And who are your customers? Your customers are the people who depend upon you for the work that you do. Your customers are those people whose satisfaction determines your rewards, your rate of promotion, your recognition, and your progress in your financial and work life.

Identify Your Key Customers

You have more customers than you know. To start with, your boss is your primary customer. Your most important job is to please your boss by doing what he or she considers to be the most important task for you at any given time. If you are a manager, your staff are also your customers. Your job is to please them in such a way that they do an outstanding job in pleasing the people they are meant to serve.

If you are in sales or entrepreneurship, the people in the marketplace who use your products or services are perhaps your most important customers. All great success, all great fortunes, come from serving people, with what they want and are willing to pay for, *better* than someone else can serve them.

Deserve the Things You Want

It is a truism in life that, "You do not get what you want but what you *deserve*."

Your central focus on your job is to do whatever is necessary to make sure that you actually *deserve* the rewards and benefits that you desire. Any attempt to get something that you do not honestly and justly deserve is doomed to failure and frustration. All corrupt or criminal activity, all laziness and corner cutting, is aimed at somehow getting rewards without honestly earning them in the first place.

The word *deserve* comes from the two Latin words, *De* and *Servus*. These two words combined mean "from service."

Many people have the uneasy feeling that they do not deserve to be successful and prosperous. But the truth is that you deserve all the good things that life has to offer as long as you honestly earn them from service to others.

Your main concern is to put in the cause, and the effects will take care of themselves. Your job is to put in the seed and nature will give you the harvest. Your goal is to do your work in an excellent fashion. Your rewards will then flow to you as the result of law, not chance.

Do Your Work Well

Dean Briggs of Harvard once wrote, "Do your work. Not just your work, but a little bit more for the lavishing sake. And if you suffer, as you will, do your work. And out of your work and suffering will come the great joys of life."

Peter Drucker once wrote that, even if you are starting a new business from your kitchen table, your goal must be leadership in your industry or you shouldn't even begin at all. If all you want to do is make a quick buck or a little extra income, you will never be particularly successful. You will probably end up losing both your time and your money.

But if your goal is to create a business that offers an excellent product or service, better than anyone else, in a competitive market, and you focus on your goal with tremendous intensity of purpose, you will eventually be a big success in your chosen field. Like Steve Jobs and Steve Wosniak, designing the first Apple computer in a garage, you may end up building a world-class organization.

But even if you don't build a huge company, your commitment to doing your job and serving your customers in an outstanding fashion is the greatest single assurance of your success in the long term.

As an individual, your goal must be to join the top 10 percent of people in your field. Any goal less than being one of the best is not worthy of you. Resolve in advance that you will overcome any obstacle, solve any problem, and pay any price to *be the best* at what you do.

Be Prepared to Pay the Price

The achievement of mastery in any field requires months and years of hard work on yourself and your job. Resolve in advance that you will invest whatever time it takes to become excellent at what you do, and be patient. Anything worthwhile takes a long time to accomplish.

I once shared an apartment with a German immigrant who was a master chef. He told me that he was required to study for seven years at the Swiss *Culinary Institute* in Geneva to become a master chef. He began by learning how to peel fruits and vegetables. He did this for his entire first year until he developed a complete understanding and a deep sensitivity for the texture and feel of fruits and vegetables in all states of freshness, flavor, and composition. In the second year, he moved on to salads and the preparation of fruits and vegetables in simple dishes. In each subsequent year of training, he spent hundreds of hours working with individual spices, sauces, ingredients, and recipes. At the end of seven years, after rigorous testing, he had graduated with perhaps the most respected culinary degree in the world.

He then worked in an internship under a master chef in one of the top restaurants of Europe. After another five years, he was in demand, receiving job offers from all over Europe and America. He was qualified to head up the kitchen of a top hotel or restaurant, if not start his own. The finest hotels and restaurants in the world are those that have been able to attract and hire a graduate of what is called the Swiss School. These chefs are highly paid and can eventually retire financially independent.

The point is this: Before they became creative, innovative cooks, such as the famous Wolfgang Puck of Beverly Hills, they had to completely master every part of the culinary art. They had to learn each stage of cooking as it had been learned and passed on over the years by the finest chefs in the world. They did not begin to innovate or change the recipes they were taught before they had reached a very high level of skill and mastery.

Many people in business today think that they can start at the top and work up. They are in a hurry, and cannot be bothered mastering the basics of their jobs. They don't realize that long-term success is the direct result of becoming absolutely excellent at what they do.

Your Attitude toward Excellence

You can tell if you are in the right field by your attitude toward excellence in that field, especially your attitude toward the people who are the very best at what you are doing or thinking of doing. All really successful people have great admiration and respect for the top performers in their industries. Because you always move in the direction of what you most admire, the more you look up to and admire the best people in your field, the more you become like them. Make the top people your role models. As you evolve and grow, compare your accomplishments to the accomplishments of the top people.

There are many people working at their jobs who don't particularly care about being at the top of their fields. They are content to be back in the pack, like average runners in a marathon race. They don't really see themselves as capable of winning and they don't particularly care. They are more concerned with security than with achievement.

Even worse, mediocre people often criticize and denigrate the successful people in their industries. They complain about them behind their backs and point out their faults and shortcomings. They get together with other average performers and gossip about the industry leaders, and tell stories. These behaviors are invariably fatal to success.

No one who criticizes the high performers in their industry ever becomes a high performer himself.

Never resent the ability or success of others. Instead, you should look up to those people and try to emulate their best qualities. The good news is that, within reason, whatever anyone else has done, *you can do as well*. The success of others is proof that you also can succeed in that field.

You Can Achieve What Others Have Achieved

You are engineered in such a way that you cannot intensely desire a goal or quality without having the ability to acquire it. You can become whatever person you want to become if you are only willing to work at it long enough and hard enough.

Some people are blessed with more natural talents than others. They learn the key skills of the craft faster and easier. Others take longer. That's the only difference. Those who take longer just require more practice. This means that, in the long run, your potential for achieving excellence in your field is only limited by your own level of commitment.

The principle of practice says, "Whatever you practice, over and over again, eventually becomes a new habit or skill." It is only a matter of time.

Bear Bryant, the great University of Alabama football coach, once said, "Success is not a result of the will to win. Everyone has that. Great success comes as a result of the willingness to prepare to win."

The only real measure of how high you can fly and how far you can go is contained in the question, "How badly do you want it?" If you want to achieve a particular level of skill badly enough, and you are willing to work at it long enough, there is nothing that can stop you. You must and you will eventually accomplish it.

Every extraordinary achievement is the result of thousands of ordinary achievements that no one ever sees or appreciates. Every great accomplishment is the result of hundreds and perhaps thousands of hours of painstaking effort, preparation, study, and practice that very few people are even aware of. But, if you put it *in*, you will eventually get it *out*. When you completely trust the principle of practice, it will work for you. And the longer you have to work to reach the heights, the greater will be the rewards when they finally come.

Longfellow once wrote, "Those heights by great men, won and kept, were not achieved by sudden flight. But they, while their companions slept, were toiling upward in the night."

Today, we would say that successful people are those who were toiling upward in the night while their companions socialized, watched television, or wasted their time on time-killing entertainment.

Preparation Puts You on the Side of the Angels

Here is a Six-P rule: Proper Prior Preparation Prevents Poor Performance. Your willingness to prepare thoroughly determines how well you will do, how far you will go, and how much you will earn.

How can you measure how much preparation for success you have put in so far? That's easy. Just look around you. The Laws of Sowing and Reaping, Cause and Effect, Correspondence and even Mental Equivalence all say that your outer world will be a *reflection* of your inner world.

Your outer world of accomplishments will exactly reflect your inner world of preparation. If at any time you are not happy with your outer world of results and rewards, you have but to go back to work on yourself. You have to change your inner world so that it is more consistent with what you want to do on the outside.

Make Skill Development a Major Goal

In the chapter on goal setting, I asked you to write down 10 goals that you wanted to accomplish in the next 12 months. I also asked you to select the one goal from those 10 that would have the greatest positive impact on your life if you were to attain it. Now, I want you to take this exercise one step further.

Once you have decided on your major definite purpose, your number one, most important single goal, you must ask yourself, "What must I be absolutely excellent at doing in order to achieve this goal?"

You know that you can only achieve a goal and hold onto it when you are thoroughly prepared for it. Therefore, what specific skills do you need to develop so that you are capable of achieving the most important goal on your list?

Just as you need a goal list, you also need a skill list. You need to make a list of the skills that you have to acquire to achieve each of the goals that you want to attain. There is no such thing as something for nothing. The horse *does* come before the cart. The development of the skill does come before the realization of the rewards.

Determine Your Key Result Areas

One of the most important concepts in business and personal success is key result areas. These are the core skills at which you must absolutely, positively be excellent if you want to achieve greatly in your field.

Your key result areas, in any job or position, are the specific outcomes or *results* that you have been hired to accomplish. Your performance in these key result areas determines your pay, your promotion, and your future. Your ability to clearly identify your key result areas and to organize them by priority is absolutely essential to your achieving mastery in your field.

All truly lucky people are very good at performing the key tasks that are critical to excellent overall performance of their jobs. A key result area can be defined as a specific outcome for which you are completely responsible. It is *measurable* and it is under your control. If you don't do it, it doesn't get done.

A key result area is an *output* of your job. It then becomes an input for someone else. It is an integral part of the functioning of the organization. For example, if you are in sales, key-result areas are getting the order and closing the sale. Once you have done this, the sales agreement becomes an input for the order department, the accounting department, and the manufacturing, distribution, and delivery departments. A key result, once accomplished, affects and influences the behavior and performance of other people.

You must begin by becoming perfectly clear about the most important results that you are expected to contribute to your organization. Then you determine the skill areas in which you must excel in order to get the results that are vital to superior performance of your job.

For What Results Are You Responsible?

One way of determining your key result areas is by asking, "What are the specific results for which I am the most highly paid and rewarded?"

Of all the things I do, which are the things that I do that are the *most important* to the organization? Why *exactly* am I on the payroll?

By determining and defining your key result areas, and then by organizing them in order of priority from the most important to the least, you now have a track to run on in your career. You must then commit yourself to becoming excellent at doing the few things by which you are most evaluated by others.

Your success in your career will come primarily from excellent performance in the key result areas that are most important to your boss and to your company at the time. All your problems in your career will come from inadequate performance in one or more of these areas.

Identify the Five to Seven Skills

There are seldom more than five to seven key result areas in any job. They are specific tasks that must be accomplished for the job to be completed successfully. In every occupation, these five to seven factors can be identified.

For example, if you are in sales, there are seven key result areas: *prospecting, establishing rapport and trust, identifying needs or problems, presenting solutions, answering objections, closing the sale,* and *getting resales and referrals.* Success in selling depends on your performing these seven functions consistently in an excellent fashion.

If you are in management, there are also seven key result areas: *planning, organizing, staffing, delegating, supervising, measuring,* and *reporting.* Excellent performance overall requires excellent performance in each of these areas. Poor performance in any area can damage and even threaten your future in your career.

If you want to be a good parent, there are five to seven key results, such as *communication, caring, consideration, courtesy,* and *complimenting.* If you are running a business, there are seven key result areas. In some jobs or areas of endeavor, there may be more or fewer key result areas that absolutely, positively determine the success or failure of the enterprise or activity.

Your Most Powerful Ability

Your most powerful ability is your ability to think. This is your ability to apply your remarkable mind to getting the critical results that determine your future. Most people operate on autopilot, doing what comes naturally. They get into a comfort zone of average performance, and seldom question their behaviors. Thomas Edison once wrote that, "There is no expedient that the average person will not go to avoid the hard labor of thinking."

For you to excel in your field, you must continually analyze and evaluate your performance, and look for ways to make it better. You must identify the individual components of skill that you will have to master to move to the top. You must engage in *continuous and never ending improvement* (CANEI).

The Determinant of Your Income

Here is a great discovery. Your *weakest* key skill determines the height at which you can use all your other skills. Your weakest important skill determines your income, your rate of promotion, and your future in your career.

Here is an example: If you were absolutely excellent in every part of selling except for *prospecting*, that weakness in prospecting would set the height of your sales and your income. If you were absolutely excellent at every key skill except for *closing the sale*, that weakness would determine your level of sales and how much money you make.

If you are a manager, and you are absolutely excellent at every part of your job except *delegating*, that weakness alone will hold you back from advancement. You will never be particularly successful in your field. You could be absolutely excellent at every part of your job except *selecting key people* to work for you, and that one weakness would hold you back and cause you to fail every time.

One of the hardest things for you to do is to honestly admit that you are not particularly good in some area. It often turns out that the areas in which you are the weakest are usually activities that you don't particularly like to do. Because you don't like them, you avoid those tasks as much as possible. As a result, you get weaker and weaker in those areas. You never improve.

Soon, you begin to engage in all kinds of rationalizations and justifications for your poor performance in that area. You blame the marketplace, the products and services, the management, the advertising, and the competition. If you are not careful, you will end up blaming every other force around you except for yourself and your performance problems in that particular skill.

The Great Question for Rapid Advancement

Here is one of the great questions you can ask to move ahead faster in your work: "What one skill, if you developed it and did it consistently in an excellent fashion, would have the greatest positive impact on your career?"

You probably know the answer to that question as soon as you hear it. What is your personal answer to this question? If you don't know the answer, go and ask the other people around you. Remember, "Feedback is the breakfast of champions." It is virtually impossible for you to get better without getting honest, candid feedback from others who can view your performance from the outside and tell you what they see.

If you are in sales, ask your sales manager if there is any skill area where you are weak. Have your sales manager or someone else accompany you on sales calls and sit quietly to observe you in action. Afterwards, ask him if he has any recommendations for you to help you be more effective. Whatever he tells you to do, give it a try at the first opportunity. Sometimes, just one small change in the way you do your work can bring about a tremendous improvement in results.

If you are in management, ask your boss, and even your staff members, if they can see anything you could do differently that would enable you to do your job better. Whatever they say, resolve to be open and accepting. Resist the urge to defend and make excuses. Instead, ask questions like, "For example?" When they give you an example, say, "Tell me more," and just listen patiently.

Be Open to Feedback

Remember, you cannot see yourself as clearly as other people can see you. You have to be willing to open yourself to constructive criticism if you want to grow. Most of us have blind spots that make us unaware of our own weaknesses. Sometimes, when someone points out a weakness of ours, we argue with that person. We try to defend ourselves and make excuses. We insist that we are indeed competent in that area, or at least better than someone else.

Don't do this. If you want to be the best in your field, you must ask for constructive feedback from others so that you can continually improve at what you do. Your goal is to excel, no matter what the price, even if the price involves your ego or your pride. Don't let vanity or fragile self-esteem stand in the way of learning what you need to know to move to the top of your field.

Ask Your Boss for Input and Advice

Here is an exercise for you: Write down everything that you feel that you have been hired to accomplish. Take this list to your boss and ask your boss to organize this list by his or her priority. Have your boss tell you what he or she considers to be the *most* important task that you have been hired to accomplish. What is the second most important? What is the third most important? And so on.

From that moment onward, use this list as your personal operating plan. Continually update it in discussions with your boss. Be sure that, every minute of every day, you are working on what your boss considers to be the most valuable task you can be doing for the organization. Whatever it is, commit yourself to doing it very, very well and getting better and better at it.

If you are the boss yourself, an entrepreneur, or a business owner, it is even more important that you discipline yourself to work on those tasks that *only you can do* that contribute the very most to your company. What one task, if you did it especially well, would make the biggest difference to your company?

The Principle of Incremental Improvement

The Japanese revolutionized their war torn economy in the 1950s and 1960s with what they called the Kaizen Principle. The word *Kaizen* in Japanese means "continuous betterment." It is based on the idea that there are always little ways to improve performance and results in a person's line of sight. Every employee at every level was encouraged to seek out and implement little improvements every single day. The cumulative effect of continuous betterment over time is the achievement of extraordinary levels of efficiency and quality.

The *principle of incremental improvement* is a key luck factor you can use in your work. This principle says that you improve step by step rather than by quantum leaps. The achievement of excellence, and then mastery, in any field is a long, laborious process of tiny, incremental advances, each one of which may be small, but when they are added together they can eventually lead to extraordinary performance in your job.

When I was growing up, like many people, I had low self-esteem and tremendous feelings of inferiority. It never occurred to me that I could be good at anything. When I saw other people who excelled at something, I admired them. At the same time, I felt inadequate and inferior in comparison to them. I felt that they were better and smarter than I was. I concluded that somehow they had been blessed with intelligence, skills, and abilities that I was lacking. It never dawned on me that I could be like them.

But then one day, I had a revelation. It suddenly occurred to me that *every one has the ability to be excellent at something*. I realized that excellence was a journey, not a destination. One did not jump from mediocrity to excellence overnight. It was a long, slow process that anyone could embark upon and eventually achieve. The attainment of excellence in your work consists more of attitude and commitment than natural talent and ability.

Everyone Starts at the Bottom

Here was the key point that changed my attitude toward myself and, eventually, my whole career. I realized that everyone who is at the top in any field was once at the *bottom*. Everyone who is at the front of the line today was once at the back of the line. Everyone who is at the top of the ladder of success was once at the bottom of the ladder, and climbed up, one rung at a time. Everyone who is doing well in your field was at one time not in your field at all.

The truth is that *you are just as good, and potentially better in many areas, than anyone else you will ever meet.* If you decide to be the best in your field, the only person who can stop you from achieving it is yourself. The limits to excellent performance are inner attitudes of mind, not the outer aspects of your life.

Remember, it doesn't matter where you are coming from. All that really matters is where you are going. And your future is only limited by your own imagination. You can learn anything you need to learn to achieve any goal you can set for yourself. You can excel at anything you really love to do if you are willing to make the necessary efforts.

Every Day in Every Way

In 1910, Emil Coué, the Swiss doctor, achieved remarkable cures by teaching patients at his clinic in Geneva to repeat the words, "Every day in every way, I am getting better and better." This repeated affirmation brought about amazing improvements in people suffering from every kind of illness. Soon, doctors and researchers were coming from all over the world to study the incredible results of what came to be called psychosomatic medicine.

You should practice the same principle as well. You should look every day for ways to become better. Continually look for ideas in your line of sight that can improve your work in some way. In your line of sight, right where you are, you can probably see all kinds of ways to do the job faster and more efficiently. In creating your own future, you should continually look for and implement new ideas that improve the way things are being done in your business and in your work.

Increase Your Productivity Daily

Imagine if you could find and apply just one idea each day that enabled you to accomplish faster, better, cheaper performance and productivity in your work. That would amount to 250 ideas each year. Even if these were small ideas, the cumulative impact of getting a little better each day over the course of a year would be extraordinary. You could double and triple your levels of productivity and output. You could move to the top of your field.

The newspapers and the politicians are always talking about the rich, and how fortunate they are to be earning far more than the average. However, *rich* is the wrong word. Instead, the better word would be *productive*. People are not paid high salaries because they are rich. They are paid high salaries because they are highly productive. They earn more because they get more and better results than the average person.

You earn greater rewards and riches by becoming the kind of person who deserves greater rewards and riches. When you become very good at what you do, and you do lots of it, you will eventually be paid extremely well for doing it. Your success will be the result of decision and determination, not chance. Luck will have nothing to do with it.

Make More Money, Guaranteed!

Do you want to make more money? Here is a guaranteed way to do it. Just become very good at what you do. The better you get at your job, the more likely it is that they will pay you more to continue doing it. And if your current company won't pay you more, some other company will come along and offer you more. One of the best ways for you to get paid more is for you to be hired away by another company that offers you more money. Just focus on building a reputation for doing such an outstanding job where you are.

Over the years, I have worked with many executive recruiters and personnel consultants. These people are continually called upon by companies to help them recruit good people for important jobs. They keep files on the best people in various businesses, and they continually upgrade their files. When a client asks them for help finding a top manager, a top executive, or a top salesperson, they check their files and ask their contacts who the top people are in that particular industry. Every one knows who the top performers are in every company. They then go after those people and try to hire them away for their clients by offering them more money.

How Many Job Offers Have You Had?

Sometimes I ask my audiences a potentially painful question. "How many people here have received a job offer in the last 30 days?" Perhaps 10 percent to 15 percent of the audience members will raise their hands.

I then point out that the top people in every field are continually receiving job offers. It is as if there is a magnetic force field around them that attracts new job opportunities into their lives. Executive recruiters, personnel consultants, and even prospective employers phone them at work and at home, in the evenings and on the weekends. The top people are constantly being approached by people who are trying to hire them away by paying them more money and giving them greater opportunities. This is the kind of person you want to be if you are going to realize your full potential in our competitive economy.

The difference between the person who earns $25,000 per year and the person who earns $250,000 per year is not ten times the skill, ability, intelligence, or hours of work. It is often a small but consistent difference in performance in key result areas that translates into enormous differences in income and rewards.

Make a Decision!

One quality that will contribute enormously to your luck is your developing *the power of decision*. Making fast and firm decisions can change your life. People are successful because they have made clear, unequivocal, do or die decisions to be successful. People are unsuccessful because they have never made such a decision.

Here is a question for you. Which person would you like to be, the top performer with the high salary or the low performer with the low salary? This seems to be an obvious question, but it is not as obvious as you think. Often when I ask this question, there are looks of confusion on the faces of the people in the audience. They are not sure how to answer. When I ask the question again, this time much louder, everyone suddenly wakes up and says that they would prefer to be the highest paid person rather than the lowest paid person.

Then I say, "Wonderful! You have just crossed the major dividing line between the top people and the average worker. You have made a decision to be one of the *highest* paid people rather than one of the *lowest* paid people." The tragedy is that most people never make that decision. They then wonder why their lives don't get any better. But nothing happens until you make a decision to do something differently.

Get Serious about Your Future

For you to achieve greatly in your chosen field, you must *get serious* about yourself and your future. The great majority of people are wandering through life. They *want* things to get better, and they *hope* that things will get better, but they have never made a clear definite decision to *make* things better.

I have spoken to thousands of successful people over the years, and the turning point for almost every one of them came when they made a clear decision to pay whatever price was necessary to be the best in their particular field. As soon as you make this decision for yourself, all the mental laws and principles begin to work on your behalf. You start to attract ideas and opportunities for personal and professional improvement. You attract people into your life who can help you with advice and introductions. Books, tapes, and articles containing great ideas to help you to move ahead faster just arrive on your doorstep. You receive seminar and course brochures in the mail. Each time you improve, you get even more opportunities to use your new skills and abilities.

Do What You Love to Do

One of the great factors influencing your present and your future is the power of love. This power, which could even be called a law or principle, says that everything you do in life is either to get love or to compensate for lack of love.

A corollary to this Law of Love is that you will only be truly successful and happy when you commit yourself wholeheartedly to doing what you most love to do.

It is almost impossible for you to get going and keep going on your journey toward excellence unless you really love and enjoy your chosen field. Without this powerful commitment, when the going gets tough, you will quit and try something else.

Here's a question for you. If you won a million dollars cash tomorrow, and you could do anything that you wanted to as a job or occupation, what would it be? In other words, if you had all the time and money that you needed, and you felt that you were free to choose any occupation, what would you most love to do?

The most successful and happy people in our world today are men and women who have thrown their whole hearts into becoming excellent at doing something that they care about, something that they feel really makes a difference in the world.

You are engineered and designed by nature in a very special way. You will only be genuinely happy and successful when you feel that you are doing something that really benefits other people in some way. This external focus, on making a difference in the lives and work of others, is the common characteristic of almost all high performing, highly paid, highly respected and valued people in our society.

Make a Difference with Your Life

What kind of a difference do you want to make? Who do you want to benefit and enrich, and how do you want to do it? What sort of activities with others gives you your greatest feeling of self-esteem and personal pride? What accomplishments in your past have given you your greatest feeling of importance? What do you enjoy doing more than anything else?

It has been said that life is the study of *attention*. Your life always tends to go in the direction of those things that most attract and hold your attention. One of the ways that you can determine the right thing for you to do with your life is by examining your past experiences. What sort of skills or abilities have been most responsible for your successes in life to date? What have you always found easy to do, but which was difficult for other people? What subjects or activities in school did you most enjoy?

If you look at your current work, what one part of your work do you like the most? What one activity in your work do you do the very best? In what area do you make the greatest contribution to your company? If you could only perform one task all day long, from morning to night, what one activity at work would you select?

Design Your Own Career

Because of the rapid rate of change today in business and industry, you are probably going to have a series of jobs and careers over the course of your working lifetime. Every couple of years, you will change jobs, either within your organization, or from company to company, or industry to industry. Your current knowledge and skills will eventually become obsolete. To remain current and to earn a good living, you will have to continually develop new knowledge and skills.

A good question for you to ask yourself is, "What is my next job going to be?" Based on the changes taking place around you, and the new and unexpected demands of your job today, what are the trends? What kind of job will you be doing in one year? Five years?

Then you can ask, "What is my next career going to be?" Since your business and industry is in a continuous state of flux, is it possible that you will have to shift into an entirely new area if you want to be successful and happy in the years ahead? What new fields most appeal to you? If you could be working in any industry at all, what industry would you like to get into?

Perhaps the most important question of all is this: "What do I have to be absolutely excellent at doing in order to enjoy a high and growing standard of living in the years ahead?"

People who do not plan for the future cannot have one. And the best way to predict your future is to create it for yourself.

Since there is a high probability that you are going to be changing jobs in the future anyway, you should start right now to define and describe your ideal job or position. You should think through and determine for yourself what you really love to do. You can then develop a plan to become excellent at doing what you most enjoy so that you can be paid at the very highest levels of your profession. If you don't do this for yourself, no one else is going to do it for you.

Mastery May Be Easier than You Think

People sometimes think that it would take them so many months or years to achieve mastery in their current field that they lose heart. They become discouraged and give up before they even begin. But often you can bring up your skill level in a particular area of weakness in a matter of weeks or just a few months. Forever afterwards, you will have that skill to use in combination with your other skills. In time, you will forget the extra effort and sacrifice that you invested to achieve that level of skill, but you will continue to enjoy the rewards and benefits of being one of the best in your field.

When you take charge of creating your own future, you accept the age-old rule that your life only gets better when you get better. This rule is both simple and inescapable. It says that any part of your life can only improve on the outside when you improve on the inside. If you want your sales to get better, you must become a better salesperson. If you want your staff to become better, you must become a better manager. If you want your children to become better, you must become a better parent. You can improve any part of your outer world if you just go to work on yourself and get busy improving yourself on the inside.

Set a Goal, Make a Plan, Get Busy

Once you have identified the critical skills that you need to master, write them down as goals, make a plan for their accomplishment, set a schedule for accomplishment, and start to work. Then, no matter how long it takes, just keep working away. Be patient with yourself. Rome was not built in a day. Important skills take a while to develop. But if you persevere, step-by-step, you will eventually become one of the most competent and highest paid people in your field.

You will earn the rewards, the recognition, and the acclaim of all the people around you. People will tell you that you were lucky to choose that particular field or how lucky you are to be so good at what you really enjoy doing. But you will know that luck had nothing to do with it.

ACTION EXERCISES
What You Can Do Now

1. Identify the key skills that are necessary for success in your field; select the one skill that can help you the most and make a plan to become excellent in that area.

2. Determine the most valuable service that you can render to your company and your boss and concentrate on that every day.

3. Identify your primary customers inside and outside your business, and make a plan to become more valuable to them.

4. Resolve to join the top 10 percent of performers in your business, and then make a plan to achieve excellence in your key result areas.

5. Project forward and decide upon the skills you will need to learn and master to lead your field five years from now. Make a plan to acquire those skills and start immediately.

6. Look into yourself and examine your past experiences; what do you really love to do, and how could you organize your career around it?

7. Go to your boss and ask him or her exactly what you can do to increase your value and make a more valuable contribution to your company. Whatever answer you get, take action on it immediately.

Principle 5—Attitude Is Everything

"The greatest revolution of my generation is the discovery that by changing the inner attitudes of your mind, you can change the outer aspects of your life."
—William James

People are described as *lucky* when they seem to move ahead faster and go further in a shorter period of time than others. Whenever someone rises to the top of his field and accomplishes wonderful things with his life, people who are not doing as well as he is always ascribe his success to luck.

When you take charge of creating your own future, rather than waiting for it to happen to you, you begin to experience more and more events that the average person dismisses as luck. You want to incorporate the principles we are discussing in this book into your life so that you can have more of the things that you want, faster and easier, than you could if you had to spend many years working for them.

Perhaps the most powerful of all luck factors, the one that can make or break you throughout your life, is the quality of your personality, the attitude that you bring to the world and to all of your relationships.

Liking is an essential luck factor. The principle of liking says that, "The more people like you, the more they will be open to your influence and the more they will help you to achieve your goals."

The most popular people tend also to be the most influential people in every field. A positive mental attitude is closely associated with success in almost everything you do. There is an old saying that, "It is not your aptitude but your attitude that determines your altitude." When you become a genuinely positive, optimistic person, people will open doors of opportunity for you that would be closed to most others.

Human beings are predominantly *emotional*. We decide emotionally and then justify logically. We are almost completely controlled by our feelings, in every situation, and especially in our interactions with others. In a contest between reason and emotion, emotion wins every time.

If you really want to experience a continuous stream of good luck and happy circumstances, you owe it to yourself to develop the kind of personality that radiates warmth and confidence, and which attracts people to you wherever you go. And your true personality is always expressed in your attitude toward others.

The One Thing You Can't Hide

Earl Nightingale, the famous radio commentator, called *attitude* the most important word in the English language or in any language. Your attitude can be defined as your general emotional approach to any person or situation. It is the one thing about you that people notice immediately. It radiates from you in your facial expression, your tone of voice and your body language. It is seen and felt immediately in every human interaction.

The people around you are affected by your attitude and react almost instantaneously. When you are positive, pleasant, and likable with people, they respond by being positive, pleasant, and likable right back.

Imagine two people calling on the same business a short time apart. One of them is cheerful, friendly, and pleasant. The other one is unsmiling, unhappy, and insecure. Which of these two people do you think is going to get past the gatekeeper and get to see the prospective customer?

If you have a choice of buying a product or service, or doing business with two different people, which one would you choose, the positive person or the negative person?

Be a Team Player

At work, the ability to get along well with others, to cooperate, and to be a good team player is one of the most admired qualities of the most respected employees. In study after study of turnover in organizations, it has been found that people are usually let go more for their inability to get along with others than for any other reason.

Even in times of recession, it is the negative people who are laid-off first. The positive people, the ones who get along well with everyone, are always the last to go, if they go at all. And if for any reason they are laid-off, they are always the first rehired, either by their previous employer or by someone else.

One of the ways to assure that you have a great life is for you to be liked and appreciated by everyone with whom you work. You will get more opportunities and steadier promotions. You will be paid more money and be given greater responsibilities. As a result of your positive mental attitude, the people around, above, and below you, and at your same level, will want you to succeed and will do everything possible to help you.

A person with a positive attitude can make more progress in a couple of years than a person with a negative attitude could make in 10 or 20 years. We all like to buy from and work with people who are pleasant and who make us feel good about ourselves when we are around them, and our words and behavior are very much under our own control.

Take full control of your words and actions, and make sure that everything you do is helping you. Resolve every day to behave like the kind of person you want to be thought of and spoken about by other people.

The Key to Your Personality

Your *self-esteem* is the key to your personality. How you genuinely feel about yourself determines your impact on others more than any other factor. Your self-esteem is best defined as *how much you like yourself*. The more you like and respect yourself, the more you will like and respect others, and the more they will like and respect you. Everything you do and say to build and reinforce your own self-esteem improves your attitude and your relationships with other people.

This is another way of saying again that your outer world will be a reflection of your inner world. Your outer world of relationships will be a reflection of your inner world of personal worth and value.

Mental fitness is very much like physical fitness; they both require regular training. Just as you become physically fit by exercising your body, you become mentally fit by exercising your mind. You build your physical muscles by working on them continuously. You build your mental muscles, your levels of self-esteem, self-respect and self-confidence, by working on them in specific ways as well.

You eat healthy, nutritious foods every day to nourish and sustain high levels of physical health and energy. In the same way, you feed your mind with healthy *mental foods* every day to keep yourself cheerful, optimistic, and upbeat, no matter what happens.

Your Mental Fitness Program

We have already talked about many of the exercises in your mental fitness program. Let's review some of them one more time:

First, to eliminate the negative emotions of anger, blame, envy, resentment, and self-pity, you make a conscious decision to *accept complete responsibility* for your life, for everything you are and everything you will ever be. You refuse to make excuses or to blame anyone else. You see yourself as the primary creative force in your own present and your own future. You realize that you are where you are and what you are because of your own choices and decisions in the past, and since you made those choices and decisions, only you are responsible.

Second, you take charge of your life by seeing yourself as *active rather than passive*. You make things happen rather than waiting and hoping for them to happen. You see yourself as a *master* of change rather than as a victim of change. If you are not happy with some part of your life, you get busy and do something about it, but you refuse to allow negative emotions to interfere with your personality or to cloud your vision.

Third, you set *clear, written goals* for yourself in each important area of your life. You create written plans of action to achieve them. You work on your major goals every day. You maintain a sense of forward momentum and progress that gives you energy and enthusiasm. You keep yourself so busy working on things that are important to you that you don't have time to worry about little irritations or situations that are out of your control.

This dynamite combination of accepting complete responsibility and then designing a clear written plan for your life gives you a foundation upon which you can build as high as you want to go. These two actions give you a tremendous sense of personal power and enable you to create your own future.

Fourth, you recognize that *knowledge and skill* are the keys to financial freedom. The more you learn, the more you earn. The more you learn about your field, the more opportunities you will have to use your increasing knowledge. You work on becoming better every day. You know that *if you're not getting better, you're getting worse.*

Fifth, you recognize that *personal mastery* in your field is absolutely essential to success, achievement, and what people call luck. Excellent performance opens every door and is the key to your earning what you are really worth.

Sixth, you have a plan for *personal and professional development* that includes reading, listening to audio programs, attending courses and seminars, and taking every opportunity to increase your knowledge and skill. The more you work on becoming better at the key skills you need to achieve your goals, the more confident and competent you feel. You know that success is not an accident. Luck is just a word that people use to explain the good things that continually happen to people who are excellent at what they do.

Seventh, and perhaps most important of all, you know that *you become what you think about most of the time*. You, therefore, discipline yourself to think continually about the things that you *want*, and keep your mind *off* of the things you don't want.

Program Your Mind for Success

There are a series of powerful *mental programming techniques* that you can use throughout the day to become a more positive and effective person. Each of these techniques is both practical and proven, and the combination of all of them together can make you both irresistible and unstoppable.

The first of these techniques is the regular use of *positive affirmations* to program your subconscious mind and to keep yourself feeling optimistic and upbeat throughout the day. Fully 95 percent of your emotions are determined by your self-talk, that is, by the way you talk to yourself moment to moment. By controlling and directing your inner dialogue, you take control of your thoughts, feelings, and actions and, ultimately, your own future.

Dr. Martin Seligman of the University of Pennsylvania calls this your "Explanatory Style." The way that you talk to yourself and explain things to yourself largely determines how you feel about what is going on around you. In other words, it is not what happens to you, but how you *interpret* what happens to you, that determines your response, positive or negative.

If you do not consciously and deliberately think and talk about the things you want, you have a natural tendency to begin thinking about the things that you don't want to happen, the people or situations that make you upset or angry. If you do not firmly take control of your own mind and keep your thoughts focused on where you want to go, you will, by default, slip into the negativity and worry that is common to most people.

The principle of affirmation says that *strong, affirmative statements repeated continually in your conscious mind will inevitably be accepted as commands by your subconscious mind.*

Whatever goal or command you program into your subconscious mind will begin to materialize in the world around you. A new goal activates your reticular activating system. This increases your awareness and sensitivity to people, ideas, and opportunities that can help you. It enables you to put your foot on the accelerator of your own potential and move more rapidly toward your goals.

Positive self-talk and positive affirmations are the tools you use to control your thinking and keep focused on achieving your goals. With positive affirmations, your potential is unlimited. You can literally talk yourself into becoming the kind of person that you want to be. The most powerful words in the world are the words that you say to yourself and believe.

The best all-purpose affirmation you can use to build your self-esteem and self-confidence are the words, "*I like myself! I like myself! I like myself!*" over and over.

When you first say, "I like myself!" you may feel a bit uneasy or uncomfortable inside. You may feel that the words are phony. This is quite normal. Psychologists refer to this feeling as *cognitive dissonance.* You experience it whenever a new, positive message you are affirming clashes with an old negative message stored in your subconscious as the result of unhappy experiences in your past.

But when you repeat the positive affirmation, "I like myself!" over and over, eventually your subconscious mind accepts these words as your new operating instructions. You begin to feel, think, and then act like a person with high self-esteem. The more you like yourself, the more you like others. You become a more positive person. And the more you like others, the more they like you and want to cooperate with you. It begins with your own self-esteem.

Another powerful affirmation you can use is the words, *"I'm the best! I'm the best! I'm the best!"* repeated over and over. Whenever you think of yourself and your work, tell yourself, in strong, positive terms that you are the best, and getting better. Tell yourself that you are excellent at what you do. Again, you may feel a little strange when you first start saying this to yourself, but after a short while, you will feel more and more comfortable with this new message. And it will start to be true. Your performance will improve day by day.

A wonderful way to use affirmations is for you to start off every day by repeating the words, *"I feel happy, I feel healthy, I feel terrific!"*

When people ask you how things are going, always reply positively by saying, "Great!" Or, "Wonderful!"

Talk about yourself and your life the way you *want* them to be, not the way they might happen to be at the moment. Remember, before you can experience it in your reality, you must convince your subconscious mind that you already have it. If you don't feel positive and enthusiastic at the moment, pretend that you do. "Fake it until you make it."

Your subconscious mind, which controls your attitude, personality, body language, emotions, and levels of enthusiasm, excitement, and energy, is mechanical, like a computer. It has no ability to think or decide by itself. It merely accepts instructions. It is as though your conscious mind is the gardener and your subconscious mind is the garden. You can plant either flowers or weeds. Either will grow. But if you don't plant flowers, your garden will fill up with weeds, all by itself.

Replace Negative Thoughts with Positive

The Law of Substitution explains one of the most powerful of all success principles in creating your own future. Many people have told me that their understanding of this simple principle has changed their entire lives. The Law of Substitution says that your conscious mind can only hold *one thought at a time*, positive or negative, and you can choose that thought. You can decide to substitute a positive thought for a negative thought any time you choose.

The way you think or feel at any time, the way you act or react, is always the result of a choice that you have made. If you are happy or unhappy, angry or exhilarated, enthusiastic or depressed, in every case, you have *decided* to feel this way. It is always a matter of choice, and the choice is always up to you.

With the use of positive affirmations, you can keep your mind centered and focused on the things you want and care about. You can choose to feed your mind with positive messages that are life enhancing rather than dwelling on things that make you angry or sad. With affirmations, you can control and improve your attitude toward yourself and others. You can use the Law of Substitution to block out negative thoughts by thinking about your goals instead.

Block Out Negative Thoughts

Ihzrat Khan, the Sufi Master, once wrote, "Life is a continuous succession of problems." At this very moment, your life is probably filled with problems of all kinds, large and small. If you don't watch out, those problems will fill your thoughts and preoccupy your mind. The more you think about your problems, the more negative you will become.

You can counter this natural tendency toward negative thinking by focusing instead on your goals. Whenever something happens that makes you angry, neutralize the negative thought by thinking about your goals, especially your biggest and most exciting goal. Repeat your goal in the form of a personal, present tense affirmation. Talk to yourself about what you want, and use that to keep your mind off of the things that you don't want.

Whenever you have a problem of any kind, discipline yourself to *think about the solution* instead. Stop reviewing the problem in your mind, thinking about who was to blame, and wondering what you could have or should have done differently. Instead, think about the solution and what you are going to do next. The instant that you start thinking about what you can *do*, your mind calms and clears. You become positive and constructive. You are back in control.

Almost all negativity requires your remembering and rehashing a past event or circumstance. Positive thinking comes from your thinking about your goals and the specific things that you could be doing right now to achieve them faster.

You can also use this principle of substitution by forcing yourself to *think about the future rather than the past.* Think about where you are going rather than where you have been. Think about your ideal life and the wonderful possibilities that lie ahead of you. Your future dreams and visions are naturally positive and uplifting. While you are thinking about them, you can't simultaneously think about something that holds you back or drags you down.

You can use the Law of Substitution by getting so busy working on goals and tasks that are important to you that you don't have any time to think about anything else. The only real antidote to worry is sustained, continuous action. I always liked Tennyson's line, "I must lose myself in action lest I whither in despair." When you "lose yourself in action," your worries disappear.

Whatever You *See*, You Will Be

Your ability to visualize your future goals as current realities, and to see yourself as you really want to be, is one of the greatest powers you can develop for success, happiness, and great achievement. To get the most from the power of visualization, you must practice feeding your mind with a continuous stream of positive images that are consistent with the person you want to be and the life you want to live.

All improvement in your life begins with an improvement in your mental pictures. If you talk to unhappy people and ask them what they think about most of the time, you will find that almost without fail, they think about their problems, their bills, their negative relationships, and all the difficulties in their lives.

But when you talk to successful, happy people, you find that they think and talk most of the time about the things that they want to be, do, and have. They think and talk about the specific action steps they can take to get them. They dwell continually on vivid, exciting pictures of what their goals will look like when they are realized, and what their dreams will look like when they come true.

Learn Any Skill

One of the keys to learning any skill is your ability to visualize yourself using that skill. One of the keys to becoming excellent in any sport is your ability to see yourself performing in that sport. One of the keys to physical fitness is your ability to visualize yourself with the kind of body you will have when you are thin, fit, and trim. An essential part of self-confidence is your ability to see yourself repeatedly performing with confidence in an important area of your life.

Send the Right Commands

Your mental pictures are a form of visual affirmations. They are accepted by your subconscious mind as commands, and your subconscious mind then works to bring them into your reality. But both affirmation and visualization are neutral processes. They work either for you or against you. They help bring about either what you want or what you don't want. They bring into your life what you think about most of the time, positive or negative.

The problem with most people is that, in the morning, they think about how much money they want to earn, and in the afternoon, they think about their financial problems. In the evening they go home and worry about their bills. They keep sending their minds a series of conflicting and contradictory messages, like giving a taxi driver different instructions at every corner. As a result, they make first a little progress, and then a little regress. Over time, they never seem to get anywhere.

Feed Your Mind with Exciting Pictures

For you to enjoy the full fruits of what people call *luck*, and to create your own future, you must fully activate the positive powers of the law of attraction. You must use it to draw into your life, from all directions, the people and circumstances that can help you to achieve your goals. You must continually affirm, visualize, and act in a manner consistent with what you want, and keep your mind off of what you don't want.

To strengthen your ability to visualize and affirm, buy magazines containing pictures of the home, car, clothes, equipment, vacation trips and furniture that you intend to have one day. Cut them out and post them all around your house and office. Think about and imagine them continually.

When my wife and I began talking about our dream house, we bought and read every magazine we could find that described beautiful homes. On the weekends, we drove around and visited beautiful houses for sale in expensive neighborhoods. We walked through them from one end to the other, noticing the various features that we liked. We went for long walks and regularly discussed what our dream house would look like. We made lists of every feature we would want in the right house when we found it.

And it worked. In less than three years, we went from a condominium to a rented house. We then bought a house, and finally another house that was perfect for us in every respect. Out of 42 items we had listed describing our perfect house, the one we bought had 41. Our house turned out to be the exact picture of the image we had created in our minds.

Get the Feeling

Perhaps the most important ingredient that you can add to the process of affirmation and visualization is the constant *emotionalization* of your words and mental pictures. The success formula says that:

Thought multiplied by Emotion = Reality (T × E = R)

The thought or image of the goal you desire, multiplied by the emotion of desire and excitement that you associate with it, will determine how fast your goal appears. The more you can emotionalize a goal, affirmation, or picture, the more energy that command will have and the more rapidly it will be acted upon by your subconscious mind. When you have an intense burning desire for a goal of any kind, you generate an inner power of enthusiasm and determination that drives you forward and enables you to overcome any obstacle that gets in your way.

Thought Creates Action, Action Creates Thought

The Law of Reversibility contains a power you can use to create your own life. It explains one of the most important luck factors of all. This law has been known for thousands of years. It has been taught by many of the great teachers throughout history. In reality, it is the basis and the expression of *faith*, the foundation principle of all religions. William James of Harvard rediscovered it in 1905 when he wrote, "Just as feelings generate actions that are consistent with them, actions generate feelings that are consistent with those actions, as well."

What this means is that you can *act* your way into feeling the way you want to *feel*. You can program your subconscious mind by behaving as if you already have the qualities and characteristics that you most desire. Your subconscious mind will then generate the emotions and energy consistent with your words and behaviors.

For example, you may wake up in the morning not feeling particularly enthusiastic about the day. You may feel reluctant to call on new customers or to visit your banker. But if you deliberately pretend to be positive and confident already, after a few short minutes, you will start to actually feel the way you are acting. You will feel happy and in control. You will feel optimistic and outgoing. Your actions will actually create the feelings or emotions that are consistent with them.

How many times does a football team that is behind in the second quarter get a pep talk from the coach in the locker room? Probably every single time. After that pep talk, the team goes charging out onto the field as though they could conquer the world. Very often, this new attitude of confidence and enthusiasm turns the game around and takes them to victory.

Become Your Own Cheerleader

You can actually become your own cheerleader by talking to yourself positively and then *acting as if* you were already the person that you wanted to be. Act as though you were trying out for the role of a positive, cheerful, happy, and likable person. Walk, talk, and act as if you were already that person. Treat everyone you meet as though you had just won an award for being the very best person in your industry or as though you had just won the lottery. You will be amazed at how much better you feel about yourself after just a few minutes of pretending.

Seek First to Understand

In your relationships with others, a vital success factor is the quality of *empathy*. This means striving to feel what the other person is feeling. As Steven Covey says, "Seek first to understand, then to be understood."

One of the fastest ways for you to overcome any shyness or insecurity you may feel is to *ask questions* of the other person and then try to understand their true feelings and concerns. While they speak, sit quietly and listen closely to their answers. Ask follow-up questions and check for understanding. Repeat back what they have said to be sure you understand. As coach Lou Holtz says, "Everyone's first question is: *Do you care about me?*" Listening shows that you do care.

Most people are so preoccupied with themselves and the details of their lives that they pay little attention to others. When you do the opposite and empathize with them by trying to understand their concerns, by asking them questions and listening to them when they talk, they will like you and will want to cooperate with you. They will open doors for you and buy what you are selling.

Make Others Feel Important

An extension of the principle of empathy is the Law of Emotional Reciprocity. This law says that *when you do and say things that make other people feel good about themselves, they will want to reciprocate and make you feel good as well*.

What people want more than anything else is to feel important. They want to feel valued and appreciated. They want to feel that what they are doing really makes a difference. They want a sense of *significance*. Your job is to give it to them in every interaction.

Just as you want people to like you, respect you, and treat you nicely, each person you meet wants the same. If you want people to say things that raise your self-esteem, look for every opportunity to say nice things to others that raise their self-esteem. Look for ways to cause people to like themselves even more.

The people that you like the most in life are the ones who make you feel the best about yourself when you are with them. The people who like you the most are the people who you make feel the same way. With every person you meet, look for something that you can say that will make that person feel better about himself or herself. This is the key to excellent human relationships.

Resolve to be a positive person in every interaction. No matter what happens, decide in advance that you will never criticize, condemn, or complain. If you can't say something nice, don't say anything at all. Silence can be golden. Even if you have a problem of some kind, it is better for you to start off by asking for help rather than criticizing when you approach another person.

Look the Part

The way you look on the outside can help you or hurt you. Your appearance is an important success factor, and can contribute immensely to your luck. Sometimes, your image can make or break you in a critical business relationship.

People are highly visual. You've heard it said that you never get a second chance to make a good first impression. People are always sorting and judging the new people they meet, trying to determine whether or not they are important. This process takes place unconsciously. We are usually not even aware of it. But often we make an instant decision when we meet a person for the first time. Ever after, that first impression exerts an inordinate influence on our thoughts and feelings toward that person.

Research shows that people make up their mind about you in the *first four seconds*. Each person's mind is like quick drying cement, and the first four seconds leaves the first impression. The cement sets fast in about 30 seconds, and after that, the observer will look for things about you to justify their initial impression. Because of the way the human mind is constructed, people use selective perception and will ignore or reject factors or evidence that is inconsistent with what they have already decided to believe.

The most successful people are usually those who look good on the outside. They do not leave their first impressions to chance. They give a lot of thought to their appearance. They carefully study other successful people and they dress accordingly. They constantly observe the top people in their field and strive to look more and more like them.

You've heard it said, "Birds of a feather flock together." Or, "Like attracts like." You'll find that, as you rise to higher levels in your business and personal life, the people at each higher level dress better than the people at the lower levels. Successful people can recognize other successful people across a crowded room. Just as birds have plumage that enables them to be recognized by other birds of their same kind, individuals have plumage as well, in the form of the clothes they wear, their grooming, and their accessories. Because of the power and irresistibility of the Law of Attraction, people who look similar seem to be attracted to each other in social and business situations.

The fact is that you are most comfortable dealing with people who are very much like you. And so is everyone else. If you want important people to be comfortable dealing with you, you must dress the way they dress and carry yourself the way they carry themselves. If you want to be taken seriously, you must look like a person who should be taken seriously.

Appropriate Dress in Business

Many thousands of experiments have been conducted on the most influential ways to dress for various situations. The ideal colors for business, for men, are navy blue, dark gray, and, occasionally, beige. These are also the ideal colors for women; in addition, women can wear hunter green. Men should wear white or pastel shirts and silk ties, carefully coordinated with the color of their suits. Women should always wear accessories that complement the main color and design of their clothes. Both men and women should wear high quality shoes, properly polished.

There is an acceptable type of grooming for both men and women in every occupation and at every level of society. If you want to drive a truck, you can wear a beard with hair down your back. If you want to be successful in business, you should have a conservative hairstyle and a clean face.

A Complete Career Turnaround

A young man working for a sales organization in Phoenix was doing poorly at his job. He had a good education, nice clothes, a pleasant personality, and a high level of energy. He was busy and active, but he was having no luck with his sales. Both he and his boss were extremely frustrated and his boss was thinking of letting him go.

The young man had a full beard and mustache. He thought it was attractive and different, but what thousands of customer interviews have revealed is that facial hair, especially a beard, is considered eccentric. Even worse, because a beard covers half the face, it is unconsciously registered as a mask. It implies that the individual has something to hide.

When the young man learned this at one of my seminars, he went home and immediately shaved off his beard and mustache. The very next day, he made a $30,000 sale. His career took off. His sales continued to increase. Within two months he was the top salesman in his company. The same prospects who had been reluctant to talk to him became his best customers and referred him to other people. He told me that if he had not learned about how facial hair on a young man could hold him back, he would probably have failed in his new career.

Everything Counts

One of the most important success principles, and a vital luck factor, is that everything counts! Everything counts, not just what you want to count. Every little thing that you do or don't do counts in some way. Everything helps or hurts. Everything adds up or takes away. Everything moves you toward your goals or moves you away from them. Everything counts.

You've heard it said, "The devil is in the details." This is as true for your image as it is for any other part of your work or personal life. Little things *do* mean a lot. You should read at least one book on how to dress for success in business. Leave nothing to chance. Study the top people around you. If you work for a salary, dress the same way the people two jobs above you dress. Spend twice as much on your clothes and buy half as many. If you are a junior clerk, come to the office looking like a junior executive. You will immediately attract the attention of people who can help you.

When you combine an excellent, professional image with a commitment to continuous growth in your knowledge and skill, you will put yourself onto the fast track in your career. The most important people in your world will be eager to open doors for you.

Feel Terrific about Yourself

One reason why image is so important is that, when you *look* absolutely excellent in a personal or business situation, you *feel* absolutely excellent as well. When you look around you and you know that you are one of the best-dressed people in the room, you experience a tremendous inner feeling of pride, confidence, and self-esteem. You like and respect yourself much more, and as a result, you like and respect others. You are more confident, courteous, and gracious in your behaviors toward them. When you dress like a winner, you think, feel, and act like a winner.

Your outer behaviors of walking, talking, grooming, and dressing like an important person have a reverse effect on you. They actually cause you to feel like an outstanding individual in everything you do. And everything counts!

Open Every Door

Your personality and your attitude are perhaps the most powerful of all luck factors. When you combine them with a commitment to doing your job in an excellent fashion, you motivate the people around you to help you move forward in your career. The nicer you are to others, the nicer they will be to you. The more positive a person you are, the more people will want to be involved with you and to do business with you.

One of the most important discoveries in the field of leadership, especially personal leadership, is that leadership takes place when other people want you to be the leader. The better you cooperate and interact with people, the more they will want you to be successful. Doors will open for you, and luck will have nothing to do with it.

ACTION EXERCISES
What You Can Do Now

1. Resolve today to develop and maintain a positive mental attitude, no matter what happens.

2. Visualize yourself continually as a positive, confident, cheerful person, likable and liked by everyone.

3. Make other people feel important; take every opportunity to offer praise, encouragement, and gratitude to the people you work with.

4. Act as if you were already one of the most popular, persuasive, and influential people in your company; fake it until you make it.

5. Dress the part of a successful person with a great future; people are highly visual and they judge you by the way you look on the outside.

6. Be a completely solution-oriented person. Whenever there is a problem, immediately start talking in terms of what can be done to solve it rather than who is to blame.

7. Be a team player; always be looking for ways to help your co-workers make a greater contribution.

Principle 6—Relationships Are Essential

"The best portion of a good man's life,—
his little nameless, unremembered acts of kindness and of love."
—William Wordsworth

The quality and quantity of your relationships with other people will determine your success as much or more than any other factor. In the last chapter, you learned several ways to become a far more positive, optimistic, and likable person. In this chapter, you will learn how to systematically expand your network of contacts and relationships. This strategy will help you increase the likelihood that you will meet the right person at the right time with the right information or opportunity for you.

The Law of Relationships explains one of the most critical success factors of all. It says, *relationships are essential; the more people who know you and think of you in a positive way, the more opportunities you will have to achieve your goals.*

Every important change in your life will involve other people. If you want to achieve big goals, you will need the active involvement and cooperation of many other people. Often, the direction of your life will be changed by a simple comment, a piece of advice, or a single action by one person. The more good relationships you have, and the more helpful people you know, the more often the right doors will open for you.

The Law of Relationships in Action

A friend of mine was growing his business in an extremely competitive market. He needed more money to expand. He began calling on local banks with his business plan. One by one, they turned him down and told him that his business would never be successful.

However, he was an optimist. He drew a series of ever expanding concentric circles around the address and location of his business and began calling on banks at ever-greater distances. Finally, he found a bank and a banker 95 miles away who liked his business plan and lent him the money he needed to expand. He is today one of the wealthiest and most successful entrepreneurs in America.

I asked him if he had ever thought about giving up his search for the money he needed. He said, "Absolutely not! I knew that I would eventually get the money if I spoke to enough people. I was prepared to visit banks even 500 miles from my office if that's what it took to find the right banker with the right attitude for what I needed."

Improve the Odds in Your Favor

This is a key luck factor and an important part of success: Remember the Law of Probabilities, which says, *the more different things you try, the more likely it will be that you will try the right thing at the right time.*

This law applies to relationships as well. The more people you know, and the more consistently you expand your range of contacts, the more likely it is that you will meet the person you need, at exactly the right time, with exactly the right resources for you. When it happens, as it always does, it will not be a miracle, and it will have nothing to do with luck.

The most successful people in our society, at all levels, are those who know and are known by the greatest number of other successful people. But this is very much a *chicken and egg* situation. Do people become successful and then meet other successful people? Or do they meet other successful people, and then become successful themselves?

The fact is that it can work either way. People make the mistake of thinking that by being around other successful people, they will be able to piggyback on their knowledge, advice, and resources. This however will only work for a short time. In the long run, you can never get and hold onto anything to which you are not entitled as the result of your own accomplishments, talents, and personality.

Focus on Attracting Key People

The Law of Attraction is perhaps the most important of the luck factors. "You inevitably attract into your life the people and circumstances in harmony with your dominant thoughts."

The opposite of the Law of Attraction is the Law of Repulsion, which says, "You automatically drive away or repel people and circumstances that are not in harmony with your dominant thoughts."

When you think positively most of the time, you set up a force field of positive energy that attracts other positive people and situations toward you. If you think negatively, you set up a field of negative energy that drives these same forces away.

Birds of a feather *do* flock together. People at similar levels of success in every enterprise or profession tend to be attracted to each other. And you cannot fake it for very long.

Implement the Law of Indirect Effort

This brings us to an important luck factor—the Law of Indirect Effort. This law says that *most often you get what you want with other people indirectly* rather than directly. In fact, if you attempt to get other people to help you or cooperate with you *directly*, you will often end up looking foolish. You will actually drive those people away.

But if you use the Law of Indirect Effort, you will be amazed at how successful you can be. For example, if you want to have more friends, how do you use the Law of Indirect Effort? It's simple. Concentrate on *being* a good friend to others. Take an interest in them. Ask them questions and listen to what they have to say. Be empathetic. Express interest and concern about their problems and their situations. Look for ways to help them, even if it is just by being a friendly sounding board. The more you concentrate on being a good friend, the more friends you will have. You will attract people into your life like bees to honey.

Do you want to *impress* other people? The worst way to do it is the direct way, by trying to impress them. The best way is the indirect way, by *being* impressed by other people. The more impressed you are with other people and their accomplishments, the more interested and impressed they will be with you and yours. Everyone has done something that is noteworthy and impressive. When you meet a new person, your job is to find it out.

Ask people what they do. Ask people how they got into their particular field. Ask people how everything is going in their business. If you listen carefully, people will tell you about both their current successes and their current problems. When a person mentions that they have just achieved something worthwhile, be sure to congratulate them.

Everybody Likes a Compliment

Abraham Lincoln once said, "Everybody likes a compliment." People love to be acknowledged and admired for things they have accomplished. Make it a policy to find out what they have achieved and then compliment them on their successes.

A successful businessman I know made a habit of sending ten telegrams every week to people he had met over the years. The telegrams contained a single word, "Congratulations!"

Over the years he built up a wide network of men and women who liked and respected him. They were always amazed that he had somehow known that they had accomplished something worthwhile and had acknowledged them with his telegram.

When he was asked, later on in life, how he managed to be aware of the accomplishments of so many of his friends, he said that he had had no idea what they were doing. He just knew that everybody is accomplishing something every day and every week. When you send them a message that says "Congratulations!" they will automatically apply that message to whatever situation in their life that has just worked out successfully for them.

By using the Law of Indirect Effort, you constantly look for ways to compliment and congratulate people on what they are doing, what they have accomplished, how they are dressed, the recent decisions they have made, or even the fact that they have lost a few pounds.

In our society, one of the best compliments that you can give to anyone is, "You look like you've lost weight!" Even if it's not true, people always enjoy having someone notice, rightly or wrongly, that they have lost weight. Why? Because everyone wants to be physically attractive, and physical attractiveness is closely associated with being thin, trim, and fit. You can never go wrong complimenting someone on how good they look.

Satisfy One of the Deepest Human Needs

Do you want people to respect you? This is one of the deepest of all needs. Almost everything you do is to earn the respect of the people you respect, or at least not to lose the respect of the people you respect. So if you want people to respect you, the best way is for you to respect them, *in advance*.

We have moved away from the era of the go-getter and we are now in the era of the "go-giver." Successful people are always looking for ways to do things for other people. The great majority of underachievers and unhappy people are those who are waiting for others to do something for them, in advance. They want to get something out before they put something in.

But this attitude violates the Law of Sowing and Reaping. You cannot reap until you have sown. You therefore concentrate on sowing good thoughts, good ideas, and good feelings in your relationships with others. You know, as a matter of universal law, that these same things will come back to you in the most remarkable ways.

Give Generously of Yourself

The Law of Giving, another key luck factor, says *the more you give of yourself without expectation of return, the more that will come back to you from the most unexpected sources.*

Many people make the mistake of thinking that their giving should come back to them from the very people that they have given to. But this very seldom happens. When you give generously to someone else, either of your time, money, or emotion, that person will very seldom be the person who repays you in kind. Instead, you will be activating the Law of Attraction, and powers will be put in motion that will bring you the good that you need and desire, usually from a completely different source and at exactly the right time and place for you.

Why should this happen? It's easy to understand. When you do something nice for another person, it raises your own self-esteem and makes you feel better about yourself. This heightened feeling of positive energy activates your powers of attraction. You become a more powerful magnet for people and circumstances consistent with your goals. Good things start to happen to you.

There is something about helping others, about giving of yourself to others in need, that makes you feel wonderful about yourself. In fact, you are designed in such a way that you can only be truly happy when you know that you are doing something that makes a positive difference in the lives of other people.

The reality is that you benefit as much, and often, much more, than the person for whom you do a kindness. You change the force field of mental energy around you by helping others in some way. You intensify the power of attraction and draw into your life helpful people and circumstances from sources that you could not imagine or predict.

Activate the Principle of Serendipity

Serendipity works in strange ways. Here is an example. Imagine you are driving from Point A to Point B. You are in a hurry but you see an old person who is stopped by the side of the road with a flat tire. Even though you are on a tight schedule, you overcome your impatience and stop your car to help the elderly person replace the tire. The person offers to pay you but you refuse. You wish the elderly person a pleasant journey and you hurry on toward your destination. The whole incident takes about 10 minutes.

Perhaps unbeknownst to you, you have just activated the powers of the universe in your behalf. You arrive at your appointment a little bit late, but you find that the person you are going to meet is even later than you. Nothing is lost. Not only that, something has happened that morning and the person you meet with, rather than being a reluctant prospect, is very much in need of what you are selling and makes an immediate decision to buy. You walk out with one of the best and easiest orders you've ever received, and if you're not careful, you will start thinking about how lucky you were. But it wasn't luck. It was law.

Generosity of all kinds triggers happy, serendipitous events in your life. Throughout the ages, many men and women have *tithed* their way to great success and fortune. They have regularly given 10 percent or more of their income to worthy causes. This attitude of generosity and the action of giving seems to set up a force field of energy that draws financial opportunities to them that are far greater than any money they give away.

Generosity Really Pays

John D. Rockefeller began his life as a clerk earning $3.75 per week. He saved 20 percent of his income and gave 50 percent to his church. He lived on the remaining 30 percent. Eventually, he got into the fledgling oil business and built Standard Oil, the biggest oil company in the United States.

There is an interesting sequel to the John D. Rockefeller story. His entire fortune was based on his obsessive drive to reduce the cost of fuel oil to the American consumer. He used every business strategy possible to acquire ever-greater quantities of gas and oil. He built complex and sophisticated systems of distribution and delivery. He was so efficient that he was able to continually lower fuel prices. He was able to take away the market from anyone who was charging more than he was. His company, Standard Oil, was called a monopoly, but it was completely customer centered. It was built on his ability to give his customers what they wanted cheaper than anyone else.

As his business interests grew and expanded, he lost sight of his original desire to share his benefits with others. In the back of his mind, he had always intended to give money to worthy causes, but he became so busy building his empire that he simply didn't have the time.

When Rockefeller was 52 years old, he was the richest man in the world. He was also a physical wreck. He was in a state of collapse. His body was falling apart. The doctors told him that he only had a few months, perhaps a year, to live. He had worked for so long, and so hard, and had taken such poor care of himself physically, that even though he could afford any kind of treatment, there was nothing they could do for him.

Rockefeller decided that if he was going to die anyway, he was going to go back to his original intention and give away some of his money. He sold half of his interests in the Rockefeller oil companies for cash, an amount of about $500 million dollars. He then set up the first Rockefeller Foundation and began giving his money away to worthy causes that he had admired over the years. And a remarkable thing happened. The more money he gave away, the healthier he became.

Eventually, his physical problems cleared up. The more dedicated he became to charitable causes, to funding churches and foundations and other needy organizations, the better he felt, and the healthier, happier, and more positive he became.

Meanwhile, the Rockefeller oil companies continued to grow. The half ownership that he retained in his companies increased in value at a rate faster than he could give the other half away. Rockefeller lived to the age of 92, another 40 years. By the time he died, he had given away hundreds of millions of dollars. But the incredible thing was that he was worth more when he died than when he had sold half of his interests at the age of 52 and began his charitable activities.

The Giver Benefits More than the Receiver

Many of the great family fortunes of the world are characterized by generosity and altruism. It seems that the more of your wealth you give away, without anyone knowing, and with no expectation of return, the more you activate the powers of the universe to work on your behalf.

The person who benefits the most from acts of kindness and generosity is always the giver, not the recipient. When you give generously of yourself, you change the kind of person you are inside. You transform the inner aspects of your mind. You create a new mental equivalent, which is more consistent with the feelings of satisfaction, joy, and success you desire. You become a truly lucky person.

Leave Nothing to Chance

Because relationships are so important, they cannot be left to chance. The great majority of people are like billiard balls banging around on the table of life. They are like bumper car drivers at the fair, continually colliding with other people, randomly, with very little control over whom they run into or who runs into them. They live by the Law of Accident. But this is not for you.

You must make a specific plan for the relationships that you want to develop and nurture in your life. You free yourself from the Law of Accident by living your life by design. Instead of things happening to you in a random and haphazard way, you deliberately plan what you want to have happen. The clearer you are in your own mind about what you want, the more rapidly you attract it into your life and the more easily you recognize it when it does occur.

Finding the Ideal Person for You

Your choice of a mate in marriage or in a key relationship will do more to determine your overall success and happiness than perhaps any other factor. You probably know lots of people who have worked hard for years to achieve material success in the work world, and then seen it all fall to pieces when the critical relationships with their spouses and children disintegrated for lack of time and attention.

One way for you to find your ideal mate is the same way that you achieve any worthwhile goal in life. You sit down with a pad of paper and you write out a description of the perfect person for you. As you do this exercise, imagine that you are putting in an order that you are going to mail and the perfect person is going to be delivered back to you, exactly the way you have described him or her.

Take the time to write out every detail. Be sure to describe the ideal person's appearance, height, weight, and level of physical fitness. Describe the person's temperament, personality, sense of humor, education, intelligence, and attitude. Be as precise as you can with regard to the person's values, beliefs, philosophies, and opinions about the important things in life. The more detailed your description, the more likely you will be to find the perfect person for you.

Read and re-read this description every day. Add new details and characteristics to the description as you think of them. Modify and adjust the existing description so that it is more and more accurate and precise.

Each time you review the description of your ideal person, you program this picture deeper and deeper into your subconscious mind. When you imagine how happy you will feel when you are in a relationship with the perfect person for you, this emotional component activates your subconscious mind and triggers the Law of Attraction. In no time at all, you will draw that person into your life.

Decide What You Have to Offer

The next step in finding your ideal relationship is for you to do an honest evaluation of yourself. One of the hallmarks of the self-actualizing person is that he or she is completely objective about his or her strengths and weaknesses. A superior person has the courage and honesty to see himself as he really is, not as he wishes he could be. He can face the truth about himself.

Make a list of everything that you have to offer in a relationship. What are all your good points? What are the characteristics and qualities that you have developed over the course of years that make you a really worthwhile catch for the ideal kind of person that you want?

Now, be honest with yourself and make a list of the areas where you still have work to do. Are you not as disciplined as you would like to be? Do you not use your time as well as you would like? Are you sometimes impatient, irritable, or demanding? Write them all down, and then resolve to go to work to improve yourself in each of these areas.

Remember, you cannot attract into your life a person who is very different from the person you are deep inside. If you want to attract an excellent person to you, you must become an excellent person yourself.

Your relationships, especially your most important relationships, will always reflect your true personality, values, beliefs, and attitudes. You will always experience on the outside what you truly are on the inside.

Finding the Best Boss for You

Once you have made some decisions about what you want in your personal life, it is time for you to decide what kind of relationships you want in your business and in your career. One of the secrets of success in the world of work is to select your boss carefully. When you go out to look for a job, remember that you are going to be exchanging your life, your most precious possession, for the opportunity to work and get results, and the income that goes along with it.

The key to your success at work is going to be the quality of the relationship that you have with your boss, your co-workers, and your customers. Choose your boss with care. Interview carefully until you find the kind of person that you would enjoy working for. Look for someone who you like, respect, and admire. You want to work for someone who has a lot to teach you, and who will encourage you and support you in doing the best job you possibly can.

On the other hand, if you find yourself working for a negative boss or working in a difficult situation, you will never be happy or successful. Eventually, you will quit or be fired and have to go out and find a new job, somewhere else, working with and for different people. Smart people are those who refuse to continue working in a situation where they are unhappy. They know that a job they don't enjoy is a waste of time and a waste of life.

I have seen many situations where a good person has left a negative work environment and joined a different company with a positive, optimistic, encouraging boss and a group of really great co-workers. In no time at all, the person who was doing poorly in one environment began to thrive and grow in the new environment.

Get Around the Right People

One of the most important decisions that you make in life is your choice of the people with whom you habitually associate. Associate with the right people. Spend time around winners, and get away from negative people. Get away from people who complain and condemn and criticize all the time. These toxic people depress you and take all the joy out of living. After you have spent time with them, you feel discouraged and demotivated.

Instead, choose your friends and associates with care. As Baron de Rothschild said, "Make no useless acquaintances." Be perfectly selfish about the people with whom you choose to work and socialize. Dr. David McClellan's research into achievement at Harvard University concluded after 25 years that the members of your "reference group" will have more of an impact on your success and happiness than any other choices you make in life.

Your reference group is made up of the people with whom you identify and associate most of the time. If you fly with *eagles*, you will think and feel like an eagle. If you associate with *turkeys*, you will think, walk, talk, and act like a turkey. The people around you have an inordinate influence on your personality, your opinions, your goals, and everything you accomplish.

Successful people are often described as loners. This does not mean that they are a-loners. They have lots of friends, but they don't go out for lunch with whoever is standing by the door at the time. They are selective in their relationships. They insist upon only spending time with people they enjoy and whose company they can benefit from. You must do the same.

Get Out and Meet People

One of the most common characteristics of self-made millionaires in America is that they are continuous *networkers*. They know that the more people they know, and who know them, the more luck they are going to have when it comes to making sales and discovering opportunities. They take every opportunity to network with other people and to expand their network of overlapping contacts in all the areas of their life that they consider to be important.

A good friend of mine, Sylvie Begin, moved from Ottawa, Ontario to San Diego to start a new business. She did not know anyone when she arrived. Within a few months, she had become one of the most active and popular people in her industry. How did she do it? The answer was networking!

She immediately got involved in her industry associations and organizations. She became fully engaged and contributed wholeheartedly to the activities of the group, and because only a few people ever do this, she soon rose to a position of prominence in planning and organizing the major committees and functions. She was soon recognized and respected by the key people in these organizations. She quickly developed a reputation for helping out and getting things done. Opportunities began to flow her way. She gained the support and backing of important people inside and outside her business, and made more progress in a few months than most other people had made in several years.

The Networking Strategy That Never Fails

The key to successful networking is for you to deliberately select one or two organizations with members who can be of assistance to you and who you can help, as well, in achieving your personal and business goals.

The Law of Credibility is a key luck factor. It says, *the more people believe you and trust you, the easier it is for them to work with you and do business with you.*

This is another area where everything counts. Everything you do in your relationships either helps or hurts your credibility and the level of trust that you have with other people. One of your main reasons for joining key organizations is to begin building your credibility with the people who can help you sometime in the future.

Here is the formula for successful networking in business. First, before you join an organization, study it carefully. Do your homework. Learn why the organization exists and what it does. Find out what parts of the organization are the most active and the most important to the success of the organization.

Second, study the roster of members and the committee structure. Be sure that you are joining an organization that has people in it who are ahead of you in your career and in your business. They must be people that you can learn from and gain from. They must be people who have the capacity to pull you up to higher levels than you have so far attained on your own. Only when you are both satisfied and excited about the organization and what it does should you join.

Third, once you are a member, find out which committees are the most important to the functioning of the organization. Ask questions and listen carefully. When you have identified a key committee where you feel you could make a valuable contribution, volunteer for that committee. Since everything that is done in business and social organizations is largely voluntary, your willingness to contribute your time and effort will always be welcome.

Most people who join associations do little more than attend the meetings and functions and then go home. They look upon the meetings as an extension of their social life rather than as a key part of their business lives.

Volunteer for Assignments

Your strategy is different. When you join, you not only take on responsibilities, you become actively involved. You volunteer for additional assignments. You raise your hand when something needs to be done, and you perform whatever tasks are given to you. You attend every meeting and contribute to every discussion. You do your homework before the meetings so that you are thoroughly prepared, and you follow up quickly.

In no time at all, the key people on the committee will take notice of you. By constantly giving of yourself with no expectation of return, you will begin to earn both their respect and their trust. Your credibility with them will increase. They will become even more confident in your ability to perform ever more important tasks. In no time at all, they will be asking you to help in vital areas and counting on you for important tasks. You will soon become a key player on the committee and a valuable member of the organization.

My Own Story of Networking

Some years ago I joined the Chamber of Commerce for the express purpose of getting involved in the business community and making a contribution of some kind. I found that the key issue that the Chamber was involved in was the *business-government-education* situation that existed at that time. I therefore volunteered for service on the business/education committee that liaised with the government.

I invested many hours doing research and writing papers for the committee. I attended every meeting. I suggested different strategies and tactics that the business community could use to take a more active role with the government in increasing the relevance and quality of education in the state. Within six months, I had been made the vice-chairman of the committee, and assigned all of the major responsibilities of the Chamber in the business-education area.

The chairman of the committee was one of the senior businessmen in the community. He was extremely powerful and linked to a variety of business and government organizations everywhere. I worked under him and followed his guidance and instruction. He began opening doors for me and introducing me to other key business people who could give me input and advice on the business and education activities of the Chamber.

Six months later, the annual meeting of the Chamber was held in a major resort. It was attended by several hundred delegates, every one of them a top executive from a major company. They asked me if I would take on the responsibility of preparing the agenda of speakers and emceeing the annual meeting.

Again, I accepted with enthusiasm. I spent many hours preparing and studying the introductions of the various speakers. At the meeting, I was front and center as the emcee and chairman for the entire day, in front of hundreds of top business delegates. Because I had done my homework, I was thoroughly prepared to do the job in a competent manner.

After the meeting, I was invited to join the inner circle of the business and government relations committee. By the next year, I was holding and chairing meetings between groups of senior business executives and senior government officials. Some of these meetings were written up in the newspapers, including some of the comments that I had made and that the politicians had made in response. A top businessman in my city read the comments and decided that he wanted me to work for him. He hired me away from my job at double the salary plus stock options.

Before the dust had settled, I was one of the best known and respected young businessmen in the state. I was on a first-name basis with senior politicians, top business people and the heads of several private and public organizations. I was invited to become a key player with the United Way in their annual fund-raising drive. This brought me to the attention of more senior business people and gave me even more opportunities to expand my contacts.

Within two years, my income doubled again. There seemed to be a direct relationship between the ever-widening circles of contacts I was forming and the opportunities that I had to work, invest, develop real estate, travel, and interact with more and more key people.

You Can Do It as Well

And my story is not unique. Countless people have had the same experience. But it depends on you. It is up to you to get out there and to get involved with what is going on in your community. There are always vastly more opportunities for you to serve your community in social, business, or charitable organizations than there ever will be talented people to fill those slots. There are no limits to the degree to which you can expand your contacts if you approach the situation as a giver rather than as a taker.

When you meet a new person who you feel it would be valuable for you to know, remember the old saying, "The person who asks questions, has control." Use the Law of Indirect Effort. Instead of trying to impress the other person, ask him or her questions and then be impressed by what he or she says to you.

Look for opportunities to help, to put in rather than to take out. Remember that the Law of Sowing and Reaping is a universal principle. It works everywhere and under virtually all conditions. If you put in long enough and hard enough, you will eventually get out all that you could possibly want.

Every businessperson that you meet thinks about his or her sales and revenues much of the time. They measure and analyze them daily, and sometimes more often. People love to talk about what they do and why it is that their companies are unique and different. They like explaining why people buy from them and the benefits they get. You can never go wrong asking, "How is your business doing these days?"

An even better question you can ask is, "What do I have to know about your business to recommend you to a prospective customer or client?"

There is nothing that will build a bond between you and another businessperson faster than referring a customer or client to that businessperson. When you help other people build their businesses and achieve their own professional and financial goals, they will be open to helping you to improve your life and business as well. Look for an opportunity to send him or her a customer or client as soon as you can.

Liking Is a Key Influence Factor

Remember, one of the most powerful success principles is contained in the *principle of liking*, which says, "The more a person likes you, the easier it is for you to influence him or her in some way."

The rule is *emotions distort evaluations*. If a person really likes you, he or she will be less concerned about the weaknesses in yourself or your product. On the other hand, if someone is neutral or negative toward you, he will be more skeptical or suspicious about anything you say.

People like to do business with people they like. People like to socialize with people they like. People like to open doors for people they like. People like to buy from people they like. People like to hire and promote people they like. The more people like you, the more doors they will open for you and the faster you will move ahead in your career.

Continually offer to help the people you meet. I have seen some of the wealthiest and most powerful business people in the world in action. I have always been amazed to notice how courteous and attentive they are when they are listening to others. And almost invariably they ask, "Is there any way that I can help you?"

You should end any conversation with a person in business by asking that same question: "Is there any way that I can help you at this time? Is there anything I can do for you?"

Sometimes he will think of something that you can do. In most cases, he will not be able to think of any way that you can help him at this time. But the fact that you offered to help will leave a pleasant memory of you in his mind. Somewhere down the line, he or she may call on you.

The Law of Reciprocity

The Law of Reciprocity is one of the most powerful and important of all human motivators. Your regular application of it will bring you opportunities that you cannot now imagine. This principle says, "If you do something for another person, that other person will want to do something for you. He will want to reciprocate in some way so that he does not feel a sense of obligation."

Most human beings are *fair* in their dealings with others. When someone does something nice to or for a person, that person feels an obligation to compensate, to pay the person back in some way. The effect of a favor or kindness is to put the equation of equality between them out of balance. As a result, they look for a way to get even. They look for a way to pay you back by doing something nice for you as well.

If you go out for lunch with a friend and you pick up the tab, he or she will insist on picking it up next time. If you invite a friend over to your home for dinner, he or she will insist on inviting you over at another time. When you send a Christmas card to someone, she will send a Christmas card back, even if she doesn't know or remember you very well.

When you organize your life in harmony with universal laws, you will always be astonished at the speed at which good things start to happen for you. And the Law of Reciprocity in human relationships is one of the most powerful principles you will ever learn.

Relationships Open Every Door

The key to success in life is for you to build more and better relationships, and for you to become more known and respected by a greater number of people. You must do this deliberately, carefully selecting the people and organizations you want to be associated with. Then throw your whole heart into making a valuable contribution to those people and organizations.

Human beings always seek to follow the line of least resistance. And the line of least resistance in human relationships is to recommend and to do business with the people whom we already know, like, and trust. Your job is to build up the widest possible network of influential contacts as you move through life.

The more people you know and who know you in a positive way, the more likely it is that you will know the right person at the right time for the right reason to take advantage of the right opportunity. Doors will continually open for you, enabling you to expand and improve every part of your life. When you reach the top of your field by gaining the respect and esteem of all the people around you, it will be because you had a goal and a plan, not because of luck.

ACTION EXERCISES
What You Can Do Now

1. Make a list of all the important people in your industry, your community, and your nation that it would be helpful for you to know; look for ways to communicate with them, either personally or by letter.

2. Look for ways to do things for other people, or to help them or their organizations in some way; it always comes back to you.

3. Fish where the fish are; join the organizations and associations frequented by the kind of people you want to know and be known by.

4. Be a *go-giver*; volunteer to help at every opportunity. Make a habit of giving of yourself with no expectation of return.

5. Select your boss with care; the person you decide to work for can have a major impact on your career and your level of satisfaction.

6. Network continually; look for ways to refer business to the people you meet. Write to them and send a book, a news clipping, or a sample of what you do. Keep in touch.

7. Practice the principle of reciprocity in all your relationships; do things for other people, and pay them back when they do something for you.

Principle 7—Money Matters

"More gold has been mined from the
thoughts of men than has ever been taken from the earth."
—Napoleon Hill

One of your most important goals in life is to be financially independent. Having enough money is essential to your enjoying the freedom, happiness, opportunity, and full self-expression that you want in your future. And there is no area where the concept of luck is more prevalent or popular than in the achievement of financial success.

The good news is that we are living in the very best time in all of human history for achieving financial success. As a result of new information and knowledge, technological innovations, and increasing customer demand, there are more opportunities today for you to achieve financial independence, and even become wealthy, than have ever existed before. The United States is the very best country, offering more paths to wealth creation than any other.

Just a few decades ago, to become wealthy, you needed land, labor, capital, furniture, fixtures, buildings, equipment, and other physical resources. Today, you can start on your way to financial independence with pure *brainpower*. You even have certain advantages over people whose entire wealth is tied up in factories and equipment. Everything they have can quickly be rendered obsolete by a change in technology or consumer demand. Who today buys betamax or beanie babies?

The True Source of Wealth

An important luck factor in acquiring wealth is explained by the Law of Abundance. It says, *we live in a universe of unlimited abundance where there is plenty for everyone who knows how to get it.*

Your ability to *think* and to generate new ideas and innovations represents your true wealth. Your financial possibilities are limited only by your own imagination and the way you apply it to the world you live in.

When I was a young man, with no high school education, living in my car, sleeping on the ground, and working at minimum-wage laboring jobs, I often felt sorry for myself because I didn't have any money. I was envious of those who seemed to be doing better than me, and I wished that I had had the same luck that they seemed to be enjoying. I had been sold the old bill of goods that "the rich get richer and the poor get poorer." I had been led to believe that people who were successful had started off with great advantages in life. I was convinced that there wasn't much hope if you didn't come from a good family, get a good education, and have all kinds of financial opportunities open to you.

Everyone Starts with Nothing

It was a real shock to me when I learned that virtually everyone who is successful in America started with little or nothing. Less than 1 percent of financially successful Americans started off with a family inheritance of any kind. Almost all financial success has been achieved in one generation. The wealthiest man in America is 42-year-old Bill Gates, who dropped out of Harvard to start his own business at the age of twenty.

People ask me regularly how they can possibly change their lives or start a new business if they don't have any money. I tell them that there are hundreds if not thousands of businesses that you can start for less than $100. But these businesses require mental and physical capital rather than financial capital to build. The most important equity that you have to invest in your career or into any new enterprise is sweat equity. This equity represents your willingness to work and to work very hard to achieve your goals. If you have *that*, everything else you require will eventually come to you.

Think About It All the Time

In creating your own future, it is vitally important that you move your goal of financial independence onto the front burner of your mind. The primary reason that people don't achieve their financial goals is that they don't think about it enough until it is too late. It is merely one of their concerns as they go about their daily lives.

Remember, *you become what you think about most of the time*. You inevitably attract into your life the material objects that you most often visualize and emotionalize. If you think about making more money and being financially independent most of the time, you will invariably attract more and more opportunities to make and keep more money.

The Way to Financial Failure

Most American families today have no savings or cash reserves. A full 70 percent of working Americans have no discretionary income. This means that they spend everything they make, every single pay check, and usually a little bit more besides on credit cards, and have nothing left over.

The average American family is only two months away from potential homelessness. If their income were cut off for any period of time, they would be in desperate straits. They would be unable to pay their rents or make their mortgage payments.

People without money are like people who have not eaten for a long time. They become totally preoccupied with food. They can think of nothing else. In the same way, people with financial problems think and worry about money all the time. They have little emotional or spiritual energy left over to spend on the world around them.

You Need Enough Money Not to Worry

The psychologist Frederick Herzberg called money a "hygiene factor." It is a motivator up to a certain point, after which it subsides in importance.

This means that you need a minimum amount of money to feel secure. If you have less than you need, you will think about money all the time. If you have more than you need, you will be able to relax and think of other things that are more important to you.

Wealthy people will tell you that money is only a way of keeping score. Once you achieve a certain level, you are aware of it, but you stop thinking about it all the time. You view money more as a measure of how well you are doing. When you have enough, you then start to think more about your health, your relationships, and making a difference in your work life. You spend more time with your family. At a certain level, money is no longer your main concern. Your whole life improves when you reach this point.

But below a certain point, you think of nothing else. You get up in the morning and think about money. You talk about money at breakfast and you worry about money all day long. Your money concerns affect your relationships and have an impact on all your choices, including what you eat for lunch. This is no way to live.

The primary reason for marital breakdown, disagreements, and divorce in the United States is arguments about money. One of the major sources of stress, anxiety, and even suicide is money worries that become all-consuming.

You owe it to yourself to do whatever it takes to achieve financial security and, eventually, your goal of financial independence. A major responsibility of adult life is to build a financial fortress of assets, properly invested so that you will never have to worry about money again.

Everybody Is Doing It

Fortunately, there is plenty of guidance around you to help you to achieve financial independence. You read numerous rags-to-riches stories in books and magazines, and you hear about them in the lives of people you know directly or indirectly. There are hundreds of thousands, and even millions, of people who have started from nothing and made it to the top financially. There are more ideas and information at your fingertips on how to achieve financial independence than you could ever apply if you lived a hundred lifetimes.

You can dramatically *increase the probability* of achieving financial success by applying the *principle of emulation* in your activities. This principle says, *you will be successful in proportion to which you find out what other successful people are doing, and then do the same things yourself over and over again.*

This is such a simple and obvious success formula that most people overlook it completely. They try to reinvent the wheel. They attempt to succeed in a career or in business without thoroughly studying the other successful people in that field. They refuse to learn from the experience of others.

Learn from the Experts

My friend Kop Kopmeyer studied successful people for more than 50 years. He read more than 6,000 books on success and derived 1,000 success principles from his research. He told me that the most important success principle he ever discovered was simply this: "Learn from the experts."

He said that there is not enough time left on earth to figure it all out for yourself. If you want to be successful, you must find out who is already enjoying the kind of success you desire and then learn what they learned, do what they do, and keep doing it until you get the same results.

Don't waste hours, weeks, months, and even years of your life trying to blaze a new trail. Instead, read the books, listen to the audio programs and attend the courses given by people who have started from nothing and achieved financial success. Learn and master the same skills that enabled them to be successful.

Create Value in Everything You Do

The principle of value creation is a vital key to your achieving financial success. It says, *all wealth comes about as the result of increasing value in some way.*

Your ability to create and add value to your work, your company, and your customers is the key to high earnings and rapid advancement. The more value you add, the more valuable you become. Your ability to acquire the key knowledge, ideas, insights, and skills that you need, and then to apply those skills in a timely fashion to improve the life or work of someone else, ultimately determines the financial rewards that you will enjoy.

To put it another way, you must always be looking for ways to increase the value of your contribution to the world around you. Customer benefit, customer value, and continually seeking ways to improve the lives of others are the true sources of real, lasting value and wealth creation.

Seven Secrets of Wealth Creation

There are seven excellent ways to increase your value in your work and in your world. Any one of these ideas can be sufficient in itself for you to become financially successful. When you put all these ideas together, you will begin to make more money and move ahead more rapidly than you ever thought possible.

Do It Faster

The first way to increase your value is to *do things faster*. Increase the speed at which you deliver the specific result that other people want. Everyone today is impatient. A customer who didn't even know that he wanted your product or service until today now wants it yesterday. As a result, there seems to be a direct correlation between the speed at which you serve people and their perception of the value of your product or service. When you do something quickly, you are considered to be more competent than someone who does it slowly. Your products are thought to be of higher quality as well. Speed gives you an edge over your competition in almost every area.

Every innovation in business and industry today is aimed at reducing the amount of time it takes to get a particular result. They are aimed at increasing the speed at which you satisfy customers with what they want. Every technological advance is aimed at accelerating the process and getting the job done faster. Most of the popular management concepts being implemented today deal with speed and time reduction. Practices such as *reengineering, restructuring, reorganization, and reinventing* are all ways of streamlining the process of creating and delivering value faster than the competition.

More and more business competition is aimed at leapfrogging other companies in finding ways to serve customers faster. Each new speed record in satisfying customers becomes the benchmark that the next competitor has to match if they want to stay in the market.

All you need is an idea for serving customers that is 10 percent faster than the competition and you could be on your way to financial independence. Tom Monaghan started Domino's Pizza with the simple idea of delivering pizza faster than anyone else. He retired recently with a personal fortune of $1.8 billion dollars. You should be thinking every day about how you could speed up the process of serving your customers faster. Speed is a real source of value that people will gladly pay for.

Improve Your Quality

The second way that you can add value and create wealth is by offering better quality than your competitors at the same price. To improve quality, you must first find out how your customer defines it, and then look for ways to please your customer in that area without increasing your costs.

Many companies do not know for sure how their customers define quality. The fact is that quality is whatever the customer says it is. Total quality management can best be defined as, "Finding out what your customer really wants, and then giving it to him faster than your competitors."

Quality does not just mean greater durability or excellence in design. Quality refers, first of all, to *utility*, to the specific need that the customer has and the use to which the customer intends to put the product or service. It is the specific benefit that the customer seeks, and how well you provide that benefit, that defines quality in the customer's mind.

Interviews with thousands of customers show that there are two parts to any offering. First, there is the product or service itself, and second, the way the product or service is delivered. This is why it can be said that McDonalds offers excellent quality in terms of satisfying the customers' desire for speed, value, cleanliness, and price. McDonalds does not try to compete with gourmet restaurants. Instead they give their customers worldwide exactly what they want in terms of fast food, at prices they are willing to pay.

Continually ask yourself, *"How could I increase the quality of what I do, in terms of what my customer really wants?"* Here is a key strategy. Listen for customer questions, suggestions, and even complaints. Invite your customers to give you regular feedback. Ask them if they have any suggestions to improve your products or services. If you invite regular feedback from your customers, they will tell you what you can do to satisfy them even more. These insights can give you the winning edge in your marketplace.

Look for Ways to Add Value

The third key to becoming wealthy is by looking for ways to add value to everything you do. If you want to stand out as a person or as a company, you have to add value to whatever you are doing so that your customer perceives you and your offering as being superior to that of your competitors.

You can add value to a product or service by *improving the design* so that it is easier to use. You can increase its value by *simplifying* its method of operation. Apple Computers did both at the same time. They transformed the personal computer industry by making them easy to use for the unsophisticated person. One of the claims of many Apple users is that they have never read the instruction books. The computers, the peripherals, and the programs are so easy to set up and use that they literally explain themselves. Better design and simplicity became enormous sources of added value for Apple, and for countless other companies that have followed the same route.

What could you do to add value to what you do each day? Salespeople add value by asking better questions, listening more attentively, and by carefully tailoring and customizing their product or service offerings to exactly what their customers want. As a result, customers consider those salespeople to be more valuable resources to their businesses than other salespeople who don't pay such close attention.

Make It Easy to Do Business with You

The fourth key to adding value is to *increase the convenience* of purchasing and using your product or service. Fast food stores by the thousands illustrate how much more people are willing to pay for convenience. Customers pay a 15 percent to 20 percent premium on most items. It is worth it to them because they don't have to drive across town to a shopping center or a large grocery store to buy the same products.

The extraordinary popularity of automated cash machines, open 24 hours per day, is a prime example of increased convenience. Banks have been able to increase their value to their customers by making it easier for them to make deposits and withdrawals. Drive-in windows at fast food restaurants are another example of how making something easier to buy increases sales. Speedy pick up and delivery of any product or service is another way of making it easier for customers to choose you over your competitors.

How could you make it easier for customers to use your products or services? How could you make it so easy to deal with you, with complete confidence, that your prospective customers would not think of dealing with anyone else?

Improve Customer Service

The fifth key to creating value and increasing wealth is by *improving customer service* and by treating customers better. People are predominantly emotional. They are greatly influenced by the warmth and friendliness of the people they deal with. Excellent customer service strategies are a great source of competitive advantage in a tough marketplace.

Nordstrom is the most successful high-end department store chain in America. Almost every Nordstrom customer you speak to will tell you that it is not because the store carries products that are different or better than those offered by other department stores. Their competitive advantage is that they give the warmest and the friendliest customer service of any major department store in the country.

Wal-Mart has gone from being an obscure bargain department store in Bentonville, Arkansas, to being the biggest retailer in the world, all based on making Wal-Mart a fast, friendly, happy place to shop. When Wal-Mart employees approach retirement, they become "Greeters." They stand inside the door of the store and welcome the customers coming in, thanking them for shopping at Wal-Mart.

Sam Walton started back in the 1940s with little more than a bankrupt store, a pickup truck and an idea to make clothes and household products available to people in small towns at fair prices. By continually seeking ways to serve his customers better, faster and cheaper, he went on to build a fortune of $25 billion dollars.

Create Customers for Life

Carl Sewell, in his book *Customers for Life*, tells how he built the most successful Cadillac dealerships in the United States. His philosophy was to continually look for ways to offer customers what they really wanted from a car dealership. He listened closely to their comments and complaints, and then he took action, even though it had never been done before.

One of his innovations was to always have sufficient *loaners* or rental cars available so that people could drop off their cars for service and leave them for the entire day. If a new car under warranty needed repairs or service, he would send out a new car of equivalent value to the individual's house for him to drive. He would then pick up the customer's car and take it back to the dealership for servicing to spare the new car buyer the inconvenience of doing it himself.

Whenever a car came in for servicing of any kind, he guaranteed that it would be fixed right the first time or there would be no extra charge for any subsequent visits for the same problem. Every mechanic was required to take personal responsibility for every job he did, and if the car came back for the same service problem, the mechanic had to fix it without additional pay.

Carl Sewell's list of service innovations goes on, chapter after chapter. The net result is that his stores have become the most popular Cadillac dealerships in the areas where they are located. His service innovations are so successful that teams of quality experts from all over the world come to study his systems.

Where do you see ways to improve customer service in your business or industry in such a way that you can gain a winning edge over your competitors? The ways that you can improve your service to your customers, your boss and your co-workers are limited only by your own imagination.

Follow the Trends

The sixth way to add value and create wealth is to recognize and cater to changing life styles. Look for ways that customer groups, young and old, affluent and average, are changing in their desires, tastes, and preferences. Study the impact that new trends are having on customer behavior and purchasing patterns in different product and service areas.

For example, millions of people are retiring each year, and retirees are living longer than ever before. There is a national trend toward *cocooning*, or spending more time at home. More people are spending more money making their home environments more comfortable. Look at the success of chains like Home Depot and Target Stores.

Teenagers and young adults have different tastes from those of their same age groups of just a few years ago. Changing lifestyles and demographics create opportunities for new products and services that did not exist before. All you need is one new idea to serve an emerging market and you can be on your way to financial independence.

Here is an example. Three businessmen got together a few years ago and started a company called California Pizza Kitchen. Because of the recession of 1990 and 1991, people were cutting back on the amount of money they were spending for food outside the home. They still wanted to eat out because of their busy lifestyles, but they could no longer afford expensive restaurants. The California Pizza Kitchen philosophy was to offer "gourmet fast food," consisting largely of high quality, well-prepared salads, pastas, and individual pizzas.

The concept was immediately popular. From one unit, they quickly grew to 42 restaurants. At that point, PepsiCo stepped in and bought out the founders for $17 million cash. They were set for life.

What trends do you see amongst your customers, in your industry or business, that you could take advantage of and exploit by offering something new or better? One of the first rules for financial success is to "ride the horse in the direction that it's going." Never try to buck the trends. Just like universal laws, try to get your business and your work in harmony with them.

Customers today are demanding, knowledgeable, sophisticated, and value conscious. How can you reorganize and redesign your offerings in such a way that you can appeal to emerging customer groups with the sort of things they want today?

Sell for Less

The seventh way to create value for your customers, and create wealth for yourself, is by *discounting*. Look for ways to sell more of your products or services to more people at lower prices. "If you want to dine with the *classes*, you have to sell to the *masses*."

The incredible successes of stores like Costco and Sam's Club are based on creating warehouse stores stacked with low-priced products. These products sell by tens of millions of dollars. Customers come from miles around, jamming the parking lots from dawn until dusk.

How could you offer a product or service of good value at an even lower price? How could you squeeze out the costs of getting that product or service to the customer and pass the savings on to him or her? How could you sell your regular products at your current prices and then up-sell each customer by offering a discount on something additional?

Putting Them All Together

You can multiply your sales and profits by combining these various ways of adding value. You can do two or more of them at the same time. If you look for ways to increase the speed at which you deliver your product or service, improve the quality, increase the convenience of acquiring it or using it, give better customer service, cater to changing lifestyles and trends, and find ways to reduce the price, you will be astonished at the incredible number of ideas and possibilities that you will come up with.

One idea or insight for benefiting customers in a way that no one has thought of can be the springboard that launches you into a lifetime of financial success and achievement.

Self-Made Millionaires

Many thousands of self-made millionaires have been interviewed at great length. Their stories are often similar. Most of them started with little or no money. Many of them came from blue-collar families and backgrounds. Many of them did not finish high school. If they went to college, many of them, like Bill Gates and Paul Allen, founders of Microsoft, dropped out before graduating.

Most self-made millionaires continue to live in the same neighborhood where they started married life. Very few people know that they are worth more than a million dollars. The neighbors on either side of them may actually be earning more money each month, but be worth considerably less. Self-made millionaires are very different from average people in their approaches toward time, money, and life.

The Way to Become Wealthy

Here is a simple process you can follow to become financially independent. It is guaranteed to work. It works for every person who ever tried it. It consists of a series of things you can do to increase the probabilities of success in your financial life and to assure that more of the luck factors work for you in making more money.

First, to become financially independent, you must begin by setting it as a goal. Get serious! Stop fooling around. You are responsible, and if anything is going to happen for you or to you, it is going to happen *because* of you.

If you want to achieve a certain net worth over the next 10 to 20 years, write it down as a goal. Decide exactly how much you intend to be worth at a certain point in the future. You can't hit a target you can't see.

Next, set a deadline on your goal. Set subdeadlines as well. Determine how much you will have to earn, save, and invest every month and every year to achieve that goal. Determine the actions you will have to take. Create specific measures so that you can track your progress every month. The more detailed your plan, the more likely it is that you will accomplish it.

Commit to Excellence

Once you have a clear goal and a plan for financial accumulation, ask yourself the key question: "What must I be absolutely excellent at doing in order to earn the kind of money that I will need to achieve the financial goals that I have set for myself?"

Whatever your answer to that question, you then set a new goal to acquire that skill, and then to become excellent at it. You resolve to pay any price, make any effort, and go any distance to become the person you will need to be to earn the kind of money you want to earn.

Change Your Thinking about Wealth

The hardest and most important part of achieving financial independence is the changes you will have to make on the *inside* to become a millionaire on the *outside*. Once you become a wealthy person in your thinking, you will be set for life. Even if you lose your money for some reason, you will have what it takes to make it all back again. You will have developed the "mental equivalent" of wealth accumulation that virtually guarantees your financial success.

Becoming a millionaire in your own thinking requires that you move from positive thinking to positive knowing. You must move from wishing and hoping to absolutely *knowing* that you are the kind of person with the skills and the attitude that it takes to achieve financial success. Once you have this mindset, no one can take it away from you.

Throughout your life, keep a long-term vision of your financial goals in front of you. Combine that mental picture with a short-term focus on the work that you have to do extremely well to deserve the kind of money that you want to earn.

Starting Over Again

I have met people who have fled from countries in Africa and the Middle East and emigrated to America and Canada. They were successful business people in their previous countries but they had lost everything as the result of wars, revolutions, and confiscation. They arrived in these countries empty handed. All they brought with them was their belief that they could start and build a new business and create the wealth they wanted.

Many of them went into businesses that they had never been in before. But in a few years, almost all of those people who had been wealthy in their countries of origin were once again wealthy in the new world. They brought the most important thing, their mindsets, with them.

Pay Yourself First

The habit of saving your money is a key luck factor that increases the probability that you will achieve financial independence. The best story of the power of saving is in Classon's famous story, *The Richest Man in Babylon.* The key lesson of this story is that, for you to become wealthy, throughout your life you must pay yourself first.

You must take a certain amount off the top of every paycheck and put it away. Invest it carefully. Almost everyone who eventually becomes financially independent has made a habit of saving part of every paycheck and putting it away for the long term.

The principle of saving says, *if you save and invest 10 percent of your income throughout your working lifetime, you will become a millionaire.*

The average annual salary in the United States today is about $25,000 per year. If you were to save 10 percent of that, or $2,500 per year, slightly more than $200 per month, and you were to carefully invest that money to earn you a return of 10 percent average each year, over the course of your working lifetime you would be worth more than a million dollars. You would actually retire *rich!*

There are various savings and investment plans available to you where you can save money and defer paying taxes. These accounts then grow with the power of compound interest. Over the course of a working lifetime, they will enable you to achieve all your financial goals.

The very act of saving money changes your character. It develops self-discipline. It makes you more controlled and confident. It gives you a greater sense of self-mastery. Saving your money rather than spending it makes you a wiser and more thoughtful person in every other area of your life.

Start Where You Are Today

You may be thinking that, because you have so many bills and expenses, you could never even think of saving 10 percent of your income. But remember what W. Clement Stone once said, "If you cannot save money, then the seeds of greatness are not in you."

If you cannot save 10 percent of your income, you can at least save 1 percent. Get yourself a piggy bank or jar and put it on your dresser. Each night when you come home, put the equivalent of $1/30$ of 1 percent of your monthly income into that jar.

For example, if you earn $2,000 a month, 1 percent of $2,000 is $20 per month. One-thirtieth of $20 is 67 cents per day. Anyone can save 67 cents per day. Instead of having that extra cup of coffee, soda, or donut, put the 67 cents into the jar. At the end of the month, take the $20 down to the bank and put it into a special savings account.

This is a special savings account because it is not a place where you save for a new car, refrigerator, or motor home. This is money that you put away for financial independence. This is money that you resolve to never touch or spend for any reason. Once you have put it away, as far as you are concerned, it is gone forever.

You then learn to live on the other 99 percent of your income until you become comfortable. This slight adjustment in your spending should not take more than a month. You then increase your savings rate to 2 percent of your income, off the top, and learn to live on the other 98 percent. The next month, you increase your savings rate to 3 percent of your income, and so on, each month.

Within a year, two things will have occurred in your financial life. First of all, you will find yourself saving 10 percent or more of your income each month, and living on the other 90 percent or less, with no inconvenience or difficulty at all.

Second, you will find yourself becoming more financially responsible in every other area of your life. You will more carefully consider each expense. You will delay purchases and, in many cases, never make them at all. You will start to pay off your bills and reduce your debts.

Activate the Law of Accumulation

But here's the most amazing thing that will happen to you. You will activate the Law of Accumulation. As you save your money, and you invest that money with your own emotions of hope and desire, that money develops a force field of energy around it and begins to attract more money into your life to go with it.

You have heard it said that "It takes money to make money." This is true. The power exerted by that money in your bank account will attract more money and more opportunities for you to increase your income and your savings. The more you save, the more money you will attract, like a more powerful magnet attracts pieces of metal from greater distances.

You will start to receive small bonuses and unexpected increases in pay that you will add to your special account. You will sell items from your garage or home and get small amounts of cash, which will go into the bank. People will pay you back old loans and you will get income tax returns that you had not expected. In each case, it will be the laws of Accumulation and Attraction at work. As you put these amounts of money away, you attract more and more money into your life.

Opportunities Will Appear When You Are Ready

As you begin to accumulate money, you will also attract opportunities to invest that money intelligently. This success principle says, *when you are ready, exactly the right opportunity will appear to you at the exactly the right time.*

As you build your financial fortress, you will attract opportunities to deploy and invest that money in situations that will enable you to grow your money more rapidly. Often you will get a business or a second income opportunity, and you will have the money to take advantage of it.

This opportunity money is one of the greatest joys of life. People with money in the bank, and their bills under control, are totally different people psychologically than people with empty bank accounts who are worried about their bills at the end of every month. By having money, you become a more positive and optimistic person. You create a force field of energy around you and begin attracting into your life more people, more ideas, more opportunities, and more resources to help you grow your money even faster.

Violate Parkinson's Law

There are two dangers that you must be alert to on your journey to financial independence. Either of them can undermine or even destroy your chances of achieving your financial goals. The first is explained by what is called Parkinson's Law. Parkinson's Law says *expenses always rise to meet income.*

To achieve financial independence, you must consciously, deliberately, and regularly break Parkinson's Law. Your expenses may rise as your income increases, but you must never allow your expenses to rise so high that they consume everything that you are earning.

Here is how you break Parkinson's Law: Whenever your income increases, resolve to save half of that increase, and spend half. If you get a salary increase of $200, save $100 (or more) of it and only spend what is left over on your lifestyle. Make this a habit and your financial future is guaranteed.

Get Rich Slow

The second danger that can sabotage your dreams of financial success is the get-rich-quick mentality. This is the desire to get money easily, without working or paying the full price for that money, in advance. An old Japanese proverb says, "Making money is like digging in the sand with a pin; losing money is like pouring water on the sand."

The only thing easy about money is losing it. Once you have begun to put your money away, begin practicing the Law of Investing. This law says, *investigate before you invest*. Spend at least as much time investigating and studying investments as you spent earning the money. Resolve to understand the investment before you part with your hard earned money.

Remember, if it takes you a year to save $2,000 and then you recklessly lose $2,000 in a bad investment, you have not just lost the money, you have lost a solid year of hard work. You have lost an irreplaceable year of your life.

The final law of money that will make you lucky is the Law of Conservation. This law says, *it is not how much you earn, but how much you keep, that counts*.

Most people will earn an enormous amount of money over the course of their lifetimes and then end up dependent on relatives and Social Security when their working lifetimes are over. They made it but they didn't keep it.

The Three Legs of the Stool

The three legs of the financial independence stool are Savings, Investment, and Insurance. Your first financial goal is to accumulate an amount equal to two to six months of living expenses. This money should be put away in a money market account or a balanced mutual fund where it can be turned into cash in case of an emergency.

The second leg of the financial security stool is insurance. You should insure against any accident or emergency that you can't write a check to cover. You should have life insurance to provide for your family if something should happen to you. You should be fully insured for medical, automotive, fire, theft, and any other potential damage. Never trust to luck or chance when it comes to insurance. Many people ruin their entire lives, and that of their families, by trying to save on insurance.

Finally, once you are fully insured and you have a financial cushion put aside, you should begin to invest carefully in areas you have thoroughly studied, or with other successful people whom you know and trust.

Don't Lose Money

Financial accumulation in your life should be based very much on the "ratchet effect." Each time you achieve a certain financial level, you should lock it in with careful money management, and by thoroughly insuring against any unfortunate event that might occur. Once you have made the money, you must use all your intelligence to hold onto it. Don't lose money!

Invest in Yourself

Perhaps the very best investment you can make is back into *yourself*, getting continually better at the skills that are enabling you to earn the money in the first place. You can get the equivalent of full-time university attendance each year by reading an hour a day in your field, listening to audio programs in your car, and attending seminars and courses on a regular basis.

Each additional year of self-directed education will increase your annual income 10 percent or 20 percent, or even more. Often you will get even better results. I have met many people who have doubled and tripled their incomes in as little as a year as the result of starting a program of personal and professional development.

When you become absolutely excellent in your field, you will eventually be paid very well for it. When you earn a good living, and you consistently violate Parkinson's Law, you will save more and more of your increasing earnings. You will then place that money carefully into investments that you know about and understand, and with people you trust.

Your money will grow and compound, year after year. You will get completely out of debt, build a financial fortress, and finally achieve your goal of financial independence. Then the people around you will nod and tell you how lucky you have been. But you will know that luck had nothing to do with it.

ACTION EXERCISES
What You Can Do Now

1. Make a decision today to achieve financial independence; set it as a goal, make a plan, set time lines, and do something every day toward your goal.

2. Become an expert at money management; this is a skill you can learn and master, and which will serve you for the rest of your life.

3. Continually look for ways to be more valuable to your company and to your customers; concentrate on results that others appreciate and are willing to pay for.

4. Pay yourself first; make a habit of saving a percentage of everything you earn or receive. Put it away and never touch it.

5. Violate Parkinson's Law by saving 50 percent of every increase you get for the rest of your career and carefully investing it for maximum safety and return.

6. Build up a cash reserve sufficient to cover 2–6 months of expenses; insure your life, health, home, car, and possessions. Don't gamble with your future.

7. Invest in yourself, in getting better and better at the key tasks you do that can pay you the most. You are your most valuable asset.

Principle 8—You Are a Genius

"The source and center of all man's creative power is
his power of making images, or the power of imagination."
—Robert Collier

Your mind is your most valuable asset. It can make you rich or poor, happy or unhappy. By applying your intelligence properly, you can create a wonderful life for yourself. There is not a problem you cannot solve, an obstacle you cannot overcome, or a goal that you cannot achieve when you begin tapping into the incredible powers of your amazing brain.

The fact is that you are a *potential* genius. You have the capacity to function at far higher levels of intelligence and creativity than you ever have before.

According to brain expert Tony Buzan, your brain has 100 billion cells. Each of these cells is connected and interconnected with as many as 20,000 other cells. This is the mathematical equivalent of 100,000,000 to the 20,000 power, or the number one followed by eight pages of zeros. Each of these connections and interconnections is capable of a new idea or insight. This means that the possible number of different thoughts and ideas you can generate is a number greater than that of all the atoms in the known universe.

Your brain has enormous reserve capacities. There are medical histories of people who have lost as much as 90 percent of their brains as the result of accidents and yet have been able to function very effectively with the remaining 10 percent, even getting straight A's in school.

The Words You Use

You have probably heard it said that average people use only 10 percent of their brains. Unfortunately, it's less than that. According to the Brain Institute at Stanford University, average people use not 10 percent of their potential, but closer to 2 percent. The remainder goes unused and unappreciated, usually for the life of the individual. It is as if you had a bank account with $100,000 in it but you never spent more than $2,000. The balance just sits there, not even earning interest.

Word knowledge is directly linked to intelligence and accomplishment. There are more than 600,000 words in the English language. The average person uses only about 1,200 of these words in daily conversation. About 85 percent of all English usage is covered by 2,000 words and fully 95 percent of newspapers, magazines, radio, and television use about 4,000 out of the 600,000 words available.

There is a direct relationship between your knowledge and use of words and your income, and between word usage and intelligence. This is because each word is actually a mental construct. It represents a thought. The more words you know and can use, the more complex and accurate thoughts you can think. People with extensive vocabularies are capable of higher level functioning, and are far more creative and insightful than those with limited word knowledge. People with limited vocabularies have limited thinking abilities as well.

Increase Your Intelligence

You can actually increase your intelligence and the effectiveness of your thinking by merely increasing your vocabulary. Each word you learn introduces you to and improves your ability to use as many as 10 or 15 other words. The more words you learn, the more words you can learn. If you were to learn one new word per day, 365 days per year, within five years you would be one of the most articulate and intelligent people in our society.

People are often considered lucky simply because they have learned how to use more of their natural brainpower than the average person. They have learned to use their intelligence and reasoning ability as a tool for success. As a result, they make better decisions and get better results, faster than other people. When you practice utilizing more of your incredible mind as well, you will begin to accomplish things that will amaze everyone around you.

The Law of Concentration says, *whatever you dwell upon, grows in your life*. The Law of Concentration, applied to brain power, says, "The more you concentrate on any thought, problem, or goal, the more of your mental capacity is activated, stimulated, and focused on solving that problem or achieving that goal."

Make a Decision

The Law of Decision says, *any clear, specific decision clears your mind and activates your creativity*. When you are indecisive, when you can't make up your mind whether to do a certain thing, you seem to go back and forth. You become easily distracted. You lose your ability to concentrate and think clearly.

But when you decide clearly upon a goal or a specific action that you can take to solve a problem, your doubt and confusion disappears. Your mind clears. You experience a surge of energy. You feel back in control of your life.

Your Most Powerful Mental Ability

We talked earlier about the relationship between your conscious mind and your subconscious mind. Your conscious mind *commands* and your subconscious mind *obeys*. Your conscious mind analyzes the information you have available to you, compares this information with your experiences, and then decides to do or not do something. Your subconscious mind accepts the decisions of your conscious as instructions and then goes to work to bring your goals into reality.

However, the most powerful faculty you have is your *superconscious mind*. Your superconscious mind is the source of all inspiration, imagination, intuition, insights, ideas, and hunches. Your superconscious mind is the powerhouse that, when properly programmed and directed, can bring you anything you really want.

The existence of the superconscious mind has been known throughout the centuries. Ralph Waldo Emerson called it the "Over Soul." The writer U. S. Anderson called it the "Universal Subconscious Mind." Karl Jung, the psychoanalyst, referred to it as "the Supraconscious Mind." He felt that the wisdom of the ages was contained within it and available to those who learned to tap into it.

Napoleon Hill described this mind as "Infinite Intelligence." He discovered in his interviews that every wealthy man in America had become rich by learning how to tap into this superconscious mind on a regular basis.

Every scientific or technological breakthrough, every great work of art, every truly great piece of music or literature, every flash of genius that leaves a lasting impression on the human race comes as the result of the superconscious mind.

The Law of Superconscious Activity

The Law of Superconscious activity is perhaps the most important success factor of all. It says, *any thought, plan, idea, or goal held continuously in the conscious mind, must be brought into reality by the superconscious mind.*

Just imagine! You can have anything you really want in life if you can think about it, dwell upon it, emotionalize it, visualize it, and affirm it, over and over again. This is completely up to you. The true test of how much you really want something is measured by your ability to think about it all the time.

The Seven Capabilities of the Superconscious

Your superconscious mind has seven key capabilities. You will recognize the occasions when your superconscious mind has worked in the past when you compare these capabilities against your previous experiences.

Goal-Oriented Motivation

Your superconscious mind is capable of goal-oriented motivation. When you are absolutely clear about something you really want, you experience a continuous flow of energy and motivation that drives you toward it.

Your superconscious mind is actually a source of "free energy." When you are excited about achieving something, you tap into this energy source, like plugging into a universal electrical outlet. You seem to need less sleep than before. You are able to work longer and harder without becoming tired. You feel happier and more in control of your life. You feel terrific about yourself for long periods. You are seldom sick or fatigued. You feel as if you are on a psychological high, and indeed you are.

The more you write and rewrite your goals, and take definite steps to achieve them, the more motivated you become and the more you trigger this free energy. When you imagine your goal as achieved and create the emotion of joy or pleasure that would accompany success, you feel more positive and enthusiastic. You perform at your very best.

The Power of Positive Affirmations

Second, your superconscious mind is activated by clear commands, in the form of personal, present tense, and *positive affirmations* to your subconscious mind. Whenever you repeat your goal as a strong, positive statement from your conscious mind to your subconscious mind, you activate your superconscious mind. Whenever you visualize your goals, exactly as you would like to see them in reality, you activate and stimulate your superconscious mind to bring those goals into reality.

There are four elements of visualization that can stimulate your superconscious mind. These are *vividness, duration, intensity, and frequency.* Each of them increases the power of visualization, and all four together bring your goals into reality far faster.

The first element, *vividness*, refers to how clearly you can *see* your goal in your mind's eye. There is a direct relationship between how clearly you can visualize your goal and how rapidly it appears in the world around you.

When you begin visualizing, your goal will often be fuzzy and unclear. But the more you visualize, the clearer your goal will become. The clearer you can *see* your goal, the more motivated and focused you will become, and the more rapidly it will come true for you.

The second element of visualization is *duration*. This refers to how long you can hold that mental picture of your goal in your mind. The *longer* you can hold your mental picture, the more deeply you will program this goal into your subconscious, and the more rapidly it will be accepted by your superconscious.

The third element, *intensity*, refers to the amount of emotion you can combine with your mental picture. The more intensely you desire the goal you are visualizing, the more rapidly you stimulate your superconscious to work for you.

The fourth part of visualization is *frequency*, which refers to how often you think about and imagine your goal as a reality throughout the day. When you really want something, you will find yourself thinking about it all the time. The more often you imagine your goal as already realized, the better your superconscious mind functions, and the faster you attract it into your life.

The more you visualize, with vividness, duration, intensity, and frequency, the more you program your subconscious mind to direct and control your thoughts and feelings. You soon begin to walk, talk, think, and act on the outside consistent with the mental pictures that you are holding on the inside. Your outer world starts to become a mirror of your inner world.

The Solution to Every Problem

Your superconscious mind automatically solves every problem on the way to your goal, as long as your goal is *clear*. In addition, your superconscious mind will actually give you the learning experiences that you will need to achieve any goal that you have set for yourself.

Often, when you set a new goal, your life will go off in a totally unexpected direction. Many people have set goals to increase their incomes in the years ahead, and then they have found themselves fired or laid off from their jobs. Later they found new jobs or started businesses. In their new positions, they made more money than they ever could have earned at the old job. In retrospect, they realized that they would never have achieved their financial goals if they had stayed where they were.

Most successful men and women in America, upon being questioned, have admitted that their greatest success in life came as the result of *unexpectedly losing a job*, or the unexpected collapse of a business. As a result, they were forced to make new decisions and do different things. They made specific changes that put them onto a new path. On that new path, they achieved the goals that they had set for themselves.

Most people achieve their great successes in unexpected ways, by doing something different, with a different product or service, or in an industry different from where they originally started. But as long as they were absolutely clear about their ultimate goal of financial independence, the superconscious mind guided them from experience to experience, providing them with the solution to every problem as they moved forward.

The Exact Answer You Need

Your superconscious mind will bring you exactly the answer you need to your most pressing problem, at exactly the right time for you. When this answer comes, you must treat it as time-dated material. You must take action on it immediately, even if comes in the middle of the night.

For example, you may suddenly get an inspiration or intuition to phone somebody that you haven't spoken to for a long time. When you phone that person, in the course of the conversation it will turn out that that person has a priceless piece of information that is exactly what you need at that moment to take the next step forward.

If you can visualize the other person clearly enough, in many cases, he will actually phone you from wherever he happens to be. How many times has it happened that you have thought of another person and within a couple of minutes the phone has rung and the other person has been on the line? This is an example of the superconscious mind in action.

Two Conditions for Maximum Functioning

Your superconscious mind operates best under two conditions. You should create both of these conditions with every goal or problem.

The first condition occurs when you are concentrating intensely, single-mindedly, with your total attention focused on solving a particular problem or achieving a particular goal. The second condition occurs when your mind is completely busy elsewhere. Later in this chapter I will give you some techniques to activate your superconscious mind using both of these approaches.

Preprogramming Your Mind

The sixth quality of the superconscious mind is that it is capable of preprogramming. It is activated via your subconscious. You can actually give a command from your conscious mind through your subconscious to your superconscious, and your superconscious will act upon that command at exactly the right time and in exactly the right way for you.

For example, you can preprogram your mind to wake up at any time you want, under any circumstances, anywhere, no matter how many time zones you may have crossed as a result of flying. You don't need to use an alarm clock ever again. If you want to wake up at 6:30 A.M., you can program it into your mind and then simply go to sleep. At 6:30 A.M., even if it is completely dark in the room, you will wake up and get up.

You can use your superconscious mind to find parking places on busy streets or in crowded parking lots. I have spoken to people all over the world who always find parking spaces wherever they go. You do this by visualizing a parking space opening up when you arrive at your destination. And in almost every case, if you have preprogrammed your mind, even for a few seconds, the parking space will either be there or open up as you arrive.

You can also preprogram your superconscious mind with a question or problem before you fall asleep. You state the problem clearly as a question and then turn it over to your superconscious mind as you drift off. The next morning, when you arise, the exact answer you need will often leap into your mind or come from another source. Sometimes it will be a sudden flash of intuition. Another time it will be a comment from your spouse or an early phone call. Often it will be something that appears in your morning newspaper.

Remember to use this programming capability at every opportunity. Every night before you go to bed, program a problem or goal into your superconscious mind and *ask* for a solution. Then, just forget about it until the solution appears.

Do and Say the Right Thing Every Time

Perhaps the most important function of your superconscious mind is that it makes all your words and actions, and their effects, fit a pattern consistent with your self-concept and your dominant goals.

Your superconscious mind will guide you to say and do exactly the right thing at exactly the right time for you. Your superconscious mind will also stop you from saying or doing things that would turn out later to be inappropriate or incorrect.

Your superconscious mind functions best when you are in a state of calm, confident, positive expectation. The more completely relaxed, trusting, and accepting you are that everything is working together for your benefit, the more rapidly your superconscious mind functions and goes to work to bring the things you want into your life.

As you have probably figured out by now, your superconscious mind is the true seat of the power of attraction in your life. As you continually affirm, visualize, and emotionalize your goals with an attitude of calm, confident expectation, you stimulate the power of attraction and begin drawing into your life the people, circumstances, ideas, and resources that you need to achieve those goals.

When you begin to unlock and unleash the power of your superconscious mind, you will achieve more in a couple of years than many people do in a lifetime. You will tap into amazing abilities that you didn't even know you had.

Using Your Common Sense

A key luck factor is good judgment, or what is often called common sense. You develop this common sense by continually comparing the results of your actions to what you expected to achieve. This regular reflection on your performance will give you lessons and insights that will help you to be more effective and successful in the future.

Common sense is often defined as an *ability to recognize patterns* in new situations that are similar to experiences that you have had in the past. As you acquire more knowledge and experience in a particular field, you memorize more patterns at an unconscious level. You soon become capable of making faster and better decisions in that area, even with incomplete information. You will be able to detect a familiar pattern in a new situation and take immediate action. You will be able to connect the dots faster.

Your superconscious mind serves an invaluable role in improving your judgment and increasing your common sense. It enables you to see a situation in its entirety and to know intuitively what to do and say the next moment.

Trust Your Instincts

Men and women begin to become great when they begin to listen to their inner voices and trust their intuitions. You begin to achieve extraordinary things when you combine your conscious knowledge, your subconscious memory of previous experiences, and your superconscious ability to organize and interpret the totality of your previous knowledge and skill into new ideas and insights.

There are two general ways to stimulate your superconscious mind into acting on your behalf. One is passive and the other is active. You should use both on every problem.

Practice Mindstorming on Every Problem or Goal

Perhaps the most powerful *active* way to stimulate your superconscious, to flood your mind with new ideas and insights, is by using the process of mindstorming on a regular basis.

More people have become successful using this creative thinking technique than by the use of any other technique ever discovered. It is so powerful that, once you begin using it, you will feel a surge forward as though you have just stepped on the accelerator of your life. Every person who has ever used mindstorming has been astonished at the incredible number of good ideas they generate to solve their problems or achieve their goals.

The mindstorming technique is quite simple, which is part of why it is so powerful. It is easy to use. Here is how it works. You take a blank sheet of paper and write down your goal or problem in the form of a *question* at the top. Make the question as clear and as specific as possible so that your mind can focus on developing practical answers to it.

For example, if you want to increase your income by 25 percent over the next 12 months, and you are currently earning $40,000 per year, you would write a question such as, "How can I increase my income by 25 percent over the next 12 months?"

An even better way of writing the question would be, "What can I do to earn $50,000 over the next 12 months?" This question expands the range of your possible answers. It includes both your current work and every other possibility you can think of.

Your choice of question will largely determine the quality of the answers that you will generate. The better the question, the more helpful the answers.

Once you have written down the question, you then discipline yourself to write down at least 20 answers to it. This is very important. You must generate a minimum of 20 answers to your question. Sometimes, the twentieth answer is the most valuable of all. Often it is the breakthrough insight you have been seeking.

When you begin writing, your first three to five answers will be fairly easy. You will think of simple ideas like, "work harder," or "work longer," or "take additional training."

The next five answers will be more difficult. The last ten answers will be the most difficult of all. But you must force yourself to persevere until you have written at least 20 answers to your question.

An entrepreneur in one of my seminars had been struggling with a problem for six months. If he didn't find a solution to it, he was going to go broke, and time was running out. Much to his surprise and delight, the twentieth answer in this mindstorming process contained the perfect solution, the very first time he tried it. He told me later that it worked perfectly, and that it saved his business.

Once you have generated 20 answers, review them carefully and then select at least one idea that you are going to take action on *immediately*. This is a critical part of the process. The faster you take action on a new idea, the more ideas you will implement to solve that problem or achieve that goal. The more ideas you generate and try out, the more likely it is that you will do exactly the right thing at exactly the right time. You will have what other people call luck.

Become an Idea Machine

If you were to apply this mindstorming technique 5 days per week on your goals or problems, generating 20 ideas per day, you would be producing 100 ideas per week. Over the course of 50 weeks, you would generate 5,000 new ideas, and that's assuming that you don't even bother to think on the weekends or on your vacations.

If you were to implement one of your 20 new ideas each day, 5 days per week, 50 weeks per year, you would be implementing 250 new ideas every single year. When you consider that the average person only thinks of three or four new ideas per year, and usually does nothing with them, this would give you a tremendous advantage. Your mind would continually sparkle with ideas and insights. You would see opportunities and possibilities all around you all day long.

Ideas are the keys to the future. Ideas are the stepping stones to the achievement of every goal. Ideas are what you use to overcome obstacles. Ideas are the tools that you use to solve problems. It is ideas that will make you richer, happier, more satisfied, content, and successful. It is within new ideas that all the key elements of luck are contained.

When you use the mindstorming technique first thing every morning, you will stimulate your mind for the whole day. You will see new possibilities and potentials all around you. Other people will be amazed at how quickly you think of new ways to achieve goals and find innovative solutions to persistent problems. And the more you develop a reputation for creativity and innovation, the more opportunities you will attract to you to use your new thinking skills.

Resolve to Take Action on Your Ideas

There are basically two ways that people respond to new ideas like mindstorming. There are those people who listen and nod and then go home and do nothing. Then there are those few, the top 10 percent, the creative minority like yourself, who learn this mindstorming method and immediately put it into action.

It is essential in the process of shaping your own future that you develop the habit of *acting quickly* on a good idea when you hear it. There is a direct relationship between how fast you take action after you get an idea and how likely it is that you will ever take any action at all. The world is full of good ideas, but there are only a few people who grab them and run with them. If you have a great idea or insight and you don't do anything with it, you should not be surprised if nothing changes for you.

By one estimate, the average person has three or four ideas each year driving to and from work, any one of which would make him a millionaire, but he does nothing with them. How many times have you had an idea for a new product or service; then, a couple of years later, you saw some other individual or company come out with the same idea and make a million dollars? The only difference between you and the other person or company is that you failed to act on your idea whereas the other individual or organization took the idea and tried it out as fast as they could. Remember, as hockey great Wayne Gretzky once said, "You miss every shot you don't take."

Believe in Your Mental Abilities

Don't sell yourself short! The very fact that you can come up with an idea or insight means that you probably have within you the ability to implement it. Because of the Laws of Attraction and Superconscious Activity, you will attract into your life everything that you need to make your idea or goal a reality. The important things are that your goal or plan is clear, and you want it badly enough.

Mindstorming both activates your reticular cortex and increases your sensitivity and awareness to things going on around you. You begin to notice all kinds of connections among different people, facts, and events. You develop a steady stream of ideas and insights that give you new answers and solutions that help you move more rapidly toward your goals.

Stimulating Maximum Creativity

Your superconscious mind is stimulated by three primary factors. These are: (1) intensely desired goals; (2) pressing problems; and (3) well-worded questions. You should use all three of these continually to maximize your creative abilities.

Intensely desired goals, backed by burning desire, enthusiasm, and excitement, activate your superconscious mind and stimulate you to higher levels of awareness of the possibilities around you.

Pressing problems, which you intensely desire to solve, accompanied by regular mindstorming exercises, stimulate your creativity and drive you to take action.

And finally, *well-worded questions* that provoke your thinking are a powerful way to stimulate new ideas and open your mind to new ways of doing things.

Be a Professional Problem Solver

Sometimes I tell my seminar audiences, often consisting of several hundred or even several thousand people, that I know what every single one of them does for a living.

I can see the faces of disbelief smiling back at me while they wonder, "How could he possibly know what *I* do?" But the answer is simple. I tell them, "Whatever your job title is, your real job is *problem solver*. This is what you do all day long. Where there are no problems to be solved, there are no jobs. The bigger, the more difficult, more complicated, and more expensive the problems, the greater the opportunities there are for you to get paid more and promoted faster."

The highest paid people in every industry are the very best problem solvers in that industry. And remember, a goal *unachieved* is just a problem *unsolved*. Your job is to find ways up, over, around, and through any obstacle or difficulty that is thrown in your path. Your ability to solve problems will determine your entire quality of life, both at home and at work.

Solve Your Problems Systematically

The regular use of a systematic method for solving problems activates your superconscious mind. This requires the practice of a simple, proven seven-step method. This method enables you to use far more of your thinking abilities than you possibly could if you simply threw yourself at an obstacle or difficulty the way most people do.

Systematic problem solving is a hallmark of genius in every field. Extensive interviews and research show that *geniuses* approach every difficulty with a specific methodology and process of problem evaluation and problem solution. When you begin to use the same kind of method, you begin to function at genius levels as well.

In addition, an *organized* way of approaching any problem enables you to use more of your mental abilities in solving it. A systematic approach activates your superconscious mind to give you the insights and ideas that you need at the moment.

Approach the Problem with Confidence

Step *one* in systematic problem solving is for you to approach the problem with a calm, confident expectation that there is a logical, workable solution just waiting to be found. This approach calms you down, relaxes your nerves and opens your creative mind to all the different ways you can go about solving this problem. You should assume, from the beginning, that every problem contains within it the seeds of its own solution. The solution is the flip side of the problem. It is just lying there, waiting for you to find it.

Be *solution oriented* rather than problem oriented. Think in terms of the positive actions you can take and what can be *done*, rather than who is to blame. When you continually think and talk in terms of possible solutions, you will be more optimistic, calm, and creative in your reactions and responses.

Change Your Use of Words

The *second* step is for you to define the problem as a *challenge* or, even better, as an *opportunity*. Words *are* important. Words have the power to create emotions, either positive or negative. The choice of certain words in describing a problem can raise or lower blood pressure, heart rate, and respiratory rate. Words can make you happy and creative or angry and reactive.

A word like *problem* is a negative word. It creates tension and anxiety. It can cause worry and stress. Imagine how you feel when somebody calls up and says urgently, "We have a real problem here!" You immediately become uneasy and anxious. But if you refer to every problem or difficulty as a *challenge* or as an *opportunity*, you will respond with greater calmness and clarity.

The Great Success Secret

Napoleon Hill, in his 22 years of interviewing successful people, looking for the secrets of success, found that every one of them had finally concluded that, *within every setback or obstacle there is contained the seed of an equal or greater advantage or benefit.*

Your job is to see every difficulty as a *challenge* sent to make you smarter and better, and then look into that difficulty for the advantage or benefit that it might contain. The good news is that you will always find something good or beneficial that can help you.

Clarity Is the Key

The *third* step in this systematic method is to define the problem or challenge clearly. Ask yourself, "What *exactly* is the problem?" Write it down. Define it clearly on paper. A problem properly defined is half solved. Accurate diagnosis is half the cure.

Once you have defined the problem clearly, ask yourself, "What *else* is the problem?" Remember, well-worded questions are a powerful stimulant to creativity. The more different ways that you can state and restate your problem in the form of questions, the more different ideas and approaches you will generate for solving it. Beware of a problem for which there is only one definition.

If your sales are down, you could define your problem by simply saying, "Our sales are down." But what if you decided to redefine or restate the problem in a variety of different ways. You could say something like, "Our sales are not as high as we would like them to be" or "We are not selling as much of our products or services as we would like."

With these definitions, new approaches to solving the problem would be indicated. You could even say, "Our competitors are selling more of our products and services than we are" or "Our salespeople are not closing enough sales for us to achieve our volume goals" or "Our customers are buying more of our products or services from our competitors than they are from us."

The more you restate the problem, the more amenable it becomes to a solution. Each new definition of the problem or goal leads you in a different, and often more helpful, direction.

Identify All the Possible Causes

The *fourth* step in systematic problem solving is for you to identify all the possible causes of the problem. Look for both the obvious causes and the hidden causes. Test your assumptions. Ask yourself, "What if we were completely *wrong* in our approach to this current situation?" If you were doing exactly the opposite to what you should be doing, right now, what changes would you have to make?

Errant assumptions lie at the root of every failure. You may have unconsciously assumed something that is not true about your product, your service, the market, the competition, or your customers. All good scientific research is based on the exhaustive testing of your hypotheses or assumptions. What are your hypotheses or assumptions? How can you test them?

Determine All the Possible Solutions

Step *five* in this systematic method is for you to determine all the possible solutions. Write down the obvious solutions and then some of the not-so-obvious solutions. Pick solutions that are opposite to the obvious solutions. Sometimes the solution is to do nothing at all. Sometimes the solution is to do something totally different. The more solutions you can generate based on your accurate definition of the problem, and your definition of the reasons for the problem, the more likely it is that you will arrive at the ideal solution or combination of solutions.

Make a Decision

Step number *six* is for you make a decision among the various solutions you have developed. Any decision is usually better than no decision. A clear, unequivocal decision of any kind stimulates creativity, generates energy, and activates your superconscious mind. Be willing to make a decision, and if you get new information, be equally willing to change or modify your decision.

Assign Responsibility for Results

Step *seven* is for you either to take full responsibility yourself or to assign responsibility to someone else for implementing the solution. You then take action on the decision. Get started as quickly as possible. Don't procrastinate or delay.

It is absolutely amazing how many people have changed their entire lives by going through this decision-making process and then taking some specific action *immediately* to solve their problem or achieve their goal.

Remember, successful people are not those who make the right decisions all the time. But, they make their decisions *right*.

As soon as you implement a decision, you will immediately get feedback from your actions. This feedback enables you to self-correct where you are off track. As you correct your course and take new actions, you will get more feedback that you can learn from. You become smarter and more competent. As a result, you start to move faster and faster toward your goal.

Unlocking Your Inner Genius

These two *active* methods—mindstorming and the systematic approach to problem solving—will enable you to achieve your goals faster than perhaps you ever imagined possible. In addition, there are several *passive* activities that you can apply to problem solving and goal attainment. These approaches enable you to use the deeper levels of your mind.

The Law of Relaxation says, *in all mental working, effort defeats itself.* This means that the more you relax and let go and turn problems over to your superconscious mind, the more rapidly it will solve them for you.

There are several passive methods you can use to activate your superconscious mind. To start with, something as simple as *daydreaming* is a wonderful way to relax your mind. In this calm state, breakthrough ideas will often dart into your consciousness. Listening to classical music, going for walks in nature, or just sitting, relaxing, meditating, or contemplating, opens up your mind to inspirations, ideas, and intuitions that can save you thousands of dollars and years of hard work.

The Practice of Solitude

Perhaps the best passive method of all for creative thinking is *solitude*. The way you practice solitude is simple. First, you find a place where you can sit alone quietly and be completely still. Second, make yourself comfortable and take a few deep breaths to relax and center yourself.

Third, in this calmness and silence, resolve to sit without moving for 30 to 60 minutes. Refrain from getting up, drinking coffee, smoking, or even listening to music. Just sit perfectly still and wait in the silence for the voice of inspiration to speak to you.

When you are clear about what you want, your superconscious mind will be stimulated into giving you ideas to accomplish it. When you precede the practice of solitude with mindstorming, you raise your mental functioning to a high state of alertness. You focus your conscious mind on a solution. Then, in solitude, your superconscious mind begins to function. As you sit quietly in the silence and listen for an answer, you will often receive insights that can change the entire course of your life.

The Key to Your Future

Unlocking the powers of your mind is the key to creating your own future. You *are* a potential genius. You have the all the brainpower you will ever need within you, right now, to achieve any goal you can set for yourself. The very fact that you can write it down and visualize it means that it is possible for you. The only questions are, How badly do you want it? and Are you willing to pay the price, in advance, to get it? Only you can answer these questions.

When you begin to generate a steady stream of ideas for goal attainment, you will start to move ahead faster than you ever have before. It will look from the outside as if you are having a run of good luck, but it isn't luck, at all.

ACTION EXERCISES
What You Can Do Now

1. Read, learn, and develop your vocabulary every day; the more words you know, the better you can think and the better decisions you can make.

2. Practice mindstorming on every problem or goal; write your goal or problem as a question and then generate 20 answers to it. Take action on at least one of your answers immediately.

3. Look into every problem or difficulty for the equal or greater opportunity or benefit it contains; you will always find it.

4. Approach every problem or obstacle systematically and logically; determine all the possible causes, define all the possible solutions, and then make a decision. Take action.

5. Become a solution-oriented person, always thinking and talking about what can be done to remove the roadblock or achieve the goal.

6. Have complete confidence in your ability to solve any problem and overcome any obstacle on the path to your goal.

7. Tap into your superconscious mind regularly by feeding it with clear goals, positive expectations, periods of solitude and relaxation, and positive affirmations. This is the greatest power of all.

Principle 9—Results Determine Rewards

> *"My success just evolved from*
> *working hard at the business at hand each day."*
>
> —Johnny Carson

People say you are *lucky* when you achieve great success faster and easier than other people, But everything that happens is based on *probabilities*. Successful people are always taking actions, large and small, to increase the likelihood that they will achieve their goals. They attribute their success to their own personal characteristics and especially to their willingness to work harder than other people. People who fail always ascribe their lack of success to bad luck and blame it on other people and circumstances.

The ultimate success principle is your ability to get results for which people are willing to pay you, promote you, advance you, open doors for you and move you up into the top levels of your profession.

Your Results Determine Your Rewards

The principle of results says, *your rewards will always be equal to the quality, quantity, and timeliness of the results that you achieve for other people.*

Everyone is selfish in that every person is always tuned in to his or her own personal radio station, WII-FM. These call letters stand for the question, What's In It For Me? This is what everyone wants to know. We evaluate other people in terms of their ability to help us to get the things we want—financially, materially, emotionally, intellectually, and politically. The people who can help us get the results or outcomes we desire are the ones who we most respect and reward.

Contribution Is the Key

The principle of contribution is closely connected to the principle of results. It says, "Your financial rewards in life will always be in direct proportion to the value of the contribution that you make to others, as they value it."

In a market economy, the customer is the king or queen. He determines the prices of all products and services by what he is willing to pay. The customer pays all wages, salaries, and commissions with his purchases. Everyone works for the customer. Sam Walton is famous for saying, "We all have one boss, the customer, and he can fire us any day by choosing to shop somewhere else."

Companies or people do not set wages or salaries. They merely administer the judgments of the marketplace. Companies create and keep customers by combining the factors of production with the efforts of employees to produce products and services for sale. If they perform this function and sell enough of what they produce at a sufficient profit, the company will continue to operate. If they don't, they won't.

Your work is a part of this process. You get paid for the contribution you make to the well being of your customers. You can increase the amount you earn by increasing the quality and quantity of the contribution that you make to your business. In the long term, there is no other way for you to do it.

The Reason for Job Insecurity

Many people suffer from job insecurity and stagnant or declining levels of income because they have not continued to *increase* the value of their contribution to their employer. Today, the most valuable component of any product or service is the amount of knowledge and skill that goes into it. If a person does not continually learn and grow, developing his skills ever higher, the value of his contribution will gradually decline over time, like the water level in a leaky bucket. He will inevitably experience terminations, lay-offs, downsizing, extended periods of unemployment, and continuous financial worry.

You achieve job security and higher income by dedicating yourself to improving and increasing the results you get for others, and by increasing the contribution that you make to their lives and work. According to the Law of Correspondence, *your standard of living on the outside will be the reflection of the value you have prepared yourself to contribute on the inside.*

Become Intensely Results Oriented

One of the fastest ways for you to come to the attention of the important people in your work is to become an intensely results-oriented person. Results orientation is a key quality of the highest paid and most respected people in every company and area of endeavor.

According to Theodore Leavitt, Dean of Business at Harvard University, the most valuable asset that a company has is its reputation. Its reputation is how it is *known* to its customers. The reputation of a company is the way its customers and other people in the marketplace talk about and describe that company to others. A company with an excellent reputation for its goods and services can always sell and charge more than a company with a poor reputation or with none at all.

Sony Corporation is a good example. The company has a worldwide reputation for quality and technological innovation. The Sony name on a product can increase the perceived value of that product by 20 percent to 30 percent, even though it may be almost identical to a similar product on the same shelf, but one with a lesser-known brand name.

Like a company, your *personal* reputation is your most valuable asset as well. Your reputation, your *brand*, is defined as the way you are perceived by the people you work with and for, and by your customers. Your reputation is summarized in the words people use to describe you when you are not there. Everything you do to improve the quality of your reputation improves your perceived value, and the value of what you do. And perhaps the most important part of your reputation is your ability to get the results for which you were hired.

Quality Work Is Its Own Reward

Whenever a company gets an excellent reputation for offering quality products and services, customers line up to buy from it. When you get a reputation for doing quality work, people will line up to purchase your services as well. The habit of doing your work well moves you into a different category from those who only do as much as they need to to avoid criticism.

Imagine that you went to the doctor with a pain or problem of some kind, and the doctor, after completing the examination, told you that you required a serious, life-threatening operation. What would be your first concern or question?

Your question would probably be, "Who would be the very best doctor to perform this kind of surgery?" If you needed a serious operation, for yourself or for a member of your family, you would never ask, "Who is the cheapest doctor I can get for this operation?" Price would not even be a factor if the product or service were important enough.

Many salespeople and business executives think that prospects and customers only care about getting the lowest price. But price is always *relative* to what you are selling and what else is available. When a customer says, "Your price is too high," he usually means that your quality is too low relative to the price you are asking. The quality of your offering in relation to the benefit he is seeking is the critical issue.

When you develop a reputation for being one of the very best people in your field, you will be paid far more than the average. You will always be in demand. You will quickly learn that what people want more than anything else is quality of results rather than merely low price.

Be Prepared to Work Hard

In addition to quality work, you must be prepared to work hard. Hard work is essential for any kind of lasting success. Good work habits go hand in hand with what people continually refer to as luck. A person who works efficiently and well, and gets a lot of high-value work done, on or before schedule, seems to get a lot of lucky breaks. He or she gets even more opportunities to do more high-valued work.

In every organization, everyone knows who works the *hardest*. Everyone knows who works the second hardest, and the third hardest, and so on. And the hardest workers are always the most respected.

Imagine your company hired an outside firm of efficiency experts to interview everyone in your business. These experts ask each person to rate each of their fellow employees, from the person they feel works the hardest, to the person they feel works the least. These surveys would then be gathered up and condensed into a single report to be presented to management. You would probably find that virtually everyone in the company knows and agrees about who works the most and who works the least, and where everyone else ranks in between.

People who rise to positions of importance are almost always the hardest working, most dedicated and committed people in that field. They are continually looking for other people who are like them. Birds of a feather *do* flock together. There is perhaps no faster way for you to attract the attention and support of the people who can help you than for you to develop a reputation within your organization as being one of the hardest working people in the place.

Most People Are Lazy

Unfortunately, most people are lazy. They do just as much as they have to do to avoid getting fired. They sometimes act as if they are entitled to a job, whether they do it well or not. Sustained affluence since World War II has created two or three generations of employees who have grown up with the idea that they can do a half job and get a full salary.

Because of the dumbing down of our educational system, with diminished course work combined with social promotion, many people have been able to coast from the first grade to the twelfth grade, and even through university, without working particularly hard to get a diploma or a degree. When they enter the world of work, they simply continue doing what they have been doing for years.

Time Wastage Is Universal

According to Robert Half International, the average person works less than 50 percent of the time for which they are paid. Even managers interviewed privately have admitted that they spend fully 50 percent of their time at work doing things that have absolutely nothing to do with the job or with the company. This average time wastage of 50 percent means that half are above and half are below. Many people waste even more than 50 percent of their time.

The primary area of time wastage is in idle socializing. According to the research, fully 37 percent of every workday is spent in idle conversation with co-workers. The other 13 percent of wasted time is the result of coming in a little later, and leaving a little earlier. It is consumed with longer coffee breaks and extended lunch breaks. It is eaten up by personal business and personal phone calls. The average person in America doesn't really start working until about 11:00 A.M. Up to that time, he or she is drinking coffee, reading the newspapers, checking the mail, talking with co-workers, and making a few phone calls.

I was recently doing a television interview on time management and personal effectiveness. When I arrived at the station I was taken through the offices and the control room. Of the 12 people that I passed, only 2 were working. All the others were chatting about their family, friends, or football games, reading newspapers, drinking coffee, or looking out the window. And *this* was in a competitive, private sector business. Think about what the work standards must be in large bureaucracies or government organizations!

Working on Low Priority Tasks

What is even worse is that when people are not wasting time, they are usually working on low priority tasks, and working inefficiently as well. As a result, they get very little done. Their work mounts up and they shuffle it around. When the pressure builds up, they rush the job to completion and hand it in poorly done. It is estimated that fully 25 percent of the costs of any business are eaten up by reworking and redoing products, services, or tasks that have been produced or performed improperly.

The average employee in America begins shutting down at about 3:30 in the afternoon, even if their working hours are until 5 P.M. or 5:30 P.M. Some companies have a sign in their staff rooms that read, "In case of fire, do not panic. Merely leave the building at the same speed that you normally leave at 5:00 P.M. each day."

Create Your Own Reputation

Here's a question for you. Do you have a reputation for being one of the hardest and most efficient workers in your company? Do people look up to you and respect you as one of the top people in your business? Are you continually being given more and bigger assignments, more important responsibilities, and more opportunities for promotion than anyone else? If the answer is no, isn't it time for you to make a decision to get serious about your future? Remember, this life is not a rehearsal for something else.

The Law of Applied Effort

The Law of Applied Effort is a key luck factor. It says, *any goal, task, or activity is amenable to the sustained effort of hard work.*

There is very little that you cannot accomplish in life if you are willing to work at it long enough and hard enough, and to persist in the face of all obstacles and difficulties until you win through. Hard, hard work is and has always been the key to great success.

Work All the Time You Work

Your goal is to be a star in your field. Your aim should be to join the top 10 percent of high performers in your business. Your plan should be to develop a reputation as one of the very best people in what you do. The key to achieving these goals is simply for you to work all the time you work!

Make a decision, right now, that when you go to work, you will *work* all the time you work. You will not waste time socializing or reading newspapers. You won't dawdle over coffee breaks or lunches. You won't waste company time on personal telephone calls, shopping, picking up your laundry, dropping off your dry cleaning, or checking out the latest sale. Instead, you will *work all the time you work.*

When people try to interfere with your new work ethic by asking you if you have a moment to talk, you simply tell them, "Yes, but not now." You encourage them to talk to you before or after working hours or at lunch. But meantime, you say, "Right now, I have to get *back to work!*"

Keep repeating to yourself, like a positive command that you program and drive deep into your subconscious mind, those powerful words, "Back to work! Back to work! Back to work!"

This way of working won't be easy at first. When you stop wasting time along with your co-workers, they will do everything possible to pull you back down to their level. They will feel threatened by your new commitment to earn your pay and get a lot done during the workday. (In unionized organizations it can be even worse. The insistence on average work performance is so strict that highly productive workers are actually punished and even fired, because they make the others look bad.)

Nonetheless, you must persist in your resolution. When you develop a reputation for working all the time you work, you will not only get more done, and be on top of your work, you will also start to get the lucky breaks. You will start to get paid more and promoted faster than anyone else.

Double and Triple Your Output

Once you have decided to become the hardest working and best employee in your organization, you will soon be producing double and even triple the output of the average person. By using a series of proven methods and techniques for personal effectiveness, you can so dramatically increase your results and the value of your contribution that you will amaze the people around you. When you begin using these techniques, which are practiced by the best performing and highest paid people in every organization, you will get more done, more easily, and have more free time than you can believe possible right now.

Time Management and Personal Performance

There are several key principles about time that you must know. First of all, time is inelastic. It cannot be stretched. It is fixed in quantity. And it goes by with an absolutely unstoppable regularity. This is a fact of nature to which you must conform, because it cannot be changed.

Time is limited. You can't get any more of it. But the fact is that you have all the time there is, 24 fresh hours every day. And the entire quality of your life will be determined by how you use those hours.

Here is an important point. You can tell your true values and beliefs by the way you spend your time. You can tell how important something is to you by measuring the amount of your time that you are willing to invest in it. Your decisions about time usage tell you who you really are, what you really want, and where you are really going in life.

You start your life with little money and lots of time. If you work hard, save regularly, and invest carefully, you will end your life with less time but ample money. Throughout your life you enter into a series of trades. You trade your *time* for the results and rewards of your life. At any given time, you can look around you at where you are today and measure how well you have traded your time in the months and years past.

An excellent trader will be worth a good deal of money by the age of 40, 20 years or so after starting work. He will have traded a substantial amount of his time for *learning*. He will have traded his time to acquire key skills. He will have traded his time for setting goals and planning his life. He will have traded his time for personal and professional development. And as a result, he will now be trading his work time for a high income. This must be your goal as well.

Saving versus Spending

Another key principle of time is that it cannot be *saved*. Time can only be *spent*. It passes by quickly no matter what you do. The only power you have is to decide to spend your time differently. You can reallocate time away from lower-value activities and toward higher-value activities, but you cannot save it.

People are successful because they spend more of their time doing things of *higher value*. They do more of the things that move them toward their goals faster. People underachieve and fail because they do too many things of low value, or no value at all. They perform tasks and engage in activities that do not move them toward the things they really want. Worst of all, they waste time doing things that actually move them *away* from their goals.

You are always free to choose how you spend your time. You are in control. You are in the driver's seat. You are the architect of your own destiny. Each moment, you can decide to spend your time on high-value activities or on low-value activities. The sum of your choices will determine the quality of your life today and tomorrow.

Your Mind Is Your Most Productive Tool

At the beginning of your career, you may have been a manual or clerical worker. Today however, you are a *knowledge* worker. As a knowledge worker, you have two main responsibilities. First, your job is to determine *what* is to be done, rather than *how* it is to be done. Second, you are measured, not on the basis of your *activities*, like a blue collar or factory worker, but on the basis of your *results*. Your job is to focus on the measurable results you have been hired to deliver.

Your most important task is to accurately identify, in advance, exactly *what* is to be done, and in what order of importance. You must then discipline yourself to work on your tasks in the order of priority that you have established. This is the key to high personal productivity. It is to do what is most important at the moment, whatever it is. This discipline is an essential part of creating your own future.

The Elements of Personal Success

The elements of personal success have been studied throughout human history, dating back to the writings of the earliest philosophers in 500 B.C. In the past 100 years, there has been more and better research conducted on the characteristics of successful people than in all the rest of history put together.

One of the most important discoveries of all, based on more than 50 years of research at Harvard by Dr. Edward Banfield, is that success is largely *attitudinal*. What he and others have found is that the most important determinant of what happens to you is your attitude toward *time*. Do you think short term or do you think *long term* when you make your key decisions?

Dr. Banfield concluded that people with *long time perspective*, as Dr. Banfield called it, are invariably more successful than people with only a short-term outlook. People with long time perspective make their day-to-day decisions based on where they want to be many years in the future. As a result, they make decisions today that are more likely to assure that they create the future they truly desire. The rule is: *Long-term thinking improves short-term decision making.*

You begin to develop long time perspective by imagining what your ideal life will look like 10 and 20 years into the future. You project forward and visualize what your life would look like if it turned out *perfectly*. You then return in your mind to the present day and ask yourself, "What would I have to do, right now, to begin creating the kind of future I really want?" You then plan your goals, priorities, and activities in terms of what you will have to do to get to where you really want to go.

Less than 3 percent of Americans have long time perspective. These people eventually become the leaders of their companies and families. They move to the top of most organizations. They end up controlling most of the money and assets in our country. They begin saving and investing early in life, and by the time they retire, or many years before, they are financially independent. They become the most respected and influential people in their communities.

The key to long time perspective is contained in the word *sacrifice*. Delayed gratification has always been the key to personal and economic progress. The willingness to engage in short-term sacrifices in order to enjoy long-term success and security is the key to happiness and prosperity. The unwillingness to delay gratification, the inability to hold yourself back from spending everything you make and a little bit more besides, virtually assures a lifetime of money worries and ultimate financial failure.

The Two Most Important Words for Success

The two most important words in achieving success are *focus* and *concentration*. Your ability to focus clearly on your highest priorities, and to concentrate single-mindedly on them until they are complete, will determine how much you achieve more than any other qualities you can develop.

You can be the most brilliant person in your field. You can be extraordinarily good looking, well educated, highly personable, and surrounded by all kinds of opportunities. But if you cannot focus and concentrate, these attributes will be wasted. You will continually lose out to even an average person who can discipline himself to focus and concentrate on his highest priorities throughout the working day.

The ability to set clear priorities lies at the heart of personal and life management. All wasted effort and underachievement comes from misplaced and misdirected priorities. All success comes from the ability to select priorities intelligently and then to stay at your most valuable task until it is completed.

The power of the sun is warm and gentle until it is concentrated through a magnifying glass on a single spot. Then it can burn intensely and create great heat. A small light bulb may give off a gentle glow, perhaps not even enough to read by, but when concentrated into a laser beam, it can cut through steel. It is the same with setting priorities. When you learn to choose your most important task, and then focus and concentrate on it without distraction, you begin to accomplish incredible things.

The Power of Personal Priorities

There are several steps to setting priorities. These techniques will enable you to get a lot more done than the people around you. The first of these is the habit of making a list of your activities and tasks *before* you begin. The very act of working from a list will increase your productivity by 25 percent or more the very first time you do it.

Top time managers and highly productive people use lists. Just as you would not think of going to the grocery store without a list of what you wanted to buy, you should never embark on your day without a written list of the things you want to do.

There are several kinds of lists. The first is a *master list*, which lies at the core of your time management program. This is a list of everything that you can think of that you want to do in the foreseeable future. As something new comes up, you jot it down onto your master list so that you won't forget it. This list can actually have hundreds of items, some of which may be scheduled for some years in the future.

Your second list is your *monthly list*, which consists of the key tasks that you have to accomplish in the next month. This list summarizes all your work responsibilities and projects, and it can include items from your list of long-term goals as well.

The third list you need is your *weekly list*. This is a more refined version of your monthly list, consisting of the things you want to do this week.

Your final list, and the key to maximum productivity, is your *daily list*. This is a complete blueprint of the present day from morning to night. It is an organized plan that you can follow to maximize your performance and productivity. It serves as a track to run on to assure that you get the very most done in the time you have.

Always start your day, your week, and your month with a list. Make lists for everything. *Think on paper*. All the most productive people think with a pen in their hands. They have lists for everything.

Plan every day in advance. Organize your plan as though *this* is the most important day of your life and every minute is precious to you. Don't make the mistake of starting with whatever task happens to be the most pleasant or the most convenient. Think before you act and then act efficiently and well.

The measure for evaluating the performance of a company or stock is contained in the letters *ROI*. These stand for Return On Investment. The formula for personal effectiveness is contained in the letters *ROTI*. These letters stand for Return On Time Invested. Your rewards in life will be a reflection of the return you get on the minutes and hours you invest each day. Your goal must be to get the highest return possible on everything you do.

Write out a list for each day, preferably the night before. This makes it possible for your subconscious mind to work on some of your tasks while you sleep. Set priorities on the list. Decide the order in which you will start work on your tasks, based on their value and contribution to your goals.

Determine the Sequence of Events

Time management is the process of determining the *sequence of events* in your life. It consists of your ability to decide what you are going to do *first*, what you are going to do *second*, and what you are not going to do at all. By choosing or changing the sequence of events, you control the entire direction of your life.

Perhaps the most popular time management technique for setting priorities is the 20/80 Rule. This rule says that 80 percent of the value of any list of activities will be contained in 20 percent of the items on that list. Sometimes 90 percent of the value of your entire list of activities will be represented by only 10 percent of them. One item in a list of ten tasks can be more important than the other nine. Your ability to decide which tasks are in the top 20 percent largely determines your productivity and performance.

Begin with the Most Important

Never give in to the temptation to clear up small things first. Once you have identified the 20 percent of tasks that can account for your most valuable results, begin with the most important. If you start off with the idea of clearing up all your small tasks, they tend to increase. They multiply. If you start working on small items, at the end of the day, you will find yourself still working on small items. Your big, important tasks and responsibilities will still be waiting for your attention.

Determine the Consequences

The potential consequences of any action determines the priority of that action. A task or activity that can have significant consequences for your life or your work is a high priority. A task or activity that has few or no consequences is a low priority.

A major task that is important to your company and to your customers is a top priority. The potential consequences of doing it or not can be significant. By the same token, personal development is a high priority. The long-term consequences of becoming increasingly better at what you do in your career can be extraordinary.

On the other hand, taking a coffee break or going for lunch with your co-workers has no real consequences at all. You could take coffee breaks and go for lunch for 40 years and it would make no difference to your level of accomplishment or income, except perhaps to reduce them both.

The ABCDE Method of Time Management

Always think in terms of potential consequences before you begin. What are the likely consequences of doing or not doing something? This is where the ABCDE method can be extremely helpful.

Take your list of daily activities and write a letter (A, B, C, D, or E) before each item. An A task is something that you must do. There are serious consequences for doing it or not doing it. It is important to your life and your career. People are depending on you and expecting you to perform it. It is a top priority. Mark an A next to all the top priority items on your list that absolutely must be done, done well, and done soon.

If you have several A tasks, list them as A-1, A-2, A-3, and so on. Then begin on your A-1 task and stay at it until it is complete.

A B task is something that *should* be done. There are mild consequences for doing or not doing it. People may be unhappy or inconvenienced if you get it done or not, but it is not as important as an A item on your list. Make it a rule for yourself never to do a B task when there is an A task still to be done.

A C task is something that would be *nice* to do, like a coffee break or lunch. These might be pleasant activities, but there are no consequences, positive or negative, if you do them or not. Socializing with your co-workers, reading the newspaper, or calling home on personal business are nice things to do, but they have virtually no consequences beyond the current moment.

A D item is something that you delegate. Resolve to delegate everything you possibly can of low priority so that you have more time to do the few things only you can do that will really make a difference. Every time you have someone else type a letter, make a phone call, file a contract or perform a clerical task, you are delegating. Every time you pick up dinner on the way home rather than cooking it, you are delegating the preparation of the dinner, and saving yourself all the time necessary for preparation and clean up. Delegation is one of the best time-saving tools of all.

The E in the ABCDE formula stands for *eliminate*. One of the greatest time savers of all is to completely eliminate certain tasks or activities. Stop doing things that may have been important in the past but that are no longer as valuable or as important as something else that you have to do in the present.

Set Both Priorities and Posteriorities

Setting priorities means setting *posteriorities* as well. A priority is something that you do more of and sooner. A posteriority, on the other hand, is something that you do less of and later, if at all.

The fact is that your schedule is already full. If you are like most people, you have more than 100 percent of your time already spoken for. This means that for you to start something new, you must stop doing something old. *Getting in requires getting out.* Starting up requires stopping off. Setting posteriorities, deciding on the tasks that you are going to discontinue, either partially or altogether, is one of the fastest ways to free up your schedule for more valuable work.

What are your posteriorities? What are all the things you are doing today that are no longer as important as other things you should be doing? These may be tasks that you have become accustomed to doing over time. But they are no longer as valuable to your life and work as other things that you should be doing. Your ability to set accurate posteriorities is a key determinant of your effectiveness as a person and your productivity in your work. What are they?

Five Questions for Peak Personal Performance

There are five key questions you can ask continually that will help you to stay focused and get better results. By organizing your work around the answers to these questions, you will leverage your talents and produce more than anyone else around you. You must ask, answer, and act upon these five questions every day.

The first question is "What are my highest-value activities?"

What are the things that you do that contribute the most value to your company, your career, and your life? If you are not sure about the answer to this question, reflect on it for a while. Give it some thought. Talk it over with your boss and your co-workers. Discuss it with your spouse. You must be crystal clear about your highest value activities if you want to perform at your best. You can't hit a target that you can't see. You cannot advance in your career if you are not sure what you must do to be paid more and promoted faster.

The second question for setting priorities is "What are your key result areas?"

What are the specific results that you must get in order to do your job in an excellent fashion? A key result area is something for which you are completely responsible. It is under your control. It is specific, measurable, and time bound. If you don't do it, it won't be done by someone else. Whatever your key result areas, you must define them clearly and concentrate on performing in an excellent fashion in each of them.

The third question for setting priorities is "Why are you on the payroll?"

Why do they pay you money for what you do? If you were trying to explain or justify the money you receive, how would you describe the results that you get in exchange for the money that you receive? Make a list of everything you do at your job. Which of the tasks on this list are vital to successful performance of your responsibilities?

If you are not sure exactly why you are on the payroll, take the list to your boss and ask him or her to set priorities on your tasks. Be sure you know exactly what you have been hired to accomplish and in what order of importance. Then, work on your most important priorities all day long.

The fourth question for setting priorities is "What can you—and only you—do that, if done well, will make a real difference?"

You should ask and answer this question continually, every single day. There is always an answer to this question. There is always one thing that only you can do that, if you do it quickly and well, will make a real difference to your company. If you don't do it, it won't get done. But if you do it, and you do it well, this is usually your top priority, your key result area, and the foremost reason that you are on the payroll.

The final question is "What is the most valuable use of my time right now?"

Your ability to ask and answer this question, and then to apply yourself to doing only that one thing, is the key to high personal performance and maximum productivity. Your ability to concentrate single-mindedly on your most valuable task is the true measure of self-discipline and self-mastery.

Zero-based Thinking

To get more of the right things done, apply the principle of Zero-based Thinking to all your activities. Continually review your life and work and ask yourself: *"If I had it to do over, is there anything that I am doing today that, knowing what I now know, I wouldn't get into again today?"*

Because of the rapid rate of change in your life, there are often things that, *knowing what you now know*, you wouldn't get into again today if you had to start over. It is almost impossible to get your time and your life under control if your time and energy are taken up in activities or relationships that you wouldn't even get into, based on your current experience. One of the worst uses of time is to do very well what you shouldn't be doing at all.

Keep asking yourself, "Is there anything in my life that I wouldn't get into again today, if I had to do it over, knowing what I now know?"

Look at your job or career. Is this the right one for you? Is this what you would choose for yourself today, knowing what you now know? If it isn't, what kinds of decisions do you have to make?

Look at your relationships, personal or business. Is there any relationship that you wouldn't get into again today, knowing what you now know? Staying in a bad relationship, one that you wouldn't get into again, is one of the greatest of all time wasters.

Look at your investments or commitments of time, money or emotion. Is there anything that is taking up a good deal of your mental, emotional, or financial resources that, knowing what you now know, you wouldn't get into? If there is, your next question is *"How do I get out of this situation, and how fast?"*

Make It Happen!

There has never been a time when we have known more about how to achieve higher levels of health, happiness, and financial prosperity than we know today. The ultimate success factor in your business and career is your ability to get results that really make a difference for your company, and for yourself.

The better you become at making a more valuable contribution to your company and your world, the more opportunities will open up for you. You will move ahead more rapidly than the other people in your field. You will soon rise to the top of your industry, with the rewards, recognition, and prestige that go along with great success. And everyone will call you *lucky*.

ACTION EXERCISES
What You Can Do Now

1. Ask yourself continually, every minute of every day, "What results are expected of me?" Whatever your answer, concentrate on those results most of the time.

2. Set priorities on everything you do; always be working on the most valuable use of your time.

3. Apply the ABCDE principle of priority setting to your list of tasks, before you begin; never give in to the temptation to clear up small things first.

4. Practice zero-based thinking in every area of your life. Is there anything that you are doing today that, knowing what you now know, you wouldn't get into again today?

5. Set clear posteriorities on those activities that contribute very little to your life or work; stop doing useless or unimportant tasks.

6. Develop an attitude of long-term perspective toward your work and your personal life; decide where you want to be in the future and then do what you need to do today to make that future a reality.

7. Carefully consider the potential consequences of each thing you do; your ability to accurately predict what might happen is a key thinking skill.

11

Principle 10—Seize the Day!

*"If your real desire is to do good, there is
no need to wait for money before you do it;
you can do it now, at this very moment, and just where you are."*
—James Allen

The Law of Probabilities makes luck predictable. It is the most critical success factor of all. The Law of Probabilities simply says that the more different things you try, the more likely it is that you will try the right thing at the right time and in the right way. This is why *action orientation* is a characteristic of all highly successful people. The more actions you take, the more likely it is that you will experience what others call luck. The more you *try*, the more you will eventually *triumph*.

Action orientation requires organizing your life in such a way that you get more done, faster, in a shorter period of time. It is based on the key luck factor of *alertness*. The more alert you are, the more likely it is that you will be aware of opportunities and situations that you can turn to your advantage. Many people's lives have been changed completely as the result of spotting a small advertisement or story in a book or magazine. It gave them an idea, which they acted on before anyone else, and it changed their lives.

Move Quickly When Opportunity Appears

Peter Thomas, a high-energy, action-oriented entrepreneur from Canada was sitting on the beach in Hawaii one day reading the *Wall Street Journal*. He came across an advertisement seeking real estate franchisees for a new company based in Newport Beach, California. He knew something about real estate and he saw the possibility of importing this concept to Canada before anyone else. He got up from the beach, went back to the hotel, packed, caught a plane for Los Angeles and took a taxi to the offices of Century 21.

The executives of Century 21 had given little thought to the Canadian market. In short order, Peter Thomas was able to purchase the exclusive rights to Canada for the Century 21 real estate franchise concept. Before the dust had settled some years later, he had opened Century 21 offices from coast to coast. He was a multimillionaire living in a penthouse suite with his yacht in the harbor below.

Thousands of people saw the same ad, and thousands of people turned the page without paying attention to it. But one man, because he was alert, quick, and action-oriented was able to take advantage of it and go on to make a fortune.

Opportunities Are Everywhere

If this seems like something that could never happen to you, you are wrong. Opportunities like this exist all around you, every day, but if you are not alert and aware to these possibilities, you can walk right past them and not notice.

Some years ago, a young man decided he wanted to start his own business. He attended a Joe Cossman seminar on entrepreneurship. There he learned that 95 percent of all products manufactured in any country are never exported. He also learned that there are thousands of new products being invented and marketed throughout Europe and the Far East every year that nobody in America ever hears about or sees.

He decided to send away for a catalog of European manufacturers who were seeking distributors for their products in the United States. He knew something about gardening and when he came across a description of a new, high quality, lightweight and inexpensive wheelbarrow with an innovative design, he was convinced that there would be a market for this wheelbarrow in the United States.

He immediately wrote to the company and asked them to send him a sample of the product, which they did. He then took that sample to a major national gardening trade show a month later. He couldn't afford his own booth so he arranged to share some booth space with another manufacturer of garden equipment.

Buyers for three major department store chains came by, saw the wheelbarrow, recognized its market potential and placed orders with him for a total of 64,000 units. He made a profit of $20 each. By the time he had filled the orders, he was a millionaire. It was less than a year from the time he set a goal, made a decision, acted on his decision, and sold the 64,000 wheelbarrows.

There are many millionaires, multimillionaires and even people worth hundreds of millions of dollars who started out with limited educations and no business experience. But one thing they had in common was the habit of moving quickly when opportunities presented themselves.

The more you study your field and learn the key skills you require for success, the more knowledgeable and alert you will be. You will more readily recognize opportunities and possibilities when they appear.

Use the Momentum Strategy of Success

One of the most important luck factors of all is called the Momentum Strategy of Success. It is based on the physical principle of *inertia*. This principle, paraphrased from Sir Isaac Newton, says, "A person in motion tends to remain in motion; it takes much less energy to keep moving than it does to stop and try to start moving again."

For example, you may require ten units of energy to get yourself moving initially, but then you only need one or two units of energy to keep moving. However, if you stop for any reason, it can take you another ten units of energy to get yourself going once more. This is why many people who stop never get going again. This principle explains why it is that successful people are moving targets. They are always in motion.

There is a famous quote: "On the beaches of hesitation lie the bleached bones of millions, who at the moment of victory, rested and in resting, lost all."

Maintaining momentum is similar to keeping the plates of your life spinning. As long as the circus performer keeps applying pressure to the stick that the plates are spinning on, the plates keep spinning indefinitely. But if the plates are allowed to slow down below a certain speed, they fall off the stick and the show is over.

You've probably had the experience of going away on vacation and coming back after a week or two. You remember how hard it was for you to get back into your job and to get up to full steam again. Sometimes it takes as many days to get back to your normal work routine as the number of days you have been away on vacation.

Keep yourself in continuous motion. Keep your personal plates spinning. Do something every day that moves you toward your most important goal. Resolve to become a moving target, difficult or even impossible to hit.

The good news is that the faster you move, the more you get done. The faster you move, the more likely it is that you will do the right thing for the right person at the right time. Get going and then keep going. Maintain your momentum. All successful people move fast.

Your Superconscious Guidance Mechanism

A guided missile, once programmed onto its target, will move unerringly toward the target, no matter where the target moves. A sophisticated weapon, such as a Cruise or an Exocet Missile, will lock onto the target and continually adjust course and direction until it hits what it was aimed at. No evasive action on the part of the target will be possible to enable it to escape destruction.

You are like a guided missile as well. You have the most incredible guidance mechanism imaginable. Once you program yourself onto a clear, specific, written, and measurable goal, your superconscious mind moves you unerringly past every obstacle and through every problem on the way to that goal. Your superconscious guidance mechanism gives you every lesson you need, exactly at the right time for you. As long as you keep in motion, moving forward, you will ultimately achieve your goal, sometimes in completely unexpected ways.

Here is the key point: The most sophisticated guided missile in the world cannot adjust course or change direction toward the target until it is *launched* and in flight. It must be in the air, in motion.

You are similar to that missile. To achieve greatly, to create your own future, you must launch toward your goal. Once you begin moving forward, with a clear idea of what you want, you will receive continuous feedback that will enable you to adjust your course. This feedback, in the form of difficulties and obstacles, will allow you to make course corrections as you move ahead. These course corrections will eventually bring you to your target. But you must keep moving.

The Special Quality of Top Performers

There is one special quality that seems to separate the most successful people from the least successful. It is the quality of *initiative*. The top performers in every study seem to demonstrate much higher levels of personal initiative than the average performers. Top people are much more likely to accept responsibility and take action when they see something that needs to be done. They are more proactive than reactive. They move quickly, usually without detailed discussion, analysis, or waiting to get permission.

In one study, average managers who had been repeatedly passed over for promotion were asked if they felt that they had the quality of initiative. These managers all agreed that they had high levels of initiative and that they demonstrated it in their work.

The researchers then asked them to define what the word initiative meant to them. The average managers defined initiative as, "answering the phone when it rang, calling up someone to remind them of a meeting or a commitment, or bringing a piece of news or information to someone else's attention."

The top performers, however, had a completely different definition of the quality. They considered the activities of the low performers to be merely part of the job. Top performers defined *taking initiative* as doing something well above and beyond the call of duty. It was taking risks, trying new things, moving out of the comfort zone, working longer hours, and volunteering for tasks that the average person would not do.

It is the same with you. The more initiative you show, the more you will be perceived as a valuable player in your organization. When you continually seek out newer, faster, better, easier, more convenient ways to get the job done for your company and your customers, you very quickly come to the attention of the people who can help you.

Trying More Things

Amoco Petroleum is a major oil company with a reputation for developing more reserves of oil and gas than any other company in the industry. The president was once asked why it was that his company was so much more successful at research and development than other companies. He said that the reason was simple. They all had similar land leases, similar geological studies, and similar drilling engineers and equipment. The reason Amoco was ahead of the other companies, he said, is because, "We drill more holes." It was no miracle. They put down more wells and as a result, they discovered more oil.

The faster you move, the more energy you have. The faster you move the more experience you get. The faster you move and the more experience you get, the more competent and confident you become. The faster you move, the more ground you cover, the more people you see. The more different things you try, the more likely it is that you will strike oil.

Get Busy on Your Key Tasks

In studies of unemployed people searching for new jobs, the researchers made an interesting discovery. They found that there are *two* types of unemployed people. There are those who quickly get back into the workplace, at good jobs with good salaries, and there are those who are unemployed for long periods of time.

The one observable quality of the people who quickly got back to work after they had lost a job was that they looked upon job-hunting as a full time activity. They got up and got going at seven in the morning. They worked steadily all day long. They continually studied the ads, made phone calls, sent resumes and went to interviews. They made 30 or 40 contacts a week.

On the other hand, the majority of unemployed people only go on an average of two job interviews per week. They send out a few resumes, post their information on a few Internet sites, and then wait around for someone to call or contact them.

Take Charge of Your Career

Not long ago, a counselor for a group of unemployed executives noticed that at every weekly meeting, the participants spent almost the entire time complaining about their past companies and blaming their boss for letting them go.

He suggested that, at the meeting next week, instead of complaining about the past, which could not be changed, everyone would share one positive interview experience that they had had in their job search in the previous seven days.

A week later, only two of the 16 executives showed up for the meeting. When he phoned around to find out why they hadn't come, he found that none of the nonattendees had had even so much as a single job interview in the previous week. They had spent the entire time sitting at home watching television or hanging around the house. He recognized immediately that the reason they were all so negative was that none of them were out in the marketplace actively talking to people and pursuing new career opportunities.

Become an Intelligent Risk Taker

When you study really successful people, you find that they are all *calculated* risk takers. They are not *gamblers*. They do not go to casinos or buy lottery tickets. They do not like games of chance. But they are always willing to take intelligent risks in the pursuit of their goals. This type of managed risk may have a likelihood of loss, but they know they can influence the outcome with their own intelligence and ability.

Fears of failure and rejection are the greatest barriers to success. The fear of failure stops people from even trying in the first place. The fear of rejection, the fear of hearing the word *no* actually paralyzes people. It causes them to make all kinds of elaborate excuses and justifications to avoid going out and talking to new people.

Risk taking requires that you move out of your comfort zone with no guarantee of success. By taking calculated risks, you eventually overcome your fears of failure and replace them with the thrill of accomplishment. Soon you become positively addicted to the sense of achievement that comes from taking chances and succeeding. You become more confident and competent as you move faster and faster toward your goals.

The more positive and enthusiastic you are about what you do, the more energy and ambition you will have. The faster you move, the more of your mental powers you will activate. When you work continuously toward your goals, your superconscious mind works 24 hours a day to attract into your life the people and opportunities you need to achieve them.

Seven Keys to Action Orientation

There are seven ways to increase your productivity, performance, and output immediately. These are the techniques practiced by the highest paid people in every field.

Work Faster

The first key to high productivity is for you to work *faster*. Pick up the pace. Get on with it. Move quickly. Develop a sense of urgency. Whatever you have to do, do it in real time. Take action on it immediately. Fast tempo is essential to success.

Repeat over and over to yourself, "Do it now! Do it now! Do it now!" You can dramatically increase your output by simply resolving to walk faster, move faster, act faster, decide faster and get on with the task, whatever it is. Successful people are quick and efficient. Unsuccessful people delay and procrastinate. The faster you move, the luckier you will turn out to be.

Work Longer and Harder

The second key to high productivity is to *work longer and harder*. A reputation for hard work will cause you to stand out immediately. Most people are lazy. They don't work very hard, even when they are at work. But when you develop a reputation as a hard worker, everyone will notice. Sustained, concentrated, applied effort is the key to high performance and high productivity.

Here is one of the paradoxes of working in an office. It is that, "You can't get any work done at work." When you go into an office environment, you are completely absorbed by telephone calls, people wanting your time, meetings, unexpected emergencies, and a dozen other things that use up your time and energy. By the end of the day, you often feel that you have been busy all day but you have accomplished very little. As the saying goes, "The hurrieder I go, the behinder I get."

However, in one hour of uninterrupted work time, you can accomplish as much as you would in three hours of normal office time. If you start one hour earlier, work at lunchtime, and stay an hour later, you will add three hours of uninterrupted, productive time to your day. These hours will enable you to produce the same amount of work that another person might produce in a full day. You will *double* your productivity, performance, and output just by making a small adjustment to your working day.

Getting a Jump on the Day

An ambitious graduate of one of my seminars took this idea to heart. She started going to bed at nine each evening and getting up at four in the morning. She went straight to work in her apartment. By 7:30 A.M., she had done the equivalent of a full day's work. When she went into the office, she did another full day's work. Within a few months, she had been promoted twice and was earning 50 percent more than a co-worker who had started on the job at the same time. Within two years, she was a member of management, and people were muttering about how lucky she had been; but it wasn't luck at all.

If you get up a little earlier and get into the office one hour before anyone else, you will immediately start to join the ranks of the top people in America. It is a truism in sales that if you want to talk to the top people, call before the receptionist or the secretary get there. The top people are always in the office earlier, sometimes by 6 or 7 A.M. If you want to avoid the receptionist, wait until the company closes and then call at 6 or 7 P.M. Very often, the person who answers the phone will be the top person in the organization. The reason he is the top person is because he gets in early and stays late.

Don't Be a Clock Watcher

Regular office hours are for average people with average futures, not for successful people who are going somewhere with their lives. Your *attitude* toward the clock is a good indicator of whether or not you have much of a future in your current job.

Your attitude toward the clock should be that it merely keeps score. It tells you how much more time you have to work before your next task or responsibility. The clock reminds you of how much time you have left to get your most important tasks completed. You use the clock to measure your results and how much time you have left to get even greater results.

People with limited futures have a different attitude toward the clock. They see it in terms of how soon they have to start work, and how soon they can stop. To unsuccessful people, the clock is the *enemy*, keeping them at work or holding them back from coffee breaks or lunch. They think only in terms of the hours they put in, not what they put into those hours. They want to get to work at the last possible moment and get away as soon as they can.

Set Your Own Schedule

There is no law that requires you to automatically get up at 12:00 noon and walk out the door for lunch with whoever is standing there. Successful people simply don't do this. They make every minute count. Take the hour between 12:00 and 1:00 P.M., close your door and concentrate on getting your top jobs out of the way. This one uninterrupted hour will enable you to produce what could take you two or three hours of interrupted time during the normal workday.

The highest paid people in America—entrepreneurs, executives, and professionals—work an average of 59 hours per week. This amounts to either six 10-hour days, or five 12-hour days. In my many years of studying successful people, I have never found a person who has achieved anything worthwhile working the basic eight hours per day. Your success in competitive business will be in direct proportion to the number of hours that you work *in addition* to eight each day, and over 40 each week. When you start working 50, 60, and 70 hours, and you use that time well by concentrating on your highest priority tasks, you will start to move to the front of the line in your career.

Do More Important Things

The third key to high performance is to *do more important things*. Since you only have a certain number of hours each day, make sure that you spend every minute doing those things that are more valuable to you and your company than anything else.

Continually ask yourself, "If I had to leave town for a month, and I could only complete one task before I left, what one task would that be?"

Whatever it is, discipline yourself to work on that, and only that, until it's finished. Single-minded concentration on one task, the most important task, will put you into the zone. It will put you onto a higher plane of performance. You will find yourself getting more done in less time. Your thinking will become crystal clear. You will activate your superconscious mind, and you will have more and more ideas and insights that you can use to get things done even faster. You will only get into the performance zone when you work faster, work harder, and concentrate on high-value tasks.

You've heard it said that, "If you want something done, always give it to a busy man or woman." This is because a busy person is working at a higher rate of output than the average employee. The really busy person is doing two or three times as much in the course of a day as a person who is working at a slower pace or lower level of activity.

Do Things You're Better at

The fourth key to higher performance and productivity is for you to *do things you are better at*. When you work on the things that you do best, you not only enjoy your work more, but you also get it done faster. You make fewer mistakes. You make a more valuable contribution.

One of the best time-management techniques of all is to get *better* at the most important things you do. This is a key luck factor. The reason is simple. Since your major rewards and recognition come from your ability to do your most important tasks and to do them well, the better and better you get at those key tasks, the more rewards, recognition and opportunities you will enjoy. By being excellent at your key tasks, you will experience more luck than the average person.

Bunch Your Tasks

The fifth key to high productivity is for you to *bunch your tasks*. Do groups of similar tasks together. Return all your phone calls at the same time. Do all your telephone prospecting in a single block of time. Fill out all your expense accounts at the same time. Write all your letters and proposals one after another.

One of the most powerful time-saving techniques in any field is what is called the learning curve. Learning-curve theory says that, "The more you do of a repetitive task, the faster and easier you will perform each subsequent task of that kind."

If it takes you 10 minutes to do the first of a series of identical tasks, it may only take you 9 minutes for the second task, 8 minutes for the third task, 7 minutes for the fourth task, and so on. You can reduce the time required to complete a group of similar tasks to as little as 20 percent of the time it would take to do them one at a time. This is a huge time saving over doing these tasks randomly throughout the day.

Many people are unaware of the learning curve. They therefore work in a haphazard way. They do one of this and one of that. They perform a task in one area and do something in another area. As a result, they never get down the slope of the learning curve. They never produce at high levels.

Do Things Together

The sixth key to high productivity is to *do things together*. Your ability to work well and function as part of a team is critical to your success. When you learn to cooperate and work effectively with others, with each person taking the part of the job that they are most suited to do well, you will be amazed at what you can accomplish.

During World War II, the U.S. government made a commitment to building Liberty Ships for carrying cargo across the North Atlantic at a faster rate than German U-boats could sink them. They created a series of industrial innovations that are still being used worldwide today. First, they reduced the time needed to build a ship from two years to 42 days. Then, in an incredible display of team work and cooperation, all the skilled workmen got together, made a plan, and built an entire ship, ready for launching, in four days.

One of the reasons they were able to build literally hundreds of Liberty Ships, one after the other, was because they used the learning curve. They bunched all their tasks together so they could do them more efficiently and they worked as a smooth, well-functioning team throughout. You should look for opportunities to apply the same principles to your work as well.

Simplify Your Work

The seventh key to increasing your productivity is for you to *simplify* and streamline your work. This is often called *reengineering*.

Reengineering and simplifying the job follows a simple process. First, you make a list of every step necessary to complete a particular job, from start to finish. Second, you examine each step and decide if it is still necessary. Third, you determine those tasks you could simplify and do faster. Fourth, you look for steps that you can combine with others or jobs that you can consolidate in a single person. Finally, look for parts of the task that you could eliminate altogether. You continually look for ways to reduce the time that it takes to complete the entire job.

Reducing the Time Required

There is a powerful productivity improvement technique called *time compression by responsibility expansion*. This requires that one person be made responsible for several steps in a particular task. This dramatically simplifies the task and makes it possible to get it done far faster.

Here is an example: In a study of the processing of life insurance policies, researchers discovered that it was taking six weeks from the time a policy was submitted from the field to the time it was either approved or disapproved.

The researchers took a policy and followed it through the various steps involved in getting it approved. They found that it went through 24 people in six weeks, but the actual amount of time spent working on the policy itself was only 17 minutes. They therefore decided to change the way the policy was processed. Instead of having 24 people look at the policy, they reduced the number of people to two.

The first person would check each detail of the policy application, from beginning to end. The policy would then be sent to a second, more senior, person who would double check the work of the first person. Using this technique of time compression by responsibility expansion, they were able to reduce the processing time of a policy from six weeks to 24 hours, and have an approval back to the agent within the week. As a result, their underwriting business increased over the next year by many millions of dollars.

Today, time is the most valuable resource in business and personal life. You must think continually about how you can reduce the amount of time it takes to get a task done. People who can do things quickly for others are always the most valued and the most rapidly promoted people in any organization. They are the ones who get all the lucky breaks.

Seven Keys to High-Energy Living

Energy is a key luck factor. For you to be at the top of your form, to be action oriented, fast moving and extremely productive, you have to have high levels of physical and mental energy. For you to be able to take advantage of all the possibilities around you, and to have the continuous enthusiasm that keeps you and others motivated and moving ahead, you have to organize your life so that you feel terrific about yourself most of the time.

Today, we know more about the health habits you can practice to enjoy higher levels of energy than we have ever known before. Here are the *seven* key factors that determine your physical and mental energy levels. You should incorporate them into your daily life.

Eat the Right Foods

The first key to high energy is a *proper diet*. To perform at your best, you must eat the right foods, in the right balance, and in the right combinations. Your diet has an inordinate impact on the amount of energy you have, how well you sleep, your levels of health and fitness, and your performance throughout the day and into the evening.

Olympic athletes have been studied extensively to find out what it is they eat to perform at world-class levels. Even though they come from more than a hundred countries, Olympic diets have three elements in common. These practices should be learned and incorporated into your life.

First, Olympic athletes eat lots of *fruits, vegetables, and whole-grain foods*. They eat ample quantities of pasta and rice, the complex carbohydrates that turn rapidly into glucose and serve as a fuel for the high performance body and mind.

Because your body is 70 percent water, you should eat foods that are composed of 70 percent water, like fruits and vegetables. In addition, you should eat whole-grain products like wheat bread, macrobiotic rice, bran muffins, shredded wheat, and bran flakes to get the roughage you need to keep your system functioning smoothly.

The second part of the high-performance Olympic diet is *lean source protein*. This type of protein comes from fish, chicken with no skin, lean beef, and tofu. You need high-quality protein to rebuild your cells and replenish your energy.

In addition, these forms of protein are lower in fat than many other foods. Fat has been found to contribute to a variety of physical ailments and health problems. If you switch to a diet that is low in fat, you will immediately start losing excess pounds and gaining energy.

When you combine a low fat diet with more fruits, vegetables, and whole grain products, you will find yourself trimming down quickly and feeling far better.

The third part of a high performance diet is drinking lots of water. Most people just sip water when they drink. But you need to drink eight 8-ounce glasses of water per day to combat the normal water loss that occurs as the result of your daily activities.

More and more people today carry water bottles around with them. They sip at those bottles continually. They are constantly hydrating their systems with lots of water. This helps their systems to function better and assures that their urine is clear or only mildly yellow.

In fact, if your urine is dark yellow, it means that you are dehydrated. If you are dehydrated, your digestion will slow down and you will tire easily. But if you drink lots of water, it will continually flush out salts, toxins, waste products, and other residues that can build up in your system and slow you down. You will feel much better just by increasing your daily water intake.

Avoiding the Three White Poisons

In addition to the Olympic diet of fruits and vegetables, whole-grain products, lean source protein, and lots of water, you should avoid the three white poisons that are the cause of many health problems in America. These are white flour, white sugar, and white salt.

Canned foods that you buy at the supermarket can be as much as 50 percent salt. Most canned soup has more salt than it has water. Most snack foods are loaded with either salt or sugar. And there is a very good reason for this.

In order to stop food from going bad on the store shelf, the very best way is to *kill* the food before you put it on the shelf in the first place. Then it cannot die and decompose before it is sold and consumed. The two best ways to kill any food substance are with salt or sugar. Therefore, much canned or snack food is inert. It is totally dead. It has no nutrients or food value at all. It has only salt or sugar and perhaps fat, which cause you either to retain water, as in the case of salt, or to gain weight, as in the case of sugar or fats.

The fact is that you don't need any additional salt or sugar in your diet. Most of the foods that you eat have too much sugar and salt in them already. At the very least, you don't need to add salt or sugar to anything you consume.

White Flour Products

There is a direct correlation between the introduction of refined, white flour and the decline of health in the industrialized countries. White flour was first introduced to the upper classes in Britain and America in the 1800s. It caught on because of its attractive appearance. But in order to create white flour out of whole grain wheat, the wheat must be ground very fine and all the kernels, which contain the nutrients, must be removed. Then, the flour that is left must be bleached for whiteness, thereby killing any nutrients that might still remain.

When a bread package claims that the contents contain products made with enriched white flour, it means that vitamins have been added back to the dough before it was baked. What they don't tell you is that the 350-degree baking process kills any vitamins that might have been added back after the flour has been rendered inert in the bleaching process.

It is only the foods that you put on or combine with the bread that give you any nutritional value at all. Probably the worst part of eating unhealthy foods is that they satisfy your appetite temporarily and steer you away from eating foods that will actually do you some good.

Resolve today to shift your diet away from fatty, sugary, salty food and toward healthy, nutritious foods. Eat for high energy and drink lots of water. Take complete control of what you put into your mouth.

Watch Your Weight

The second key to high energy is proper weight. Proper weight is essential for health, happiness, and long life. Being slightly under your ideal weight is best. As they say, you can never be too rich or too thin.

One of your primary goals should be to look and feel great. You can begin by getting your weight and physical appearance under control. If you are not happy with your current level of physical health, you need to set specific goals for yourself for the weeks and months ahead.

Take Charge of What You Put into Your Mouth

You are completely responsible for what you put into your body; no one else is. More than 50 million Americans are seriously overweight today.

Carrying too many extra pounds is one of the fastest ways to reduce your energy levels.

Exercise Is Essential

The third key to high energy is *proper exercise*. The best activity for high energy and physical fitness is aerobic exercise. This type of exercise requires that you get your heart rate up into what is called *the training zone* three times per week. This training zone is about 120 to 160 beats per minute, depending on your age. You then keep it there for at least 20 minutes or more each session.

You can get all the physical and aerobic exercise you need by walking two to three miles, three to five times per week. You can get your essential exercise from swimming, cycling, exercise equipment, at gyms or at home, and jogging. You should build exercise into your lifestyle as much as you include eating and sleeping if you want to perform at your best.

Your muscles are meant to be used every day. Every joint should be fully articulated. You should stretch your legs, back and arms regularly. You should use light weights to keep your muscles strong and supple. Most of all, you should be getting aerobic exercise on a regular basis if you want to feel and look terrific.

Regular exercise is the key to the high, sustained levels of energy and stamina that you absolutely have to have to be strong, alert, and capable of taking continuous action toward your goals.

Get Lots of Rest and Recreation

The fourth key to high energy is *proper rest*. You need an average of seven to eight hours of sleep each night to be fully rested. You need to take off at least one full day each week during which you don't work at all. You should take regular miniholidays of two or three days each, every couple of months. You should take one and two week vacations each year when you relax completely and get your mind totally off your work.

In the day or two after you come back from a complete rest, you will be far more productive than if you had continued to work. You will have more ideas and produce better results than you ever would if you allowed yourself to become exhausted and burned out. Make regular rest and recreation a key part of your lifestyle.

Take Vitamin and Mineral Supplements

The fifth key to high energy is to add *vitamin and mineral supplements* to your diet. No matter what you eat or what anyone says, most foods today are deficient in the essential vitamins and minerals you need to function at your best. The healthiest people in our society are those who take high-quality vitamins and minerals in addition to their regular diets.

The very best supplements are those from natural sources. Natural-source vitamins and minerals are usually bound with *chelates*. They may cost more, but more of the vitamins and minerals contained in them are absorbed by the body and made available to you for higher levels of health and vitality.

One of the great breakthroughs in recent years is the discovery of the importance of *antioxidants*. These chemicals remove free radicals, the disease causing substances, from your blood stream. Antioxidants are contained in proflavenols, green vegetables, and some absolutely excellent vitamin formulations. They make your whole body function better. They add considerably to the overall quality of your life, and to your energy levels.

Develop a Positive Mental Attitude

The sixth key to high energy is the *elimination of negative emotions*. This can be the most important thing you do to assure a long and happy life. Your ability to keep your mind on what you want and off what you don't want will determine your levels of health and happiness more than any other decision you make.

The more you think or talk about the people and situations that make you angry or unhappy, the angrier and unhappier you become. Negative emotions actually depress your mind and body. They rob you of energy. They disempower you. They depress your immune system and make you more susceptible to illnesses of all kinds. They tire you out and discourage you. They undermine your confidence and enthusiasm and lower your ability to perform effectively in the important areas of your life. One unrestrained outburst of anger can consume as much energy as eight hours of regular work.

The way that you overcome the temptation to complain and criticize, which almost everyone does on occasion, is by using the Law of

Substitution. Since your conscious mind can only hold one thought at a time, you can cancel out a negative thought by replacing it with a positive thought. Perhaps the most powerful way to neutralize the emotions of anger, fear, or worry is with the affirmation, "I am responsible! I am responsible! I am responsible!"

You cannot accept responsibility for a situation and continue to be angry at the same time. Most negative emotions are triggered by *blame*. Anger and resentment almost always requires you to blame someone for something. The instant that you stop blaming others, and start accepting responsibility, the negative emotion stops. Accepting responsibility puts you back in control. You begin thinking clearly again and then you get busy doing something constructive to solve the problem or resolve the situation.

If you are still bothered by negative experiences from your past, you should practice *the principle of forgiveness*, perhaps the most important of all decisions for mental health and spiritual development. The principle of forgiveness says, "You are mentally healthy to the exact degree to which you can freely forgive anyone who has hurt you in any way."

Whenever you think of someone that you still feel angry toward, cancel the feeling by saying, "I forgive him or her for everything." It is not possible to be angry and unhappy about another person and forgive him or her at the same time. In forgiving, you not only let the other person go, you set yourself free as well. You cannot accept responsibility on the one hand, forgive on the other, and still be angry or upset in the middle.

Start a Personal Mental Fitness Program

The seventh key to high energy is for you to go on a 21-day positive mental attitude diet, one day at a time. Resolve that, for the next 24 hours, you are going to keep your mind on what you want and keep it off the things you don't want. You are going to think and talk positively and optimistically about your goals, other people, and everything that is going on in your life.

Once you complete your first 24 hours on this mental diet, resolve to do it for 24 hours more. Say to yourself, "Just for today, I am going to think and talk about my goals, and I refuse to think or talk about anything that I don't want to see in my life." After you have kept your words and thoughts on what you want for one whole day, then do it for one more day. After the second day, do it for a third day, and then another and another, until you've kept your thinking positive for three whole weeks. This exercise will change your life.

By going on a 21-day positive mental attitude diet, one hour at a time, one day at a time, one situation at a time, you can gradually make yourself such a positive person that you will be able to bounce back from any reversal or negative situation.

Become a Personal Powerhouse

The more you practice the health habits we have talked about, the more energy and vitality you will have. The more you keep your conversation focused on your goals and on the things you want, the greater the amount of strength and power you will feel. You will be more alert and aware. You will feel more positive and action oriented in every situation.

You will step on the accelerator of your own potential. You will find yourself racing forward faster than you ever have before. You will get more done; make more money; earn more rewards, recognition, and esteem; have more doors opened for you; and experience more of the things that everyone refers to as luck.

ACTION EXERCISES
What You Can Do Now

1. Resolve to become intensely action oriented from now on; whenever you get a good idea or something needs to be done, move quickly.

2. Look for opportunities everywhere, and when you find one, move quickly; one good idea is all you need to start a fortune.

3. Develop momentum and then keep it up; once you get into motion, stay in motion. Do something every day that moves you toward one of your key goals.

4. Create a sense of urgency in everything you do; fast tempo is essential to success. The more things you do and the faster you do them, the more doors will open for you.

5. Maintain high energy levels by taking excellent care of your physical health; eat the right foods, watch your weight, and get lots of rest.

6. Develop a reputation for speed and dependability; become known as the person who can be depended upon to get the job done fast.

7. Continually reengineer your work, looking for ways to reduce the steps in a task or process so that you can get the job done faster.

Principle 11—Character Counts

"Honesty is the first chapter in the book of wisdom."
—Thomas Jefferson

In about 340 B.C., the Greek philosopher Aristotle laid out a series of principles that became the foundation for much of Western thought for the next two thousand years. His original ideas and insights still affect much of modern thinking today. An understanding of his basic ideas enables you to think and act with greater clarity and effectiveness than others who do not know them.

Perhaps Aristotle's most important contribution to philosophy was contained in his *principle of causality*. He taught that we live in an orderly universe and that, therefore, *everything happens for a reason*. There exists a cause-effect relationship among all events. Even if you do not know the reason for a particular effect, this does not mean that a reason does not exist. Success in any area comes from finding out the cause-effect relationships between the things you do and the things you want, and then organizing your activities so that they are in harmony with what you are trying to achieve.

The Ultimate Goal

One of Aristotle's great breakthroughs was his conclusion that all human behavior is *purposeful*. It is aimed at a goal or result of some kind. He said that everything you do, you do for a reason, and behind every smaller or intermediate goal, there is a larger goal that you are striving toward. Aristotle was the first to declare that the ultimate goal of every person is the desire to be happy.

For example, you say that you want to get a good job. Why? So that you can earn a good salary. Why? So that you can have enough money. Why? So that you can buy a house and a car and have a nice standard of living. Why? So that you can have happy relationships and a good life with other people. Why? The final answer is always the same: So that you can be happy.

No matter what you do, your ultimate goal is to achieve your own happiness, however you define it. You are, therefore, successful to the degree to which you can organize your life in such a way that you are genuinely happy. You are a failure to the degree to which you cannot attain your own happiness.

The only difference between people in this area is that some people are better at achieving their own happiness than others. Some are good at it and others are not. Some people do the right things and get the desired results. Other people make choices and decisions that leave them unhappier and worse off than they ever would have been if they had done nothing at all. But in every case, each person is aiming at his or her own happiness.

The Role of Virtue in Happiness

Aristotle moved forward from this powerful and profound insight. He studied the human condition and came to another remarkable conclusion: "Only the good can be happy, and only the virtuous can be good."

This is a major breakthrough in human thought. Just imagine! You can only be happy if you are a good person, and you can only be a good person if you practice the virtues that are associated with goodness.

What this means is that, to have a happy life, you must continually strive to become a *better* person. Each time you act consistently with the highest good that you know, you feel happy inside. You enjoy higher levels of self-confidence and self-esteem. You become more effective in your relationships and in your work. In this sense, virtue *is* its own reward. It pays for itself with the inner feelings of happiness, contentment, and personal power you feel when you do and say the things that are good and noble and true.

The Central Role of Character

Character is the greatest guarantee of good luck. The universal truth is that you inevitably attract into your life the people, circumstances, ideas, opportunities, and resources that are in harmony with your dominant thoughts. You can never achieve on the outside what you have not earned on the inside. Your outer world, by the Law of Correspondence, is always a reflection of your inner world.

If you want to change your outer world, you must begin by changing your thinking, by reprogramming your subconscious mind. You must build within yourself a structure of values, beliefs, and inner convictions that are consistent with the kind of life you want to enjoy on the outside. You must develop your own character.

Your Personal Definition of Success

You are reading this book because you want to be more successful in life. You want to be happier. You want to have better relationships, make more money, and more fully express yourself in everything you do. You want to have a great life. And what makes you superior to the average person is that you are willing to constantly learn more and more about how you can be better and better.

But what is success? How do you define it? The Gallup Organization interviewed 1,500 members of Marquis's *Who's Who in America* some years ago. These people were among the most prestigious of all living Americans—company presidents, leading politicians, top academics and authors, Nobel Prize winners, and others who have made a significant contribution to American life and who have been acknowledged and rewarded by their peers and others.

They asked these highly successful men and women what they considered to be the chief rewards of success. The first four answers they gave might surprise you.

The first reward of success mentioned by 86 percent of them was that they felt they had earned the respect of their parents; the second was that they felt they had earned the respect of their spouses and children; the third was that they felt they had earned the respect of their peers and colleagues; and the fourth benefit was that they felt that what they were doing was making a difference in the lives of other people. Finally, the fifth reward of success they identified was that they no longer worried about money, even though many of them were not particularly wealthy. They had simply reached a point where money didn't matter that much in comparison to the work they were doing and to the other aspects of their lives.

Gaining the Respect of Others

When you think of success in your own life, you will find that it is closely tied to the respect you get from the people that you respect. Almost everything you do is done or not done with a view toward how other people will think about you. Your consideration of the opinions of the important people in your world has a major effect on your behavior.

Your reputation is your greatest asset, both in your business life and in all your personal relationships. Your reputation can best be defined as *how people think about you and talk about you when you're not there*. As you know from your own experience, whatever people say about you has a positive or negative impact on your thinking and your emotions when you learn about it.

Successful people are always thinking about how a particular decision or behavior will be judged or evaluated by others. They are concerned not only about doing the right thing, but about doing what *appears* to be the right thing from the perspective of others, especially others whose opinion they care about.

The law of attraction is very powerful. You develop your character, as the result of living more and more by the highest and best virtues that you know. As a result, you will inevitably attract into your life other men and women of quality and character as well. Like *does* attract like.

The Development of Virtue

Aristotle taught another principle as well. He taught that the primary purpose of education is to teach virtue to the young. This would give them a solid foundation to build on and would assure that they would be good people as adults. By becoming good people, they would be able to create and maintain happy, successful lives when they grew up.

What do you do if your education or upbringing has been deficient? What if you have grown up without being thoroughly trained in the virtues that you must have to be an outstanding person as an adult? What if you are not satisfied with your current level of character development? What if there are additional virtues and qualities that you would like to incorporate into your personality?

Aristotle concluded that virtue is a *practice*, not simply a feeling or belief. Virtue is expressed in action, not in words. It is not what you hope, wish, or intend; it is only what you *do* that demonstrates your true character.

Aristotle said that, if you do not possess a particular virtue, you could develop it in yourself by practicing the virtue whenever it is called for. You can become virtuous by disciplining yourself to *act as if* you already have the virtue that you desire.

The Law of Reversibility says that *you can actually act your way into feeling and believing something that you sincerely desire to feel or believe*. In this way, you can take complete charge of the development of your character. You can become a truly excellent person by resolving to think, talk, and behave consistently with the very highest and best that you know, under all circumstances.

The Law of Concentration says that *whatever you dwell upon, grows*. You can use this powerful law to shape your character by dwelling upon a particular virtue that you want to be known and respected for. You can read about it and look for it in the stories and lives of other people. You can visualize and imagine yourself practicing this virtue in everything you do.

You Are a Social Animal

Aristotle also taught that man is a *social animal*. He has no identity separate from his position in society. He taught that everything in life involves relationships with other people. The quality, quantity, and complexity of your relationships defines you and shapes your life. We are all both dependent and interdependent. No one lives on an island, completely to himself or herself.

The highest virtue in life and relationships is the virtue of *integrity*. The dictionary definition of integrity includes, "Absolute truth, oneness, wholeness, perfection, fully integrated, without blemish or fault." You can develop within yourself this quality by meditating or dwelling on the quality of integrity. You can think about what it means to be a person of integrity. You can think of other people, those you know personally or historical characters, who are known and respected for their integrity.

You Become What You Do

Do you remember the nickname of Abraham Lincoln? It was Honest Abe. When he was a young man, working in a general store, he walked several miles to return a couple of pennies that he had overcharged a woman. People heard about this and told the story to others. Over time, he developed a reputation for complete honesty. He was so highly respected for his character that he was nominated to be the presidential candidate of the new Republican Party at the convention in Chicago in 1860, even though he never left Springfield, Illinois. His name and reputation carried the delegates. The qualities of his character made him one of America's most revered and respected presidents.

The more you dwell on a virtue like integrity, the more you will behave consistently with it. The more you turn it over in your mind, as you would turn over a precious piece of artwork in your hands, the more the practices of that virtue will be programmed into your subconscious mind. The more you imprint this virtue into your subconscious mind, the more likely it is that you will act as a person of integrity when the situation demands it.

As your reputation for integrity spreads, more people will trust you and want to be associated with you. Doors will open for you. You will start to experience the kind of *luck* that people with weaker characters never seem to enjoy.

Trust Is the Critical Bond in Society and Relationships

Francis Fukiyama wrote a book in 1995 entitled *Trust*. In this book, he reported on the results of studies of various nations over the centuries. Each of these nations was examined on the basis of the level of trust that existed within their societies. Fukiyama concluded that *high-trust* nations are prosperous and offer ever-greater opportunities for more and more people. Low-trust nations, on the other hand, have lower levels of prosperity and development. What is the reason for this?

It turns out that the greater the levels of trust amongst the people, the government, and the business community in any particular nation, the greater was the level of economic activity, growth, development, and prosperity that occurred. The lower the level of trust, the higher was the level of corruption and dishonesty. People were reluctant to invest or tie up their money in that country or economy.

The fundamental glue that holds any relationship together is trust. It is impossible for us to proceed in any kind of a relationship unless we trust the other person. All intimate relationships are based on trust. All good friendships are based on trust. All strong families are built on trust. In businesses and organizations, trust is the essential ingredient that holds the organization together. The success of the enterprise is virtually impossible without it.

The very best companies to work for have high-trust environments. In a great company, everyone, at every level, absolutely trusts and believes what other people say is true. In a good company, telling a lie can be enough to cost you your job.

In general, Americans place an inordinate emphasis and value on the element of trust. You cannot even drive down the street without absolutely trusting that the person coming toward you will drive on his or her side of the road. Trust is the binding ingredient that holds our entire society together.

The Foundation of Trust

The ultimate expression of trust is *truthfulness*. Your very best friends and closest associates in life will always be those who tell you the truth. Your willingness to be completely honest with yourself and others is the real measure of character. If integrity is the core quality of character, then truthfulness is the most obvious expression of integrity.

If the inner expression of integrity is truth, then the outer expression of integrity is quality work and quality behavior under all circumstances. You must be true to the very best that is in you. In your work, this commitment to honesty requires that you do your very best in every situation, especially when people are counting on you.

Be Honest with Yourself

At a very minimum, you must always be true to yourself. The psychologist Abraham Maslow studied successful, self-actualizing people for many years. He found that a predominant characteristic of the best people he interviewed was that they were extremely objective and truthful about themselves. They were perfectly honest about their strengths and weaknesses, and about their situations in life. They never tried to convince themselves of things that weren't true. They lived in truth with themselves and as a result they were able to live in truth with others.

Shakespeare wrote, "And this above all, to thine own self be true. Then, it must follow, as the night the day, thou canst not then be false to any man." Refuse to play games with yourself. Refuse to pretend or wish or hope that something is other than it is. Deal with the world as it really is, not as you wish it were. Practice *the reality principle* in everything. Always ask, "What's the reality?"

Listen to your inner voice. Trust your intuition. Do and say only those things that feel right to you. Refuse to compromise your integrity for any reason. As Ralph Waldo Emerson once wrote, "Nothing is at last sacred but the integrity of your own mind."

Live in Truth with Everyone

The practice of integrity means that you live in truth with everyone around you. You state your truth simply and honestly. You do not stay in relationships that are wrong for you or do things that you do not agree with or believe in. You do not say things to people that are not honest and sincere expressions of your true beliefs. You insist on living in truth in every area of your life.

The roots of self-esteem and self-confidence lie deep within your own character. The more you practice impeccable integrity in your relationships with yourself and others, the more you will like and respect yourself. The more you like and respect yourself, the more you will like and respect others, and the more they will like and respect you. Both the quantity and quality of your relationships will increase.

Integrity is the one value that guarantees all the others. You are honest to the degree to which you live consistently with every other principle that you know to be right and good and true. Consistency in behavior is the measure of your integrity.

Self-Discipline Is the Key to Character

Elbert Hubbard, a twentieth century writer, once wrote, "Self-discipline is the ability to *make* yourself do what you should do, when you should do it, whether you feel like it or not."

Self-discipline is the iron quality of character. It is the foundation stone of integrity and courage. Your level of self-discipline has a major impact on what you accomplish in every area of endeavor.

Other definitions of self-discipline are *self-mastery* and *self-control*, and control is a critical element in happiness. You feel good about yourself to the degree to which you feel you are in control of your own life. When you make a decision to do or refrain from doing something, and you discipline yourself to stick to your resolution even when you *don't* feel like it, you feel much better about yourself. You feel in control.

There is a direct correlation between self-discipline and self-esteem. The more you discipline yourself to do the things you have resolved to do, the more you like and respect yourself. And the more you like and respect yourself, the more capable you become of disciplining yourself to do the things that you know you should do. Each quality reinforces the other.

Your Choices and Decisions

You are where you are and what you are today because of the choices and decisions that you have made in the past. You have either thought carefully and made your decisions based on good information and sound judgment, consistent with the highest values you know, or you have *not*.

Your choices and decisions of the past do not have to dictate your future. That was then and this is now. You are in a constant state of growth and evolution. You made decisions when you were a child that you would never think of making as an adult. You made decisions last year, that you would not make this year, knowing what you now know. When you made those choices and decisions, you were a different person. Today, you are someone else.

Don't be held back by the mistakes you have made in the past. The person who made those mistakes was an earlier version of yourself. Today, you are a more mature and wiser person. You can make new choices based on the person you are today. You can make new decisions, based on your ever-growing storehouse of knowledge and experience. Today, you can put your hands on the wheel of your own future and steer in whatever direction you want to go.

The E-Factor in Personal Performance

Why is it that everyone does not live a life of high character? Why is it that every individual does not practice the essential virtues of integrity and truthfulness in all their dealings, especially since these virtues are so closely correlated with success in every aspect of life?

The answer is contained in what I call the expediency factor in human personality. This E-factor is the primary reason for failure in life. It is only when you understand how and why this E-factor works that you can counteract it. It is only when you do the opposite of what the E-factor suggests that you become the person you most desire to be.

The E-factor is based on the basic characteristics of human nature. There are many elements of what is referred to as *human nature*, but I will just describe the basic seven. Any one of these qualities, improperly directed, is enough to cause a person to fail. The great tragedy is that most people are practicing the negative side of all seven of these characteristics much of the time. They therefore accomplish very little in life, and they seldom know why.

People Prefer Easier to Difficult

The most common quality of human nature is that people prefer *easier to difficult* in accomplishing any task. You always attempt to conserve energy in doing any job. The reason for this is that your time and your energy represents your life, and you place a value on your life. You are designed in such a way that you cannot consciously choose a harder way to do something if you can see an easier way to do it. This means that, for better or worse, you and everyone else are lazy.

There is nothing wrong with laziness if it is directed constructively toward finding more efficient ways to accomplish the same task. The entire history of human progress has been the story of men and women applying their creativity to achieve the same goals, for themselves and others, with a lower expenditure of effort and energy.

Laziness is neither good nor bad. It is *value free* in itself. It is normal and natural. It is only when people practice laziness in ways that end up being counterproductive and even hurtful to themselves and others that laziness becomes a negative quality.

Everyone Prefers More to Less

The second quality of human nature is that everyone prefers *more to less*. If I were to offer you $5 or $10 for the same apple, with no other conditions, you would choose $10. This is normal and natural. It is human nature to seek to get the most for the least. All human beings prefer more to less, all things being equal.

What this means is that everyone is "greedy." Again, greediness is neutral, neither positive nor negative. If greediness is channeled productively toward improving your life and increasing the well-being of yourself and others, it can be a positive influence for good. It can be a great motivator of creativity and enterprise.

If however, greediness is aimed at getting *something for nothing*, or something that a person does not deserve, it can be harmful and destructive. It is only the way that greediness is practiced that determines whether it is a good or bad quality of the individual.

Everyone Is Selfish

The third quality of human nature is that everyone *desires things for himself or herself*. Only you can feel your own happiness, your own pleasure and your own dissatisfaction. Only you can experience your own hunger, thirst, contentment, or joy. As a responsible adult, no one can feel these feelings for you or decide what is best for you. You are a unique individual with special likes and dislikes that only you can determine for yourself.

This simply means that you are naturally selfish or self-centered. When you go to a buffet, only you can determine the ideal combination of foods that will satisfy your appetite and your palate, based on your personal tastes at that moment. You want what you want. And again, this is neither right nor wrong. It is just a fact of human nature, like being lazy or greedy.

A minister working in a rescue mission in the inner city can be totally selfish in that he is determined to satisfy his deepest needs and beliefs by helping as many people as he can with the resources that he has available. This minister can be lazy, greedy, and selfish in a very healthy, positive, and constructive way that benefits other people. In this sense, even Mother Teresa of Calcutta was *selfish*. She wanted to help and comfort as many people as she possibly could.

Everyone Is Ambitious

The fourth quality of human nature is that every act that we engage in is aimed at *improvement* of some kind. We act to be better off than we would have been if we had not acted in the first place. Consciously or unconsciously, everyone seeks improvement of some kind in everything they say or do. What this means is that everyone is ambitious. Everyone wants to improve his or her life, work, relationships, health, or financial status in some way.

The opposite of being ambitious would be to be indifferent or complacent. If you had no ambition, you would be completely satisfied and not care at all whether your life got better or worse. Ambition is a very healthy quality and is the great stimulus that drives people to overcome obstacles and achieve goals that no one might have believed possible.

Of course, if a person's ambition causes him to engage in dishonest or hurtful behaviors, then ambition becomes a negative quality. But in and of itself, it is neither positive nor negative. Like the other characteristics of human nature, ambition is *neutral*.

No One Knows Everything about Anything

The fifth characteristic of human nature is *ignorance*. No one can ever know everything there is to know about anything. This means that, no matter how much you learn or experience, every decision you make or action you take is a speculation of some kind. Because you can never know all the facts, there can never be a guarantee that your action will bring about the results that you desire. You must always decide and act with a certain degree of uncertainty.

This means that everyone is ignorant to a certain degree. Some people are far more ignorant than others. But everyone is ignorant because no one can ever know everything there is to know about even his particular area of specialization.

The drive to know, to find out, to minimize risk by increasing the amount of knowledge available on a particular subject, is the primary reason why the totality of human knowledge is doubling every two or three years today. More people in more fields are generating more information and knowledge today than has ever been done in all of human history, and the rate is accelerating. This is because we intuitively recognize that we are all ignorant, to some degree.

Vanity, Vanity, All Is Vanity

The sixth quality of human nature is that people take pride in themselves, their appearance, their accomplishments, their family, their work, and their possessions. People like to be attractive and be thought well of by others. This means that everyone is vain to a certain degree.

The opposite of vanity is indifference. Vanity can, therefore, be a good thing. It leads us to strive for beauty, health, wealth, success, and material attainment. Vanity is the driving force behind the clothing industry, the furniture industry, the home industry, the automotive industry, the cosmetic industry, the entertainment industry, the sports industry and the desire to start and build successful enterprises. It is the driving force behind political activity and exerts an inordinate influence on all your choices and decisions.

When vanity leads to your doing things that earn you the respect and esteem of others, it is a good quality. If vanity leads you to do or say things that are harmful to yourself or others, it is a negative quality. But in itself, it is neither good nor bad. Human vanity is merely a fact, like the weather.

The Need for Speed

The seventh characteristic of human nature is *impatience*. This is based on the fact that everyone prefers *sooner to later*. Everyone wants things done now rather than at some later date. If I offered you $100, and I could give it to you today or one year from today, which would you choose? If you were normal, you would probably choose to have it immediately. This is just human nature.

Why is this? It is because you value your life, and your life is made up of time. If you can have a reward or benefit sooner rather than later, especially since the future is uncertain, you will always prefer to have it sooner. Who knows what might happen tomorrow?

Our entire economy today is driven by the desire of consumers to have the things they want faster, easier, newer, better and cheaper than ever before. Every competitive business is driven by the *need for speed*. They are driven by the need to service customers faster and better than their competitors or risk being put out of business.

Basic Human Nature

Let us summarize the essential qualities that make up human nature and determine individual behavior. The normal person, including yourself, is *lazy, greedy, selfish, ambitious, ignorant, vain, and impatient*. This is quite a combination of characteristics! But there is nothing wrong with these qualities in themselves. They are just a fact of life, common to all human beings, in all cultures, races, religions, and nationalities.

The average person is, therefore, *expedient*. The normal individual constantly seeks the fastest and easiest way to get the things that he or she wants, immediately, with little or no concern for secondary consequences or for what might happen as a result.

The only constraints on the negative manifestations and runaway impulses of the E-factor are self-discipline, self-control, and self-mastery. It is only by practicing the essential virtues, especially that of self-discipline, and by insisting on doing the right thing, that you can withstand the irresistible pull of expediency, but the tendencies are always there.

The Noble Virtues of Character

It is only the persistent practice of the noble virtues that develops self-discipline, character, and great reputation. Let us look at some of these virtues.

Be True to Yourself

First, *integrity* is the core virtue, the one that guarantees all the others. Your level of integrity determines how consistently you live by the virtues you espouse, by what you know to be right and true.

Accept Responsibility for Your Life

The second key virtue of successful people is *responsibility*. When you take complete responsibility for yourself, you accept that you are the primary creative force in your own life. You acknowledge that you are where you are and what you are because of yourself, because of your own thoughts and behaviors. You say continually, "I am responsible." You say, "If it is to be, it is up to me."

When you practice the virtue of responsibility, you stop blaming other people for your problems, or for what they did and said that made you unhappy. You stop making excuses for your failure to make progress. You stop complaining and justifying. You take complete charge of your life and you accept responsibility not only for yourself, but also for all those who look up to you and depend upon you to fulfill your commitments.

Treat Each Person with Compassion

The third great virtue is *compassion*, one of the finest of all human qualities. Like all virtues, compassion is expressed in action. You become more compassionate by seeking to understand and empathize with other people rather than judging or dismissing them. You try to understand them and their situations.

When you think about and practice compassion toward others, you become a better person. You become more patient, more tolerant, more understanding and more sympathetic, especially toward those who are unhappy or less fortunate.

Instead of trying constantly to get the things you want faster and easier, you put yourself into the situation of others who are struggling in life. You keep reminding yourself, "There, but for the grace of God, go I."

Practice Kindness in Every Situation

The fourth great virtue is that of *kindness*. Everyone you meet is carrying a heavy load. When you go through your day expressing kindness, and thinking kind thoughts toward everyone you meet, you will create a feeling of warmth and good cheer wherever you go. Remember, in life, you can never be too kind or too fair.

The best payoff of all for becoming a kindly person is that you feel better about yourself. When you express compassion and kindness at every opportunity, without judging or blaming other people, you begin to walk with the saints. You become a finer person. You develop spiritually and shape your character in a very healthy way.

Be a Friend to Others

The fifth great virtue is that of *friendship*. You know that to have a friend, you must be a friend. You can make more friends in a few days by being a good friend to others than you could in years of trying to get people to like you.

Dale Carnegie once wrote that the very best way to build friendly relationships with others is to become genuinely interested in them. The easiest way to overcome any shyness or insecurity you may have is to ask questions of the other person: "What sort of work do you do?" "How did you get into that field?" "How is everything going for you?" "How are you feeling today?"

Once you have asked these open and honest questions about another person and his or her life, listen quietly and attentively to the answers. Listen without interrupting. Nod, smile, and pay attention.

The more you forget yourself and focus your attention on others, the better you will feel about yourself, and the better others will feel about you. These positive feelings become self-reinforcing. The more you do and say the things that make others feel good about themselves, the more you program these behaviors into your personality and make them a permanent part of your character.

The Quality of the Strong

The sixth virtue is that of *gentleness*, especially with the important people in your life. The fact is that only the strong can be gentle. People who are rough or indifferent toward the feelings of others are usually weak and insincere people. They commonly have low levels of self-esteem. They often feel inadequate and insecure.

Great men and women are often the kindest and gentlest people that you will ever meet. When you are gentle, patient, tolerant, kind, and compassionate toward others, no matter what the circumstances, you become a better person *inside*. You will have a more positive impact on them. You will be more admired and respected. Your influence will be greater. Practice these qualities with your spouse and children, with your friends and with your employees, and you will be amazed at the effect you have on them.

The Greatest Human Good

The greatest good in life is *peace of mind*. This should be your main aim in every decision you make. It is the true measure of how well you are doing as a human being. When you set peace of mind as your central goal, and you organize your life around it, you will probably never make another mistake.

You attain your own peace of mind only when you are living consistently with the highest values and virtues that you know. Peace of mind comes when you discipline yourself to resist the pull of the E-factor. Peace of mind arises naturally when you know that you are being impeccably honest with yourself and others. Peace of mind emerges when you listen to the still, small voice within you. You trust your intuition. You go with the flow of your own nature. You do what you know to be right and good and true.

When you live consistently with the very best that you know, you attract into your life people and opportunities that enable you to make more progress in a couple of years than many people make in a lifetime. And everyone will call you *lucky*.

ACTION EXERCISES
What You Can Do Now

1. Decide for yourself what makes you truly happy and then begin to organize your life and work around those activities; no one else can or will do it for you.

2. Make a list of the people you most respect, and who you most want to respect you; how would you have to behave to earn their respect?

3. Be true to yourself in everything you do and say; live in truth with others at all times.

4. Take charge of the development of your own character; choose a virtue that you admire and would like to have. Practice it wherever and whenever it is called for.

5. Resist the temptation to seek the expedient way to achieve your goals or accomplish your tasks. Be patient and do each thing well.

6. Practice the noble virtues of generosity, patience, kindliness, and honesty with everyone you meet, starting at home.

7. Self-discipline is the key to character and the master key to riches; apply it to every part of your life, especially when you don't feel like it.

Principle 12—Fortune Favors the Brave

*"Courage is rightly considered the
foremost of the virtues, for upon it all others depend."*
—Winston Churchill

Perhaps the most important of all luck factors is the quality of courage. The development of self-confidence, courage, boldness, and the willingness to move forward toward your goals, with no guarantees of success, is the essential requirement for high achievement. With courage, you can do virtually anything in life. And without it, none of the other qualities will help you.

The opposite of courage is fear. The emotion of fear will be and has always been the deadliest enemy to success. Fear and doubt have done more to undermine and sabotage the hopes and possibilities of individuals than any other force. It is not what is going on around you but what is going on within you that is determining everything you are and everything you will ever accomplish. The development of high levels of courage and determination is essential to your putting your entire life into high gear.

What Do You Really Want?

Is your goal to be financially independent? Do you want to be rich? Do you want to become a millionaire over the course of your working lifetime? These are reasonable goals. There are no obstacles stopping you from achieving them. Hundreds of thousands and even millions of men and women over the years have achieved these goals, starting from nothing. Many successful people today started broke or deeply in debt. Often, they started later in life. What others have accomplished, so can you.

The only question you need to answer is this: How badly do you want it? Once you have decide exactly what you want, you can activate the *principle of courage* to increase your luck. This principle says that *when you move boldly in the direction of your goals, unseen forces will come to your aid.*

Many people hesitate or quit altogether because they cannot see exactly how they are going to get from where they are to where they want to go. They forget that a journey of a thousand leagues begins with a single step. It is only when you step out in faith, when you move boldly in the direction of your dreams, that things begin to happen for you.

Make a Commitment

Charles Murray, a mountain climber, wrote these words:

Until one is committed, there is hesitancy, the chance to draw back, always ineffectiveness. Concerning all acts of initiative and creation, there is an elementary truth, the ignorance of which kills countless ideas and splendid plans; that the moment one definitely commits oneself, then providence moves, too.

All sorts of things occur to help one that would never have otherwise occurred. A whole stream of events issues from the decision, raising in one's favor all manner of unforeseen incidents and meetings and material assistance, which no man could have dreamed would have come his way.

Are you in earnest? Seek this very minute. Whatever you can do, or dream you can; begin it. Boldness has genius, power and magic in it. Only engage and the mind grows heated; begin and then the task will be completed.

The Golden Mean of Courage

When Aristotle wrote about courage, he described it as the *golden mean* between rash behavior on the one extreme, and cowardliness on the other. The quality of true courage is located in the middle of the scale. He defined courage as the ability to master and control fear in the right way at the right time. He said that the way to develop courage, as with any other virtue, is by practicing courage in every situation where courage is required.

All Fears Are Learned

There is only one good thing about the fears that hold you back. They are all *learned*. They can, therefore, be *unlearned*, by practice. You did not come into the world with any fears. When you were born, you and every other child had two wonderful qualities. First, you were completely *unafraid*. The infant has no natural fears, except for the fears of falling and loud noises. Second, you were completely *spontaneous*. The infant expresses himself freely and openly, without any thought or concern about what anyone else says or thinks.

But, as you grew up, your parents and the people around you began teaching you to be afraid. They began programming the fears into you that can hold you back for the rest of your life. For example, when you began exploring the world around you, they began saying things like, "Stop!" "Get away from there!" "Don't touch that!" "Put that down!" "Get out of there!" And perhaps the most powerful negative words of all, "No! You can't do that!"

The Fear of Failure

As a child, whenever you tried to touch, taste, smell, feel, or get into something, there was always someone there telling you to stop doing it. "It's too dangerous." " You are too small." "Get away from there." As a result, at an early age, and at an unconscious level, you developed the belief that you were too small and too weak to do anything new or different. You started to believe, "I'm not good enough."

Soon you began to develop the first signs of the fear of failure, which is always expressed in the words, "I can't!"

When you became an adult, you took personal control of the negative reinforcement process begun by your parents. Whenever something new or challenging came up, you began saying to yourself, "I can't do that." "I'm not smart enough." "I'm not creative enough." "I'm not educated enough." "I'm not good enough." "I can't."

As an adult, your first reaction to anything new or different may now be to think of a reason why it is not possible for you. If you are not careful, you will go before the court of life and become the prosecutor against yourself in your own case. You will immediately think up all the reasons why you cannot achieve your dreams and goals. You will talk yourself out of doing the very things you need to do to enjoy the success and happiness you most want. Henry Ford once said, "If you believe you can do a thing, or you believe you can't, in either case, you're probably right."

The Fear of Rejection

The second major fear that you develop is the fear of rejection. This fear comes about when your parents make their love for you conditional upon your behavior.

A child needs love like roses need rain. The child needs security and approval as much as the child needs food, water, and comfort. The child is completely emotional and interprets every word and gesture emotionally. He is inordinately affected by the emotional environment in which he grows up. If your parents constantly criticized and disapproved of you because you did or didn't do certain things, you learned very early to change your behaviors so that you were always doing what you thought they wanted and would approve of.

Destructive Criticism Holds You Back

If you grew up with a lot of criticism and disapproval, as an adult you will often be *hypersensitive* to the opinions of other people. You will constantly seek their approval, whether they are members of the opposite sex, co-workers, your boss, or even people you hardly know or care about.

Some people are so traumatized by criticism in early childhood that they cannot make any decision at all in adult life. If they think anyone around them might disapprove, even people they don't know, they become paralyzed. They are frightened of making a mistake and triggering the criticism of others.

The obstacle that holds most people back from starting their own businesses, or changing careers, is the fear of disapproval or ridicule from others. Rather than to have someone else not like them or admire them, they would rather do nothing at all.

Unfortunately, when you do nothing at all, you accomplish nothing at all, as well. The greatest guarantee of failure is to be overly concerned about failure in the first place.

Fears of Disapproval

The fear of rejection is characterized by the feeling that, "I have to!" It is the compulsive feeling that you *have* to do things that others will approve of, and that simultaneously, you cannot do anything that others may disapprove of.

Mild fears of failure and rejection are healthy. They can motivate you to do what is necessary to succeed. Mild feelings of inadequacy and inferiority can drive you to become the kind of person that others will admire and respect. In this sense, they act as positive stimuli to constructive behavior.

Fears of rejection, when they are manifested in a valid consideration for the feelings and opinions of others, can be helpful to your position in society. The desire to be liked and accepted by others lies at the basis of our respect for the rule of law, common courtesy, manners, politeness, and the social customs and norms that make civilized life possible.

Aristotle was known for having said, "Moderation in all things." There is nothing wrong with moderation in the area of fears as long as it does not have the effect of sabotaging your potential, which unfortunately is the case for most people.

Eliminating the Fears That Hold You Back

The way you get over the fear of failure is this: Whenever you think of a person or circumstance that is making you tense or fearful, you cancel out these emotions by using the *principle of substitution*. You repeat the words, "I can do it! I can do it! I can do it!"

To overcome the fear of rejection, you repeat to yourself, *"I don't have to! I don't have to! I don't have to!"*

Tell yourself that you don't *have to do* anything that you don't want to, and that you *can do* anything that you really want to do. When you repeat these affirmations, you begin to take full control of your emotions. You override your conditioned fears and build up your self-confidence. You begin to become unstoppable.

Unlocking Your Mental Powers

The more boldly you act and the more confidently you move in the direction of your dreams, the more your mental powers will work for you. You will attract the people and resources you need to achieve your goals. You will become more positive and optimistic. Your superconscious mind will work to affect the world around you. You will have regular experiences of serendipity and synchronicity.

Here is a great question you can ask to blast through the barriers of fear and doubt that hold you back: *What one great thing would you dare to dream if you knew you could not fail?*

If you could have anything you really wanted in life, what would it be? If you could wave a magic wand and change anything about your life, what would you want to happen? What would you dare to attempt if you had no limitations at all? If you were absolutely guaranteed success in any one great thing, what one big goal would you set for yourself?

Almost everyone knows the answers to these questions. But the instant you think of your answer, your fears will attack you from all sides. They will appear like a mob of subconscious demons, arousing your doubts and misgivings, and undermining your belief that these goals are possible for you.

Getting Rid of Your Excuses

Here's a good way to test the mental obstacles or excuses that you have used in the past to hold yourself back. Ask yourself, *"Is there anyone any-*

where who has experienced the same limitations that I have but who has gone on to be successful, anyway?"

This question forces you to be honest with yourself. It forces you to face the realities of your current situation. This question immediately reveals your *excuses* for not doing and being what you really want.

Whatever your favorite excuse might be, you can be sure that there are thousands of people who have had far worse circumstances than you could ever dream of having. Yet these people have gone on to accomplish wonderful things with their lives. They have made great contributions to their families and their communities. And what others have done, so can you. What is holding you back?

Releasing Your Brakes

Psychologists today have identified two major factors that make you afraid and undermine your self-confidence far more than is justified by the facts in any situation. The first brake on your potential is the feeling of learned helplessness.

Dr. Martin Seligman of the University of Pennsylvania, in his book *Learned Optimism*, explains, on the basis of 25 years of research, that perhaps 80 percent or more of the population has this feeling of *learned helplessness*, to a greater or lesser degree.

Learned helplessness is the feeling that there is nothing you can do to change or improve your situation. You feel trapped. Whenever you get an opportunity to change, you say, "I can't! I can't!"

Psychologist Abraham Maslow said that the history of the human race is the story of men and women *selling themselves short*. The reason you settle for less than is possible for you is because you have unconsciously accepted that there is very little that you can do to change things. You feel helpless.

The Only Real Limitation

However, this is not really true. You can create your own future, almost without limitation. You can bring about dramatic changes, and sometimes very quickly, by practicing the principles we have talked about throughout this book. In reality, the only limitations on your abilities are the ones that exist in your own mind. Remember Napoleon Hill's famous words, "Whatever the mind of man can conceive and believe, it can achieve."

The fact that you can clearly define a goal for yourself, write it down, and make a plan for its accomplishment, means that you probably have within you and around you everything you need to achieve that goal. Your ability to describe what you really want means that you have the ability to attain it, as long as you want it long enough and you are willing to work hard enough. The only real limit is the intensity of your desire.

Your Comfort Zone

The second factor that holds people back from great success, and makes them afraid to reach for higher goals, is that they get stuck in a comfort zone. We are all creatures of habit. We form habits and then our habits form us, even if we are not particularly happy with the results we are getting.

The Law of Habit is a key luck factor. It says, *your behavior is governed by your habits; in the absence of a clear decision on your part, or some external stimulus, you will keep on behaving the same way indefinitely.*

The Law of Habit is another expression of Sir Isaac Newton's Law of Inertia. He said, "A body in motion tends to remain in motion unless acted upon by an external force."

This law, applied to your habits and behavior, says that you will continue to do the same things you are doing today unless something happens to change your direction. You will continue to associate with the same people, earn about the same amount of money and live very much at the same level of accomplishment. Nothing will change for you unless you make a clear decision to change your situation or unless something happens to you that forces you to change.

This is why losing a job, the breakdown of a marriage or relationship, or the loss of all of your money in a bad investment can actually be a good thing. It can jar you out of your complacency and knock you out of your comfort zone. A shock of any kind can wake you up and open your eyes to other possibilities you can pursue and other directions you can go in.

The "Act as If" Principle

The writer Dorothea Brande felt that this was the most important of all success principles. She said, "Whatever you sincerely desire, *act as if it were impossible to fail*, and it shall be!"

Churchill said, "The best way to develop any quality is to assume that you already have it, and act accordingly."

Aristotle said that the best way to develop the quality of courage was to practice courage in every situation where it was required until it became a habit.

The Brave Person and the Coward

Here is a discovery that changed my life some years ago. It was my realization that *everyone is afraid*. You are afraid, and I am afraid, and everyone you meet is afraid of certain things. As the result of our childhood conditioning, we all grow up with a variety of fears. These fears sometimes help us, but mostly they hurt us or hold us back. But we all have them.

If everyone is afraid, what then is the difference between the brave person and the coward? And the answer is simple. The brave person is the person who acts *in spite of* his fears. The coward is the person who allows his fears to overwhelm him and control his thoughts, feelings, and behaviors.

Ralph Waldo Emerson once wrote that one of the most important lessons he ever learned was, "Do the thing you fear and the death of fear is certain."

One of the hallmarks of brave people is that they make a habit of confronting their fears whenever they arise. When you confront something that is making you afraid, and you move toward that fear, the fear diminishes and loses its hold over you. But if you back away from the fear, the fear grows until it dominates your whole life. The actor Glen Ford once said, "If you do not do the thing you fear, the fear controls your life."

Mark Twain wrote, "Courage is not lack of fear, absence of fear; it is control of fear, mastery of fear."

Develop the Habit of Courage

The Law of Habit says that whatever you do *over and over* again becomes a new habit. If you make a habit of confronting your fears, of doing the thing you fear, of acting as if you had no fears at all in a difficult situation, your fears diminish and your courage increases. Soon you reach the point where you are not afraid of anything.

Here is an exercise in developing courage: Take your dream list and use the worry-buster method on each of your dreams and goals.

Make a list of all the things you want down the left-hand side of the page. Draw a line down the center of the page. In the right-hand column, opposite your goals, write out the worst possible thing that could happen if you immediately took action toward the achievement of that goal. In almost every case, the worst possible consequence will not be very serious at all. You will wonder what has been holding you back.

Then resolve to do something immediately to achieve one or more of your goals. The very act of taking the first step increases your confidence and motivates you to take the next step, and then the next. The key is to get started.

Eliminating the Worry That Holds You Back

One of the symptoms of fear is worry. Worry is a sustained form of fear caused by indecision and doubt. Worry has been defined as *negative imagination*, or negative goal setting. It is thinking about and imagining exactly the things that you *don't* want to happen. But when you take action toward your goals, your worries disappear and your entire attention shifts to the results you are trying to accomplish. You are on your way!

People who worry about money all the time always have money problems. People who think and talk negatively about other people always seem to have problems in their relationships. People who complain about their companies or their jobs are surprised to find that they are always having problems at work. By the Law of Attraction, you get more of whatever you think and talk about most of the time.

When you worry, you attract into your life more of those things that you are worrying about. You must be careful to think about, talk about, and imagine only the things that you want. You must refuse to dwell upon the things that you don't want. You must do everything possible to assure that these mental principles and laws are working for you and not against you. This is essential for creating your own future.

Three Steps to Developing Courage

How do you develop the quality of courage? Here are three steps that you can practice over and over again.

First, when you think of a situation that makes you afraid for any reason, try to identify the worse possible thing that could happen as the result of that situation. Once you have identified the worst possible thing that could happen, resolve to accept it, should it occur. Then, you can stop worrying about it and put it out of your mind.

You can then focus all your attention on doing everything possible to assure that the worst doesn't happen. John Paul Getty used this philosophy to become one of the richest men in the world. When he was asked his secret of success, he said that it consisted of two parts. "First," he said, "Whatever business situation you are thinking of getting into, identify the worst possible thing that can happen in that situation."

"And number two," he said, "Make sure that it doesn't happen!"

Once you have identified the worst possible thing that can happen in any situation, your fears and your worries tend to evaporate. Your mind becomes calm and clear. You can then focus all your energies and enthusiasm on success rather than spending half your time thinking of failure.

Dare to Go Forward

When I was in competitive karate some years ago, I learned an important technique from one of the top karate masters in the world. He taught me that if I advanced toward my opponent in a karate match, even half an inch at a time, my opponent would move backward to keep the relative distance the same between us. While I was moving forward, 100 percent of my energy and attention was focused forward. But when my opponent was backing up, fully half his energy was taken up by thinking about what was behind him and the edge of the mat.

I was able to compete successfully and win prizes in several national championship matches because I always moved forward, even against a better opponent. This gave me the psychological edge, and that made all the difference.

Focusing 100 percent of your energies *forward* gives you that critical edge as well. It can spell the critical difference between success and failure.

Think About Success

One of the best ways to build up your courage is for you to dwell upon all the *rewards and benefits* that you will enjoy as the result of achieving your goals. Write them down. Think about them continually. Convince yourself that the rewards of success are much greater than the potential costs of temporary failure.

The more *reasons* you have for wanting to achieve your goals, the more motivated you will be. The more rewards you can think about enjoying when you overcome the obstacles in your path, the more power and energy you will have. Since you can only think about one thing at a time, if you're thinking of the rewards of success, you cannot simultaneously think about the penalties of failure.

The more you think about what you want, the more motivated you will become. The more confident you become, the more courage you will develop. Eventually you will reach the point where you are not afraid of anything. You will become unstoppable in your pursuit of your goals.

Be Willing to Do What It Takes

One of the most important luck factors is *willingness*. This is your resolution to do whatever it takes to achieve your goal. The quality of willingness is an expression of courage, and depends upon it.

Of course, you will only do what is legal and within reason. You would not take senseless risks, endanger your life, or attempt things where the cost of failure is unacceptable. But within these boundaries, the quality of being willing to do whatever is required will dramatically increase the likelihood that you will achieve your goals.

Many people, when they set a goal for themselves, are willing to do *almost* everything that it takes to achieve the goal. But this is not sufficient. You must be so committed to your goal that you are willing to pay any price, go any distance and make any sacrifice if that's what it takes to get from where you are to where you want to go.

What is the price you will have to pay to achieve your goals? Do you know? What extra efforts and additional sacrifices will you have to make to succeed greatly? Most people have not thought through the answers to these questions. They have no idea the price they will have to pay. When they start out on the journey to success, they soon find out what it will cost. Then they turn away. They give up on their dreams. They are not really willing to pay the full price. Don't let this happen to you.

The Two Parts of Courage

The first part of courage is the willingness *to begin*, to act in faith, and to step out boldly in the direction of your goals with no guarantee of success. The second part of courage is your willingness *to endure*, to persist, and to keep on working longer than anyone else.

Sometimes, the greatest advantage you can have is your determination to succeed. It can be your decision that you will never give up. The person who is the most resolute and determined in any competitive situation is the person who will almost invariably win.

Persistence Gives You the Edge

Perseverance, persistence, and determination are the essential qualities that make you a *lucky* person. Every great triumph is usually preceded by weeks, months, and even years of hard work that often result in very little success. The average self-made millionaire has worked 22 years to get from a zero bank balance to net worth of more than a million dollars.

Most people don't know this. Many people think that it is possible to get rich quickly, which is seldom true. Instead, it is patience, resolution, and determination, backed by indomitable willpower and unshakable persistence that will ultimately guarantee your success.

In a study conducted in New York on goal orientation not long ago, the researchers found that 95 percent of the goals that people set they ultimately achieved, as long as they didn't give up.

The primary reason that people fail is not because of lack of ability or opportunities. They fail because they lack the inner strength to persist in the face of obstacles and difficulties.

Be Prepared for Reversals

As soon as you set a big goal for yourself, your life will often hit a storm. You will be tossed and turned by a whole series of unexpected reverses and difficulties. When you set new, big, challenging, exciting goals, your superconscious mind will often trigger changes in the world around you. These changes will all have one thing in common. They will conspire together to bring you the experiences and the opportunities you need to ultimately achieve the new goals you have set for yourself.

The Golden Questions

Here are two powerful questions you can use to turn failure into success. They will help you to persist in the face of adversity. I call these the *golden questions*. I learned them from a self-made millionaire, and I have taught them to many people who have used them to become self-made millionaires themselves.

The first question that you ask yourself, no matter what happens is, "*What did I do right?*" Carefully analyze every single thing that you did right in that situation. Even if the situation turned out to be a disaster, there were certain things that you did that were worthwhile and worth repeating.

Then, ask yourself, "*What would I do differently if I had this situation to do over again?*" This forces you to think about the valuable lessons that this situation contains for you. It forces you to think about the future and what you could do next time rather than about the past and what may have happened.

Both of these questions require *positive* answers that enable you to extract the maximum value out of every situation. Both of these questions require you to keep your mind focused and your future oriented. Both of these questions enable you to learn and grow at a more rapid rate.

When you ask these two questions, "What did I do right?" and "What would I do differently?" after every situation, you will learn and grow more in the next month than another person might learn and grow in two or three years, if at all.

If you work with other people, you should conduct a review with these questions after every important situation. "What did we do right in this situation? What should we do differently next time?" You will be amazed at how much you can learn. These ideas and insights will help you to move ahead faster than you can imagine. Just try it once and judge for yourself.

Great Success Is Preceded by Failure

One of my favorite quotes is from Phil Knight of Nike shoes. He said, "You only have to succeed the last time."

This is a great observation! You can fail over and over again, but all it takes is one big success to wipe out all your previous failures. This explains why many of the most successful men and women in history have also been the biggest failures in history as well.

Thomas Edison, the greatest inventor of the modern age, was also the greatest failure in the world of invention. He experimented and failed more times in the development of his various products than any other inventor of the twentieth century.

But Thomas Edison had a special way of thinking about his work that we can all practice. When he began working on an invention, he started with the belief that finding the correct solution was only a matter of time. Success was inevitable. Failure was not an option. All he had to do was eliminate all the ways that didn't work until all there was left was the one way that did work.

Edison carefully recorded the results of every experiment. He extracted every lesson he could learn from each experiment that could be applied to subsequent experiments. He was thoughtful and methodical. He did not make the same mistakes by failing to learn the first time.

Assume That Success Is Inevitable

Practice this approach yourself. Begin with the assumption that your ultimate success is guaranteed. Whatever setbacks or difficulties you have, resolve to extract every possible lesson from them. Think on paper. Make careful notes. Analyze every single part of your performance and write down what you learned from that situation. Lock in the lessons so that you don't have to repeat them.

Thomas J. Watson Jr., president of IBM, once said, "We don't mind if people make mistakes around here. It is normal and natural to make mistakes. If you're not making mistakes, you're not trying hard enough. But what is unforgivable," he said, "is to make the same mistake more than once because you haven't learned from it."

Prepare for the Persistence Test

Emerson once said, "Nothing great was ever accomplished without enthusiasm." We could paraphrase that by saying nothing great was ever accomplished without persistence. The development of persistence is the price that you pay to enjoy the kind of life that is possible for you.

No one ever accomplishes greatly without having passed *the persistence test*. It is like an exam that you must take over and over again. You can only move ahead in your life and your career as you develop ever-higher levels of persistence. This quality is one of the greatest luck factors of all!

Most people achieve their greatest successes one step beyond where anyone else would have quit. But because they persisted, they finally broke through. Continually remind yourself that you could be only one step away from success. Remember the poem:

> Don't give up though the pace seems slow;
> You may succeed with another blow.
> And you never can tell how close you are,
> It may be near when it seems so far.

Sometimes your greatest failure can be the springboard to your greatest success. Sometimes the complete collapse of an idea or an enterprise is the final piece of the jigsaw puzzle that enables you to make the breakthrough that enables you to achieve your goal at last.

Persistence and Stubbornness

There is a difference, however, between persistence and stubbornness. Persistence is the quality of persevering toward a clear goal in the face of the obstacles and difficulties that inevitably arise. Persistence requires that you remain flexible regarding the means of attaining the goal. You always keep your eye on the ball. You always know where you are going. But you are willing to turn and change and try a variety of different ways to get there. You never give up.

Stubbornness is something else. It is the quality you demonstrate when you fly in the face of the facts. You try to make something work that is obviously unworkable. The evidence against you is overwhelming. You are simply not being realistic or honest with yourself and the situation.

You must remind yourself of the difference between persistence and stubbornness while you work on your goals. You should be sure that it is persistence that is driving you forward, and not stubbornness.

Becoming an Unstoppable Person

You become unstoppable by refusing to stop. You develop the qualities of courage and persistence by practicing these qualities whenever they are called for. Your goal is to reach the point where you believe in yourself with such resolution and confidence that nothing can ever stop you or hold you back for very long. This is where persistence is so important.

The more you persist, the more you believe in yourself, and the more you believe in yourself, the more you persist. Your persistence is actually your *measure* of how much you believe in yourself and your ability to succeed. You can increase your belief in your ability to succeed by acting as if your success were guaranteed, as long as you keep going.

Self-Discipline in Action

Persistence is self-discipline in action. Each time you persist in the face of adversity, you strengthen your self-discipline. You build your character. You become stronger and more capable of practicing all of the other virtues and values. You attract helpful people and situations into your life. The greater your level of self-discipline, the more capable you become of persisting in the overcoming of ever-greater obstacles and difficulties.

Because of the direct relationship between self-discipline and self-esteem, whenever you discipline yourself, whenever you force yourself to do the things that you know you should do, you feel better about yourself. You like and respect yourself more. You become more confident and optimistic. You become more determined. Eventually, you become unstoppable.

When you develop the twin qualities of courage and persistence, you will begin to experience luck in ways that you never thought possible. The more you practice courage and persistence, the more confident you become. If the first part to success is "get-to-it-iveness," the second part is "stick-to-it-iveness." Once you launch toward your goal, you resolve in advance that you will never give up until you finally get there.

Both success and luck are predictable. They do not happen by accident. Your goal is to put the natural laws and principles to work on your behalf. Your aim must be to do everything possible to increase the odds in your favor. You must work every day to develop the winning edges of courage and persistence that will enable you to accomplish extraordinary things in the creation of your own future.

ACTION EXERCISES
What You Can Do Now

1. Resolve to confront your fears, whatever they are, until you have mastered them and developed the habit of courage.

2. Make an absolutely unshakable commitment to your goals and resolve in advance that you will never give up.

3. Break the bonds of *learned helplessness* by eliminating the words *I can't* from your vocabulary. Instead, keep reminding yourself "I can do it! I can do it!"

4. Analyze the worst possible thing that can happen in any worry situation, resolve to accept it, should it occur, and then get busy making sure it doesn't happen.

5. Become unstoppable by resolving in advance that you will never stop until you have achieved your goal; remember that no one can stop you but yourself.

6. Turn failure into success by always asking, "What did I do right?" and "What would I do differently next time?"

7. Motivate yourself to act courageously and persist indomitably with poems and quotations that inspire you to push forward, no matter what happens.

The Summing Up: Make Your Life a Masterpiece

The great secret of success is that there are no secrets of success. From the beginning of recorded history, the principles of success have been discovered and rediscovered over and over again. Here they are, once more:

Principle 1: Your Potential Is Unlimited—Take complete control of your mind, and learn to unlock your special powers to attract whatever you want into your life.

Principle 2: Clarity Is Critical—You must be absolutely clear about the things you want to achieve and the person you want to become.

Principle 3: Knowledge Is Power—Learn everything you need to know to be an expert in your field. Read continually, listen to audio programs, and take every course you can to stay ahead of your competitors.

Principle 4: Mastery Is Magical—Resolve today to become absolutely excellent at what you do. Develop your skills to a high level, and resolve to be among the top 10 percent in your field. This will help you more than anything else.

Principle 5: Attitude Is Everything—Become a totally positive person, so that people like you and want to be around you and help you. Think and talk only about the things you want, and refuse to think or talk about the things you don't want.

Principle 6: Relationships Are Essential—Develop a strategy for expanding your network of contacts and improving your key relationships in every part of your life. The more people who know you and like you, the more doors they will open for you.

Principle 7: Money Matters—Make a habit of saving your money. Start with 1 percent of your income, and then gradually build up to 10 percent, 20 percent and 30 percent. A person with money in the bank attracts more opportunities and good fortune than a person who is broke most of the time.

Principle 8: You Are a Genius—Unlock your inborn creativity by constantly looking for ways to get results faster, better, and cheaper. There is no problem that you cannot solve, and no goal that you cannot achieve by applying the incredible power of your mind.

Principle 9: Results Determine Rewards—Concentrate single mindedly on getting the most important results possible in everything you do. Focus continually on your highest priorities, on the most valuable use of your time, every minute of every day.

Principle 10: Seize The Day!—Develop the habit of action orientation, the essential quality of all successful people. Get going, get busy, move fast. Practice a sense of urgency. Stay in continuous motion in the direction of your goals.

Principle 11: Character Counts—Become a thoroughly good person. The better a person you become on the inside, by practicing the qualities of character that you most admire and respect, the better will be the quality of your life on the outside.

Principle 12: Fortune Favors the Brave—Have the courage to begin and the persistence to continue. Resolve in advance that you will never give up.

When you combine all these factors together, you will become a totally positive, future focused, highly energetic, likable, talented, skilled, intelligent, and optimistic human being. You will become completely unstoppable. You will start to have lucky experiences in every area of your life. You will achieve every goal that you ever set for yourself.

Later on, when people say that you were *lucky*, you can smile humbly, and agree that you have indeed been fortunate. But in your heart you will know. It wasn't luck at all. You did it all by yourself!

Brian Tracy's Focal Point
Advanced Coaching and Mentoring Program

Brian Tracy offers a personal group coaching program in San Diego for successful entrepreneurs, self-employed professionals, and top salespeople. In the course of this program, you learn how to double your productivity, simplify your life, and double your time off.

You complete a detailed personality profile to help you identify your major strengths, areas of interest, and the steps you can take to be more effective in getting your most important results. Then you learn a step-by-step process of personal strategic planning that will enable you to take complete control of your time and your life.

You learn how to develop absolute clarity in each of the important areas of career, family, finances, and health. You learn how to set and achieve your key goals, simplify your life, take more time off with your family, and maximize your personal potential. You learn how to identify the major opportunities in your life and how to take advantage of them.

During the program, you meet with Brian Tracy one full day every three months. As a result of a process of powerful self-analysis exercises, you will identify those things you do better than anything else. You will learn how to excel in your most profitable activities.

You will learn how to delegate, outsource, and eliminate those tasks and activities that contribute very little to the achievement of your most important business and career goals.

You learn how to determine your special talents and how to focus and concentrate on the key activities that can move you to the top of your field.

Who Should Attend?

This program is designed for successful entrepreneurs, executives, top salespeople, and self-employed professionals who want to move to the next level in their careers and their personal lives.

Coaching sessions are small and personal with ample opportunity for interaction and brainstorming with other successful people. You learn how to develop your own personal strategic plan, how to implement your plan with daily, weekly, and monthly goals, and how to update your plan as you move forward.

If you qualify for this program (minimum income $100,000 per year), you will learn how to apply the *Focal Point Process* to every part of your work and personal life. You will make more progress in one year than someone else might make in ten years.

Focal Point Advanced Telephone Coaching Program

We offer an intensive 12-week advanced telephone-coaching program that you can take in the convenience of your home or office. You work with an expert coach who has had many years of experience in helping successful people get the most out of themselves and their lives.

You receive a detailed 410-page, 12-part study guide plus a complete outline of the program on audio for your review. Each week, you complete one session and answer several questions in preparation for your telephone meeting with your coach. After each coaching session you then develop an action plan for the coming week that keeps you moving forward.

During the course of this program, you learn how to set and achieve goals in each part of your work and personal life. You learn how to identify your most profitable and enjoyable activities, and how to delegate and eliminate all those things that clutter up your life.

You learn how to clarify, simplify, maximize, and multiply your results. At each stage, your coach will guide you and advise you to help you realize more and more of your potential. At the end of 12 weeks, you will be performing on a new high level of effectiveness and personal satisfaction.

For more information or to apply for the next live or personal telephone coaching program, visit www.briantracy.com and click on Coaching, or phone 858-481-2977. We will send you a complete information package.

To book Brian as a speaker, please contact:

Brian Tracy
Brian Tracy International
462 Stevens Avenue, Suite 202
Solana Beach, CA 92075
Phone: 858-481-2977, ext. 17
Fax: 858-481-2445
E-mail: briantracy@briantracy.com

Index

About the Author

Brian Tracy is one of the world's most successful speakers and consultants on personal and professional development. Each year he addresses some 450,000 people in the United States and abroad. His corporate clients have included IBM, McDonnell Douglas, Arthur Andersen, the Million Dollar Round Table, and dozens more. Brian Tracy is also the best-selling author of *Maximum Achievement*, *Advanced Selling Strategies*, *The 21 Success Secrets of Self-Made Millionaires*, *Eat That Frog*, and *The 100 Absolutely Unbreakable Laws of Business Success*. His firm, Brian Tracy International (www.briantracy.com), is based in San Diego, California, with affiliates across the United States and in 31 countries.